W9-AFW-808

Witold Gombrowicz was born in Warsaw in 1903 and died in the South of France in 1969. His family were of Polish aristocratic origin. Finding himself unexpectedly in Argentina in August 1939 he was forced to stay there throughout the war and only returned to Europe, finally settling in France, in the early 1960s. In 1968 he won the prestigious International Publishers' Prize (Formentor) and today he is regarded as one of the most important European writers (Susan Sontag called *Ferdydurke* 'one of the most important overlooked books of the twentieth century'). Gombrowicz's novels include *Pornographia* (1960), *Trans-Atlantic* (1980), *The Possessed* (1980) and *Cosmos* (1967). His plays *Princess Ivona*, *The Marriage* and *Operetta* are performed worldwide. An autobiographical account of his life and work, *A Kind of Testament*, was published in 1973.

Other books by Witold Gombrowicz

Novels include:
Cosmos
Pornographia
The Possessed
Trans-Atlantic

Plays include:
The Marriage
Operetta
Princess Ivona

Autobiography:
A Kind of Testament

Ferdydurke

Witold Gombrowicz

Translated by Eric Mosbacher

MARION BOYARS
LONDON · NEW YORK

Reissued 1979 by
MARION BOYARS PUBLISHERS LTD
24 Lacy Road, London SW15 1NL

www.marionboyars.co.uk

Distributed in Australia and New Zealand by Peribo Pty Ltd
58 Beaumont Road, Kuring-gai, NSW 2080

First published in Warsaw in 1937
First published in English by MacGibbon and Kee 1961

Printed in 2005
10 9 8 7 6 5 4 3 2 1
© Witold Gombrowicz 1961, 1979
© MacGibbon and Kee 1961
© This translation Eric Mosbacher 1961

A CIP catalogue record for this book is available from the British Library.
A CIP catalog record for this book is available from the Library of Congress.

ISBN 0-7145-3403-X
13 digit ISBN 9780-7145-3403-9

Set in Sabon 11.5/14pt
Printed in England by Cox & Wyman Ltd, Reading, Berkshire

Contents

The History of Ferdydurke   7

   1   Abduction   13

   2   Incarceration and Further Rejuvenescence   27

   3   The Duel   51

   4   Introduction to Philifor Honeycombed with
       Childishness   70

   5   Philifor Honeycombed with Childishness   88

   6   Further Inveiglement into Childhood   102

   7   Love   117

   8   The Fruit Salad   129

   9   Through the Keyhole   143

  10   Escape and Recapture   162

  11   Introduction to Philimor Honeycombed with
       Childishness   187

  12   Philimor Honeycombed with Childishness   193

  13   Out of the Frying Pan   196

  14   Zenith and Culmination   230

The History of Ferdydurke

1937   Publication in Warsaw. Literary sensation. Scandal. Controversy. Some critics predict an international career for the work.

1939   War, and invasion of Poland. *Ferdydurke* buried and forgotten. Gombrowicz arrives in Argentina.

1947   *Ferdydurke* published in Buenos Aires, translated into Spanish by the author in co-operation with a committee of South American writers under the aegis of the Cuban novelist Virgilio Piniera.

     Some years later Gombrowicz notes in his *Journal*: '*Ferdydurke* has been drowned in the sleep-walking immobility of South America.'

1957   Things begin to move at last. For the first ten years of the Communist régime in Poland Gombrowicz has been taboo and it has been forbidden to publish him, but now, after the events of October 1956, with Gomulka in the saddle, a little liberty is allowed.

     Ferdydurke is republished in Warsaw after twenty years. The Communists think they have let a canary out of its cage, but it turns out to be a wolf.

     The edition of 10,000 copies is sold out in a few days. Popularity? Success? Yes, such is sometimes the fate of books. . . . During the war years, under the Nazi occupation and after, under the Stalinist terror, *Ferdydurke*, i.e., the few pre-war copies that escaped destruction, never ceased to circulate from hand to hand. People, reading all this crazy stuff about making people faces, violation by the ears, tyranny of backside, said to themselves: Our

7

situation precisely! For *Ferdydurke* contained, not only a premonition of existentialism, but an intuition of the deepest workings of totalitarianism. The novel becomes successful overnight. Its repressed popularity, long-suppressed laughter, burst out into the light of day.

Other works by Gombrowicz appear in Poland: *Transatlantic*, a novel; *Bakakai*, a volume of long short stories; *The Marriage*, a play; *Yvonne*, a comedy. They are warmly received by the press. Artur Sandauer, the best Polish critic, speaks on Warsaw radio of 'great literature', 'one of the greatest contemporary writers', and says: 'This writer is the pride of the nation'.

Works by Gombrowicz start appearing on the stage. *Yvonne* is a huge success in Warsaw; the critics compare it with Beckett and Ionesco. *The Marriage*, one of Gombrowicz's best works, is about to be produced at Cracow when . . .

1958   . . . a button is pressed, and Gombrowicz's name vanishes from publishers' lists, theatrical announcements and the press. It has been decided in high places that there has been too much Gombrowicz, and too much liberty in general. After that there is silence.

1959   But now the West starts taking an interest. When the French edition appears in Paris, François Bondy is the first to speak of the 'brilliant author of *Ferdydurke*, recently discovered by western Europe'. The French literary press, almost without exception, is enthusiastic. Mario Maurin in *Les Lettres Nouvelles* compares it to Sartre's *La Nausée*, the *Nouvelle Revue Française* speaks of a work 'of capital importance', and Jelenski of a 'strange masterpiece'.

★

Here, in conclusion, are two comments by Gombrowicz, the first an extract from his *Journal* and the second the concluding passage of his introduction to the Spanish edition of *Ferdydurke*:

I.   What a bore is the everlasting question: What did you mean by *Ferdydurke*? Come, come, be more sensuous, less cerebral, start dancing with the book instead of asking for meanings. Why take so much interest in the skeleton if it's got a body? See rather whether it is capable of pleasing and is not devoid of grace and passion. . . .

II.   . . . at worst the book will pass unnoticed, but friends and acquaintances when they meet me will certainly feel under an obligation to say to me the sort of thing that is always said when an author publishes a book. I should like to ask them to do nothing of the sort. No, let them say nothing, because, as a result of all sorts of falsifications, the social situation of the so-called 'artist' in our times has become so pretentious that whatever can be said in such circumstances sounds false, and the more sincerity and simplicity you put into your 'I enjoyed it enormously' or 'I like it very much indeed', the more shameful it is for him and for you. I therefore beg you to keep silent. Keep silent in hope of a better future. For the time being—if you wish to let me know that the book pleased you—when you see me simply touch your right ear. If you touch your left ear, I shall know that you didn't like it, and if you touch your nose it will mean that you are not sure . . . thus we shall avoid uncomfortable and even ridiculous situations and understand each other in silence. My greetings to all.

FERDYDURKE

★ 1 ★

Abduction

THAT Tuesday I awoke at the still and empty hour when the night is nearly over but there is still no sign of dawn. I lay in the dim light, while mortal fear lay heavy on my body and invaded my mind, and my mind in its turn lay heavy on my body; and the smallest particles of myself writhed in the appalling certainty that nothing would ever happen, nothing ever change, and that, whatever one did, nothing would ever come of it. The explanation of my terror was contained in the dream which had troubled me during the night and had ended by waking me.

What had I dreamt? By a regression of a kind that ought to be forbidden to nature, I had seen myself at the age of fifteen or sixteen, I had reverted to adolescence. Standing in the wind on a stone at the edge of a river, I had said something, heard myself saying something, heard my shrill, long-since-buried, adolescent voice, seen my excessively big hands and the immature nose on my soft, provisional, adolescent's face, felt the unprofitable content of that passing and intermediary phase of myself; and I had awoken between laughter and fear, for it had seemed to me that the adult, the thirty-year-old who I am today, was apeing and mocking the adolescent that I was then, while the adolescent was mocking the adult; and that each of my two selves was thus taking the rise out of the other. Hapless memory that forces on us knowledge of the paths that we followed in order to become what we are! Half-asleep, I even imagined that my body was not entirely homogeneous, and that parts of it were not yet mature, that my head was laughing at and mocking my thigh, that my thigh was making merry at my head, that my finger was ridiculing my heart and my heart my brain, while my eye made sport of my nose and my nose of my eye, all to the accompaniment of loud bursts of crazy laughter—my limbs and the various parts of my body violently ridiculing each other in a general atmosphere of caustic and wounding raillery. But when I came to myself completely and started looking at my life, my terror, far from vanishing, increased, though a little laugh which it was impossible to restrain kept turning up to interrupt (or perhaps stimulate) it. Half-way along the path of my life, I found myself in a dark forest; and the worst of it was that the forest was *green*.

For in reality I was as vague and uncoordinated as I was in my dream. I had recently crossed the unavoidable Rubicon of my thirtieth birthday; according to my papers and my appearance, I was grown up. But I was not mature. What was I then? Where was I? I wandered from bar to café, from café to bar, met people, exchanged words and sometimes even thoughts with them, but my situation was by no means clear, and I did not know myself whether I was a man or an adolescent. The result was that in confronting the second half of my life I was neither one nor another, I was nothing at all, and that I was rightly treated with suspicion by those of my generation who had married and had settled positions, if not exactly in relation to life, at any rate in offices of one kind or another. My aunts, those numerous, devoted, clinging, but kind semi-mammas, had been trying for a long time to use their influence to get me to settle down in some suitable occupation, say, as a lawyer or in business, for the prolonged nondescript nature of my life was torture to them. Not really knowing who I was, they did not know what to say to me, and at best their conversation with me was at a level of sad twaddle. 'Johnnie,' they would say to me between one twitter and the next, 'the years are passing, and what will people think? If you don't want to be a doctor, be a *bon viveur* or a collector, but be something, you must be something'; and I would hear one of them whispering to another that I lacked polish; and then, desperate because of the void which thereupon appeared in their heads, they would revert to their twitterings. This situation could not of course be prolonged indefinitely; the hands of nature's clock are inexorable and exact. My last teeth, my wisdom teeth, having come through, I had had to accept the fact that my development was complete, and that the hour had struck for the inevitable murder; the man must slay the youth and take wing like the butterfly, leaving the dead body of the chrysalis on the ground. I had had to enter the grown-up world.

Enter it? But with pleasure. I had made the attempt, and when I looked back on it now I split my sides with laughter. To prepare my entrance into the world of adults I had sat down to write a book, primarily to explain myself and obtain its favours in advance. I had assumed that, if I succeeded in causing a definite idea about my personality to germinate in the minds of others, that idea would itself contribute to my development, with the result that willy-nilly I should attain maturity. But why did my pen betray me? Why did a sanctimonious modesty prevent me from writing a manifestly and tediously mature novel? And why, instead of begetting from my mind and my heart lofty sentiments and noble thoughts, was I able to produce these only from the lower part of my person? Why did I introduce into the text all those extraordinary frogs and legs and things, all that fermenting matter, isolating them on the page only by the style, the cold and disciplined tone, and demonstrating to the reader how completely I dominated the ferment? And why, to the detriment of my own purpose, did I call the book *Memoirs of a Time of Immaturity*? In vain my friends advised me to drop that title, and in general to refrain from all reference to immaturity. 'Don't do it,' they said. 'Immaturity is a very drastic idea. If you yourself don't think yourself mature, how can you expect anybody else to?' But I actually thought it unseemly to pass over in silence the callow youth inside me, and I thought grown-ups far too perspicacious and clear-sighted to be so easily taken in, and, finally, I thought that anyone so closely beset by the callow youth inside him had no right to make a public appearance without him. Perhaps I took serious matters too seriously; perhaps I overestimated the maturity of mature persons.

Memories! My head buried in the pillow and my legs under the blankets, caught between terror and uncontrollable laughter, I looked back at my entrance into the world of grown-ups. I thought of the sad venture of my first book, recalled how instead of giving me the desired stability it had got me more bogged down than ever, while the wave of people's stupid opinions broke over me. What a curse it is that there is no permanent, stable order of things in our life on this planet, that everything in it is in perpetual motion, continual flux, that it is a necessity for everyone to be understood and appreciated by his neighbour, and that what fools and simpletons and oafs think of us is as important as the opinion of the wise, the subtle, the acute! For at heart man depends on the picture of himself formed in the minds of others, even if the others are half-wits. And I protest with all my strength against those of my colleagues who adopt an attitude of aristocratic contempt for the opinions of the ignorant and say: *Odi profanum vulgus*. What a cheap evasion, what a wretched shirking of reality is that high and mighty affectation! I claim, on the contrary, that the more inept and petty criticism is, the more constricting it is, like a tight shoe. Oh! those human opinions, the abyss of views and criticisms of your intelligence, your heart, every detail of your being, which opens up in front of you when you have incautiously clothed your thoughts in words, put them on paper and spread them among men! Oh! paper! paper! Words, words! And I am not talking here of the mild and gentle domestic opinions of our beloved aunts. No, I refer rather to the opinions of our cultural 'aunts', the innumerable author-aunts (I am not here concerned with their morals) who express their opinions in the press. For seated upon the culture of the world are legions of good women, tied and bound to literature, deeply initiated into intellectual values, aesthetically awake, supported by ideas, concepts, and all the rest of it, who are already aware of the fact that Oscar Wilde is out of date and Bernard Shaw a master of paradox. They know very well that you should be independent, simple, and profound, so they are independent, simple, and profound,

16

and full of an entirely domesticated mildness. Aunts, the whole lot of them! Ah! he who has never been taken into the cultural aunts' laboratory and been dissected by their trivial and pettifogging mentalities which dissect the life out of life, he who has not read in the papers what one of these aunts thinks about him, does not know what triviality, what auntiness, really is.

And more; there are the criticisms of country gentlemen, the opinions of pensioners, the petty criticisms of clerks, the bureaucratic opinions of high officials, the criticisms of provincial lawyers, the extremist opinions of young people, the infatuated judgements of old men, to say nothing of the views of doctors' wives, children, female cousins, housemaids and cooks, a whole tidal wave of opinions which describe and portray us as we appear in the minds of others. It is like being born in a thousand rather narrow minds. But my position was even more difficult and painful, because my book, in comparison with conventionally mature writing, seemed drastic and difficult. True, it gained me a handful of picked friends, and if the cultural aunts and other representatives of the vulgar could have heard how I was coddled and saturated with praise in the course of intellectually very elevated conversation in select gatherings of the eminent, the *élite*, inaccessible to them even in dreams, they would probably have fallen on their knees in front of me and kissed my feet. On the other hand there must have been something green, something immature, about my way of writing which attracted the confraternity of the immature and sanctioned their familiarity with me. For it often happened, when I emerged into the street from one of these sacrosanct places in which I was so agreeably treated with lavish respect, that I would run into some engineer or schoolboy who would treat me as if I were his brother in folly, his accomplice in immaturity, and bawl at me, to the accompaniment of hearty and repeated slaps on the back: 'What rubbish you write, old man! How can you write such a lot of tripe!' Thus I was mature to the mature and immature to the immature, with the result that I did not know which side I was on: that of those who treated me with respect or of those who regarded me as half-baked.

But the worst of it was that, though I encountered a fierce and, I imagine, unprecedented hatred on the part of the vulgar, the semi-intelligent, it was with the latter that I sided; I fled from the cordially extended arms of the *élite* into the coarse embrace of those who thought me a fool. A question of primary importance, affecting the whole development of the personality, is that of the reality in relation to which a man fashions himself. Does he, for instance, when he talks, acts, rants, writes, pay attention and take into account only grown-up, fully adult persons? Or is he haunted by the phantom of the vulgar and the immature, the shadow of a dubious and murky half-world, in the green darkness of which you slowly stifle, suffocated by the lianas, the creepers, and other African growths? Never for a moment was I able to forget the sub-world of sub-humanity and, though panic and terror seized me at the mere thought of its swampy verdure, fascinated as I was by it, like a bird by a snake, I could not shake it off. It was as if, in defiance of nature, I sympathized with and even loved the vulgar world, was grateful to it for causing the child in me to survive. Oh! living on the threshold of the lofty, adult world and not being able to go in! Being but one step distant from wisdom, dignity, distinction, ripe judgement, mutual respect, a hierarchy of proper values, and being able to savour these things only through the window, having no access to what was inside, being second-rate! Living among grown-ups and still having the feeling, as at the age of sixteen, of only pretending to be one of them! Playing the writer, the man of letters, mimicking literary style and grown-up expressions! Fighting, as an artist, a grim public battle for one's own 'ego', but at the same time secretly sympathizing with one's mortal enemies!

True, during the first days of my public life I had received a semi-consecration, been generously anointed, by the lower world. But what still further complicated the situation was that my social behaviour left much to be desired; I turned out to be completely helpless and defenceless in the semi-brilliant social world. Some sort of laziness, born of fear and timidity, prevented me from adjusting myself to any kind of maturity whatever, and sometimes, when someone made a flattering intellectual approach to me, I felt like giving him a good, hard pinch. How I envied those men of letters unquestionably predestined to superiority from birth, to sublimity from the cradle, whose minds moved perpetually towards the heights, just as if their backsides had been pricked with a pin! Serious writers who took their souls seriously, had an innate aptitude for creative suffering on the grand scale, and moved freely in a world of ideas so exalted and for ever sanctified that God himself seemed to them vulgar and devoid of majesty! Why is it not given to everybody to write yet another novel about love, or to denounce some social injustice and thus transform himself into a defender of the people? Or to write verse, become a poet, and believe in the 'noble mission of verse'? To have talent and feed the non-talented on it? Ah! How satisfying it must be to suffer and torment oneself, to sacrifice oneself on the altar, to burn oneself alive at the stake, always higher than the heights, in such a sublimated, adult world! How satisfying, to oneself and to others, to launch oneself, with the aid of age-old cultural institutions, with a confidence equal to that with which one puts money in the bank! But I, alas, was an adolescent, and adolescence was my only cultural institution, and I was doubly cornered and trapped, by a childhood which I could not get rid of and by the childishness of the ideas which others formed of me, the caricature of myself which existed in their minds. So I was the slave of greenness, an insect prisoner of the thick foliage.

This situation was not only awkward; it was dangerous too. For nothing horrifies and disgusts the mature so much as immaturity. They have no difficulty in tolerating the most destructive intelligence so long as its field of activity lies within the framework of maturity. They do not fear a revolutionary who opposes one mature ideal to another mature ideal, e.g. overthrows a monarchy in favour of republicanism, or makes mincemeat of republicanism in the interests of royalism. They even look with favour on such a happy, adult, sublimated way of behaving. But if they detect immaturity in someone, discover the youth in him, they fall on him, annihilate him with their sarcasms, peck him to death with their beaks, like swans with a duck.

Where, then, was all this going to end? Where was this road leading me? How, I wondered, had I come to be so subjected to, so fascinated by, the green and the unripe? Perhaps because I was the native of a country rich in individuals at the crude, primitive, transitional stage, a country in which collars do not suit anyone and the countryside is haunted by the lamentations of laziness and incompetence rather than those of Chopinian melancholy. Or perhaps it was because I lived in a period which was itself continually inventing new devices, new grimaces, its face twisting under the influence of a thousand convulsions. . . .

The pale dawn entered the window, and as I lay under the blankets looking back at my life I was seized by an indecent, uncontrollable, embarrassed fit of laughter; it was a helpless, bestial, mechanical laugh, a leg laugh, just as if somebody had tickled the sole of my foot, as if it were not my face but my leg that were laughing. I must make a clean break, put childish things behind me, make up my mind, make a fresh start, do something!

It was then that I had a simple but wonderful idea—to be neither mature nor immature, but simply myself; to express myself in my own proudly sovereign fashion, ignoring everything except my own inner truth. Ah! to shape oneself, express oneself, express not only that part of oneself which had reached clarity and maturity but also that which was still fermenting and obscure. Let my own shape be born of me, let me not owe my formation to anyone. Excitement impelled me towards pen and paper. I took the paper from the drawer, and by now it was full morning. The sun came flooding into the room, the maid brought the coffee and rolls, and I, surrounded by shining and finely modelled forms, started writing the first pages of a book, my book, a book resembling myself, identical with myself, born of myself, a book which was to be the supreme affirmation of myself in the face of everything and everybody. Suddenly the bell rang. The maid opened the door, and there appeared on the threshold T. Pimko, the doctor, the professor, or rather the master, the distinguished Cracow philologist, small, puny, bald, and bespectacled, in striped pants and tailcoat, his yellowish nails projecting under his light-yellow gloves.

'Do you know the professor?'

'The professor?'

Stop! Stop! Panic-stricken at the appearance of this platitudinously dull and dully platitudinous human being, I made hurriedly to hide what I had written. But he sat down, so I had to do the same; and as soon as he was seated he started condoling with me on the death of an aunt who had died some time previously, an aunt whom I had totally forgotten.

'Remembrance of the dead,' he began, 'constitutes a fraternal arch connecting past years with those to come, just like folksong (Mickiewicz). We live the life of the dead (Auguste Comte). Your aunt is dead, so we can, nay must, devote to her some erudite thoughts and lofty ideas. She had her faults (he enumerated them), but she also had her qualities (which he enumerated too), qualities which were useful to society, which enables us to say that we are dealing here with not a bad book, I beg your pardon, aunt; we may even say that the deceased deserved good marks, for, to put it in a nutshell, she was an influence for good, and it follows that the verdict is favourable, and assuring you of that fact is an agreeable duty to me, Pimko, guardian of the cultural values of which your aunt herself formed part, particularly in view of the fact that she is dead. Besides,' he added indulgently, '*de mortuis nil nisi bene.* True, some criticisms might be made here and there, but why discourage a young author, I beg your pardon, nephew? But, good gracious!' he exclaimed, noticing on the table the sheets of paper covered with my scrawl, 'not only nephew, but author as well! I see that we are trying our chances with the Muses. Well! Well! Well! An author! Let me immediately criticize, encourage, advise!' Still seated, he drew the sheets of paper towards him across the table, putting on his spectacles at the same time.

'No!' I muttered. My world collapsed in ruins. Aunt and author had utterly confounded me.

As Pimko spoke he rubbed one of his eyes. Then he took out a cigarette, held it in his left hand while he smoothed it with his right, and started to cough, for the tobacco irritated his nose. Then he sat back and started to read. He sat and read very learnedly. I paled as I watched him, and thought I was going to pass out. I could not use violence on him, because I was seated because he was seated. Heaven knows why the fact that we were seated was fundamental, was the cardinal obstacle. So I shifted in my seat, not knowing what to do; I started moving my legs and biting my finger-nails, while he, composedly and at ease, remained seated, that position following logically from and being completely explained by the fact that he was reading. The reading went on for an eternity. The minutes lasted for hours and the seconds were unnaturally extended, and I was ill at ease, like a sea that somebody was trying to suck up through a straw.

Not the master! I groaned. Not the master! Anything, but not the master!

His masterly composure crushed me; he went on reading in masterly fashion, assimilating my spontaneous outpourings with his typical master's personality, holding the paper up to his eyes. . . . Through the window you could see the block of flats opposite, twelve horizontal windows and twelve vertical. Was it dream or reality? Why had he come here, why was he sitting down, why was I sitting down? By what miracle had all that had been happening previously, dreams, memories, aunts, sufferings, thoughts, work, led to the master's sitting here like this? No! No! It was impossible. As he was reading, he had good reason to be seated, but I had no reason whatever, it was absurd.

I made a convulsive effort to rise to my feet, but at that moment he looked up at me, gazed at me indulgently over his spectacles. And then suddenly I dwindled, my ears grew small, my hands contracted, my body shrank, while he grew enormous and remained still seated, taking in and assimilating what I had written *in saecula saeculorum amen.*

Have you ever had the sensation of dwindling in size inside someone? Ah! Diminishing inside an aunt is most indelicate, but diminishing inside an eminent and famous master is the height of indecency. I could see him feeding on my greenness like a cow. It was an extraordinary sensation: the master grazing in a field, feeding on one's greenness, but at the same time seated in an armchair, and yet grazing, grazing. Something terrible was happening inside and yet outside me, something absurd, something impudently unreal. I muttered that I had a mind of my own, that I was not a mere hack, that I was alive, that I had a mind and a spirit of my own. . . . But he remained seated, so firmly and inexorably seated that the fact of his sitting, though intolerably stupid, was nevertheless all-powerful.

He removed his spectacles, wiped them with his handkerchief, and put them back on his nose . . . and his nose was a thing both indescribable and impregnable. It was a commonplace, pedagogic, rather long, nasal nose, consisting of two parallel tubes, obvious and final.

'What spirit are you talking about, please?'

'Mine!'

'Yours? You refer, no doubt, to the patriotic spirit of the motherland?'

'No! Mine is no patriotic spirit.'

'Yours?' he said benevolently. 'So we think we have a spirit? Do we at least know what the spirit of King Ladislas was?' He remained rooted to his chair.

What King Ladislas? I felt like a train that had been suddenly shunted to King Ladislas's siding. I braked and opened my mouth, realizing that my ignorance of King Ladislas was total and complete. He went on:

'But you must be acquainted with the spirit of history? And the spirit of antiquity? And the spirit of French civilization? And the spirit of the sixteenth-century bucolic writer who used the word 'navel' for the first time in literature? And with the

23

spirit of the language in general? Is "meander" masculine or feminine?'

With that question a hundred thousand spirits swept down on mine and I was utterly confounded; stammeringly I admitted that I did not know. He asked what I could tell him about Mickiewicz, and what that poet's attitude had been towards the people. He also asked me about Lelewel's first love affair. I coughed, and glanced furtively at my fingers, but nothing was written on my nails, they were clean. I looked all round, hoping that somebody would prompt me, but nobody was there. Was it dream or reality? Heavens, what was happening? Good Lord! I looked up, but it was not I who looked at Pimko, but a schoolboy darting a stealthy, furtive, look at his master. Anachronistically, I wanted to screw up a sheet of paper and throw it in his face. Feeling that something ghastly was going to happen, I made a desperate effort to control myself and say to him casually, like a man of the world: 'Well? How are you? What's the latest?' but my voice had lost its ordinary tone, had become shrill and raw, as if it were still breaking, so I held my peace. Pimko asked me what I knew about adverbs, made me decline *mensa*, *mensam*, *mensae* and conjugate *amo*, *amas*, *amat*, pursed his lips disapprovingly, said: 'Well, then, you'll have to revise,' took a notebook from his pocket, and gave me a bad mark. All this while he remained seated, and his sitting had now become immutable, permanent and absolute.

What was all this? I wanted to shout that I wasn't a schoolboy, that it was all a mistake, and I jumped up to run away, but something caught me from behind, a kind of hook which dragged me back, and there I was, caught by my childish, schoolboy's little behind. It was my little behind that stopped me from moving, because of it I could not budge, and the master still sat there, and such an overwhelmingly, schoolmasterly spirit emanated from his posture that instead of crying out I raised my arm like a schoolboy in class. Pimko frowned, and said:

'Keep quiet, Kowalski! Do you want to leave the room again?'

And he remained seated and I remained seated in a situation as absurd and unreal as a dream . . . I, seated on my childish little behind which paralysed me and deprived me of my senses and he seated on his as if on the Acropolis while he noted something in his book.

Eventually he said:

'Come along now, Johnnie, let's go to school.'

'What school?'

'Mr Piorkowski's. It's a first-class establishment. There's still room in the second form. Your knowledge leaves a lot to be desired. The first thing to do is to fill the gaps.'

'But what school?'

'Mr Piorkowski's. He's short of pupils, and, as it happens, has been asking me to find him some. The school has got to be a success, and to be a success it must have pupils. To school then, to school!'

'But what school?'

'That'll do. Come along now!'

He rang for the maid and asked for his overcoat. She started grumbling, not understanding my being taken away like this by a stranger, but Pimko pinched her and she stopped, because when she was pinched she had no choice but to burst out laughing like a servant girl when she has been pinched, showing her teeth. And the schoolmaster took me by the hand and led me out into the street where, in spite of everything, the houses were still standing and people were going and coming.

Help! Police! It was too stupid to be true. It was impossible, because it was impossibly stupid. But it was too stupid for me to be able to stop it. . . . I was powerless against the schoolmaster, paralysed by my childish, idiotic little behind, which hamstrung all possible resistance. The colossus advanced with a giant's stride, I trotted along beside him, and there was nothing I could do against him because of my little behind. Farewell, spirit which was mine, farewell, my work! Off with my true, my real shape, and on with this terrible, puerile, green and grotesque shape!

25

Cruelly dwindled and diminished, I trotted along beside the huge schoolmaster, who muttered:

'Well, well, well, little doggie! Tiny nose, tiny ears, tiny hands! Well, well, well! Little behind, what a pretty little behind!'

In front of us a woman was taking her puppy for a walk. It growled, jumped at Pimko, and tore the bottom of his trousers. Pimko expressed an unfavourable opinion about the puppy, pinned up the tear in his trousers, and led me away by the hand.

* 2 *

Incarceration
and Further Rejuvenescence

AND here—was I to believe my eyes?—was that very ordinary building, the school to which I was dragged by Pimko in spite of my tears and protestations. We arrived during the morning break; young persons varying in age between ten and twenty were walking about the playground, eating bread and butter or bread and cheese. Mothers were insatiably gazing at their little darlings through the gaps in the fence. With his double-barrelled nasal appendage Pimko voluptuously sniffed the atmosphere of school.

'Boys, boys, boys!' he exclaimed. 'Boys, boys, boys!'

Meanwhile a member of the staff, a man with a limp, probably an usher, came towards us, showing every sign of exceptional and profound respect.

'Here,' Pimko said to him, 'is little Johnnie, whom I want put in the second form. Johnnie, say good-morning to the gentleman. I'll leave Johnnie with you to get used to the place while I have a word with the head.'

I wanted to reply, but instead bowed slightly to the professor. A slight breeze sprang up and moved the branches of the trees, as well as a lock of hair on Pimko's head.

'I hope we'll behave ourselves,' the usher said, patting me on the head.

'And how are all these young people progressing?' Pimko asked in a low voice. 'I see that they walk very well. They walk, they talk, and their mothers watch them. There's nothing so

27

effective as a mother strategically placed behind a wall to bring out a pair of fresh young buttocks.'

'All the same, they're still not guileless enough,' the usher started lamenting. 'We still can't get them to be fresh and innocent enough. You will never imagine, my dear colleague, how headstrong and obstinate they are. They just don't want to be as fresh and innocent as spring carrots. They just don't want to be!'

This earned him a sharp rebuke from Pimko, who informed him severely that he was lacking in the schoolmasterly virtues.

'What?' he said, 'they don't want to? They don't want to? We must make them want to! I'll show you how to stimulate innocence straight away. I guarantee that within half an hour the whole atmosphere of the place will be twice as innocent and guileless as it is now. What I shall do is this: I shall spend some time watching the boys, and shall then give them to understand that I consider them innocent and guileless. The effect will be highly provocative; they will immediately try to show that they are the very reverse of innocent, and in so doing will automatically relapse into that innocence and naïveté which is such a delight to us pedagogues.'

Pimko hid behind a big oak tree, while the usher took me by the hand and led me among the schoolboys without giving me a chance to open my mouth.

The boys were walking about in the playground. Some were energetically scrapping or exchanging blows; some had stopped their ears and had buried their heads in their books; others were making faces at each other, or trying to trip each other up, or pushing each other about, and their stupefied, lifeless, sheeplike eyes rested on me without seeing that I was a man of thirty. Believing it was time to put an end to this farce, I went up to the nearest boy, and said:

'Excuse me, but as you see, in view of my age . . .'

'Hi, chaps!' he shouted. '*Novum companerum!*'

A group gathered round me. Somebody said:

'*Deo gratias.* What *capricius* of the *tempum* caused your *excellentissimum personus* to arrive so much in *retardus?*'

Somebody else, to the accompaniment of loutish guffaws, improved on this by saying:

'Would our *estimadus colegus* by any chance have been suffering from chronic lymphatic flemingitis, or was it a flame for some damsel that delayed his so eagerly expected arrival?'

This horrible gibberish shut me up like a clam, but they didn't stop, it seemed to be impossible for them to stop; and the more appalled I was, the more pleasure did they take in it, the more exultantly did they wallow in it, the more obstinately and crazily did they persist. Their gestures were half-baked, their faces pasty and callow. The principal subject of conversation of the small boys was sexual organs, and of the big boys sexual intercourse; a horrifying dish served up in their pseudo-archaic, Latinized jargon. They seemed somehow awkward and ill at ease, and they kept looking at the usher and convulsively clutching their behinds, and the feeling that they were under constant observation prevented them from eating their lunch.

The effect on me of this farce to which no end seemed in sight was that my head was swimming and I found it utterly impossible to explain myself. But when they noticed Pimko, who was watching them and missing nothing from his hiding-place behind the oak-tree, they became nervous in the extreme; the news spread quickly that the inspector had arrived, and was spying on them from behind the tree.

'The inspector!' some of the boys said, taking out their books, and moving over towards the tree. But neither they nor the others escaped the eagle eye of Pimko, who started taking notes.

'He's taking notes!' boys muttered all round me. 'He's spying on us and writing everything down!'

Pimko thereupon caused the sheet of paper on which he had been writing to flutter towards them in such a discreet and unobtrusive manner that it seemed to have been blown by the wind. On it he had written: 'On the basis of my observations made at X School during the long break I am able to state that the boys are absolutely innocent—of that I am profoundly convinced. It is demonstrated by their appearance, their innocent chatter, and, finally, their attractive and innocent little backsides. Signed, Pimko, Warsaw, 29th October, 193 . . .'

This put the whole ant-heap in a ferment. 'What! We boys innocent? We who knew everything when we were ten?' There were roars of laughter all round, suppressed, violent, yet secret laughter. What an old fool! What a naïve old fool! But I suddenly realized that the laughter was lasting too long, that it was growing angrier as it grew more violent, that the anger was directed at the laughers themselves, and that the angrier they grew the more hollow and artificial it was. What was happening? Why didn't they stop laughing? It was only later that I understood what sort of poison the diabolical, Machiavellian Pimko had fed them with. For the truth of the matter was that these boys shut up in school away from life were innocent. They were innocent though they were not. They were innocent in their determination not to be. They were innocent when they held a woman in their arms, when they fought, recited poetry, or played billiards. They were innocent when they ate and when they slept. They were innocent when they were innocent. Even when they swore, seduced, tortured, drew blood—all things they did to avoid being innocent—they always had innocence hanging over their heads.

That was why their laughter grew and grew; it was like being on the rack. Some of the boys started using the filthiest language, the language of drunken cabbies. Quickly, feverishly, quietly, they started mouthing oaths and obscenities, some of which they illustrated with chalk on the walls; and the pure air of autumn was filled with language even more appalling than that which had greeted me on my arrival. I thought I must be dreaming, for it is only in a dream that you find yourself in situations more stupid than anything you could imagine awake. I tried to restrain them.

'Why do you say c——?' I asked one of them frantically. 'Why do you use that word?'

'Shut up, you fool!' the brute replied, hitting me. 'It's a whale of a word! Say it! Say it yourself!' he whispered, and stamped on my toes. 'Say it at once! Don't you see that it's our only defence against backside? Don't you see that the inspector's behind the oak-tree, and that he intends to fit us out with little backsides? If you don't start straight away saying all the bad words you know, I'll land you one! Come on! Say them, and we'll say them too! Come on, he wants to give us little backsides!'

This crude individual (known to his intimates as Mientus) thereupon made his way furtively over to the oak-tree and wrote the four-lettered word on it, where neither Pimko nor the mothers could see. This exploit was greeted with a horrible, smug burst of laughter. When they heard it the mothers on the other side of the fence and Pimko behind the tree laughed too— they were delighted that their boys were having such a good time; and the gay laughter of the grown-ups and the sly laughter of the boys, delighted at this successful *coup*, clashed in the quiet autumn air, among the leaves falling from the trees, while the old school porter went on with his sweeping and the sun shone palely and the lawn turned yellow. But Pimko behind his tree, and all these louts convulsed with laughter, and, indeed, the whole situation, were suddenly so terrifyingly naïve that I found myself, with all my unexpected protests, being sucked into the general puerility, and I did not know to whose aid to go to—my own, my comrades', or Pimko's. I went over to the tree and whispered:

'Professor!'

'What is it?' Pimko replied, also in a whisper.

'Don't stay there, professor! They've written a bad word on the other side of the tree, and that's what they're laughing at. Don't stay there, professor!'

While talking this rubbish I felt myself to be the very high priest of idiocy. I was startled at what I found myself doing— muttering from behind the back of my hand to Pimko standing behind the tree in the school playground.

'What did you say?' the professor asked from behind his tree. 'What did they write?'

There was the sound of a motor-horn in the distance.

'A bad word!' I said. 'A bad word! Come out from there!'

'Where did they write it?'

'On the other side of the tree! Come out from there, professor! That's enough! Don't let them make a fool of you! Sir, you tried to make them out to be naïve and innocent, and they've written a four-lettered word.... Don't go on provoking them, professor, it's gone far enough. I can't go on talking into the air like this, professor, I shall go mad! Come out from there, please! I can't stand it any longer!'

While I said this summer declined slowly into autumn and the leaves fell silently.

'What's that?' the professor exclaimed. 'What's that? You expect me to doubt the youthful purity of the youthful generation? Never! In all matters of life and pedagogy I am an old fox.'

He came out from behind the tree, and the boys, seeing him standing there in the flesh, let out a yell.

'My dear young people,' he said after they had calmed down a little. 'I am not ignorant of the fact that among yourselves you use very coarse, indecent, expressions. Don't imagine for a moment that I don't know what goes on. But you have no cause for anxiety. No excess, however lamentable in itself, will ever affect my profound belief that at bottom you are innocent and pure, and that is what you are to me. Your old friend will always believe you to be pure and innocent, and he will always have faith in your decency, your purity, your innocence; and, as for bad words, I know that you use them innocently, without understanding, just for effect—no doubt one of you picked them up from his nurse. That's quite all right, there's no harm in it at all, it's far more innocent than you think!'

He sneezed, blew his nose and, feeling very pleased with himself, went off in the direction of the headmaster's study to talk about me to Mr Piorkowski. Meanwhile the mothers and aunts on the other side of the fence flung themselves into each other's arms and exclaimed with delight:

'What wonderful ideas the professor has! What a wonderful faith in innocence!'

Among the boys, however, Pimko's speech caused consternation. Silently they watched him walk away; and it was not until he was out of sight that the storm broke.

'Did you hear that?' Mientus exclaimed. 'Did you hear that? We're innocent! Innocent! He thinks we're innocent! Whatever we do, we're innocent! Innocent!'

The word was a thorn in his side; it paralysed, tortured, killed him, imposing naïveté and innocence upon him. At this point a boy named Pylaszczkiewicz, but known to his intimates as Siphon, seemed to succumb to what had become the prevailing atmosphere of naïveté; he said to himself, but in a voice which resounded in the pure and limpid air as clearly as a cow-bell:

'Innocent? Why not?'

And he stood there plunged in thought. Why not, indeed, be innocent? He could not have asked a more sensible question. For who is more mature, he who flees from sin, or he who seeks it out? But the thought, though rational and mature, sounded innocent, and Siphon realized this himself, because he flushed.

He tried to slip away, but Mientus had heard what he said, and was not going to allow it to pass.

'What?' he said. 'You admit you're innocent?'

Mientus was so startled by the innocence of what he had just said that he stepped back. But now Siphon was upset too, and was not prepared to allow this remark to pass either.

'Admit it?' he said. 'Why shouldn't I admit it? I'm not a child!'

Mientus laughed sneeringly in the diaphanous air.

'Did you hear him?' he jeered. 'Siphon's innocent! Wah! Wah! Siphon the innocent!'

'*Siphonus innocentus!*' boys started calling out. 'Has our worthy Siphon no knowledge of women?'

Others took up the chorus of this green raillery, and the world became disgusting again. The growing hubbub infuriated Siphon. He glared all round.

'And even if I were innocent, what of it?' he exclaimed. 'What's it got to do with you?'

'So it's true, then!' they jeered back at him. 'So it's true!'

And the unhappy lads did not realize that the further they went, the more deeply they engulfed themselves in innocence.

'Would you believe it?' they sneered. 'He doesn't even know the facts of life!'

They started jeering and booing again.

'And even if I didn't, what business is it of yours?' Siphon burst out. 'What business is it of yours, I should like to know?'

There was such a strange, icy tone in his voice that for a moment they were intimidated, and silence prevailed. Then voices started calling out:

'Come off it, Siphon! So it's true that you don't know, is it?'

And they stepped back a pace. Siphon would obviously have liked to have stepped back too, but could not. Then Mientus called out:

'Of course it's true! Look at him! It's obvious!'

And he spat. Bobek called out:

'But that's disgraceful, he ought to be ashamed of himself. I'll tell you everything, Siphon, you really ought to know!'

Siphon: 'But I don't want to!'

Hopek: 'You don't want to?'

Siphon: 'I don't want to, because I don't see the necessity.'

Hopek: 'You don't want to? You don't want to? But it isn't just a matter of what you want or don't want, it's a matter that concerns all of us. It's not a situation we can be expected to tolerate. If we did, how could we ever look girls in the face again?'

'So that's what's getting you, is it?' Siphon burst out angrily. 'Girls! Girls! You want to cut a dash with the girls! I don't give a fig for your girls! So you want to be boys with the girls!'

He had realized that he could no longer retreat, and, moreover, he no longer wanted to.

'Girls!' he exclaimed. 'Girls! And why not decent girls? Why not adolescents and decent, respectable girls? So you want to be boys with the girls! Well, I like being an adolescent for decent girls. Why should I be ashamed of using words which are decent and honourable? Anyway, that's how it is, I want to be an adolescent for decent young women.'

He stopped. But what he said was in reality so true, sensible, and convincing that many of his listeners were left perplexed.

'Doesn't he speak well?' some of them said, and others remarked:

'He's quite right, purity is better than girls!'

'One ought to have some ideals, after all!' another pointed out, and someone else remarked:

'If he wants to be an adolescent, let him!'

'Adolescents!' Siphon announced. 'Up the adolescents! Let us found a society to preserve the purity of youth and oppose everything that soils it! Let us swear never to be ashamed of beauty, purity and nobility! Forward!'

And before anyone could stop him he raised his hand and swore a solemn oath, with a grave, inspired expression on his face. Several juveniles, surprised by his gesture, raised their hand and followed suit. Mientus rushed angrily at Siphon in the pure and transparent air; Siphon's blood was up too, but fortunately they were separated in time.

'Why don't you fellows kick his arse?' said Mientus, struggling with those who were restraining him. 'Have you no blood in your veins? Have you no ambition? Only a good kick in the arse can save you! Just let me get at him!'

He was in an ungovernable rage. Sweating and pale, I looked at him. I had had the shadow of a hope that with Pimko out of the way I might somehow manage to recover my adult personality and explain myself in everybody's eyes. But what chance was there of this while innocence and naïveté were increasing and multiplying in the fresh and limpid air? The backside was split between Boy and Adolescent. The world was being shattered and re-formed on the basis of Boy and Adolescent. I stepped back.

The tension increased. Boys, red-faced and furious, set on one another. Siphon stood motionless, with his arms crossed, while Mientus shook his fists. The mothers and aunts on the other side of the wall were in a highly exalted state too, though they did not have too clear an idea why. But most of the boys remained undecided. They went on stuffing themselves with bread and butter, reciting remorselessly:

'Can the *dignissime* Mientus be a *sensualus luxurius*? Can Siphon be an *idealistus*? Let us work hard, or we shall fail in our exams!'

Others, who did not wish to compromise themselves, talked sport or politics, or pretended to be interested in a game of football. But every now and then one or other, unable to resist the fascination of the heated and piquant controversy, would break away, start listening to it; he would ponder, blush, and join either Mientus's or Siphon's party. Meanwhile the usher sat drowsily on his bench, feasting himself from a distance on the spectacle of youthful naïveté.

'Ah! the pretty little backsides, the innocent little backsides!' he muttered.

In the end only one boy failed to be dragged into the super-heated ideological conflict. He stood aloof, quietly sunning himself, wearing a shirt and white flannel trousers, with a gold chain round his left wrist.

'Kopeida, come over here!'

Everyone seemed to want him, but he took no notice of anybody. He raised one leg and dangled it in the diaphanous air.

Meanwhile Mientus was struggling in the net of his own words.

'But don't you realize that we shall be an object of contempt to every working-class lad, every hall-porter's son and apprentice and agricultural labourer of the same age as ourselves? We must defend the Boy against the Adolescent!' he declared with passion.

'We're not interested in what apprentices, hall-porters' sons and street boys think of us, they've got no education,' replied Gabek, who was one of Siphon's friends.

Mientus went over to Siphon and spoke to him haltingly.

'Siphon, this has gone far enough,' he said. 'If you withdraw what you said, I'll withdraw what I said. That's fair, isn't it?

Let's drop it! I'm ready to withdraw everything I said on condition that you withdraw everything you said . . . and agree to be told everything. It's not a matter that concerns you only, after all.'

Pylaszczkiewicz gave him a look that was full of light, dignity, and inner strength. After looking at him in this fashion, it was impossible to reply other than in vigorous fashion. He stepped back.

'There can be no compromising with ideals,' he announced.

At this Mientus dashed at him, with clenched fists, shouting: 'Come on! Come on! Death to the Adolescent!'

'Adolescents, rally round me!' cried Pylaszczkiewicz in a penetrating voice. 'Rally round me, rally to the defence of your purity!'

This appeal caused many to feel the Adolescent in themselves rising against the Boy. They formed a thick barrier round Siphon and faced up to the partisans of Mientus. The first blows were exchanged. Siphon leapt on a stone and shouted encouragement to his supporters, but the Mientus party began to gain the upper hand, and Siphon's men beat a disorderly retreat. How dreadful! The Adolescent seemed lost. But Siphon, faced with inevitable defeat, gathered his last strength and struck up the innocent, adolescent song:

> *Youth! Lift the world*
> *On your shoulders . . .*

This made his supporters shudder. Was this a song to sing in this situation? Surely it would have been better not to sing that song. But they could not let Siphon go on singing by himself, so they started joining in, and the song grew, spread, multiplied, became enormous, and took wing. . . . They sang, standing still, their eyes, like those of Siphon, fixed on a distant star; they sang in their assailants' teeth. The latters' arms dropped helplessly to their sides; there seemed no way of getting at the singers, of making any sort of impact on them. Meanwhile the singers went on singing, with a star right in front of their noses, and with gathering strength and piety. Members of the Mientus gang started grumbling, coughing, or muttering, making awkward or idle gestures, and moving away. In the end Mientus had no alternative but to cough and move away himself.

A flight of pigeons shone in the sunlit autumn air, lingered over the roof, came to rest on the oak tree, and flew away. Mientus, who could not stand Siphon's triumphant song, went to the opposite end of the playground, accompanied by Bobek and Hopek. After a time he regained sufficient self-control to be able to speak. He looked down at the ground, and was embarrassed.

'Well, what do we do now?' he said.

'Just the same as we did before,' replied Bobek. 'There's nothing else for it. We go on using the same bad words more vigorously than ever. Our only weapon is the four-lettered word....'

'Go on using that?' Mientus exclaimed. 'It's enough to make you sick, repeating the same thing—playing the same old tune, just because the other fellow goes on playing his!'

He was shaken. He stretched his hands, fell back a few paces, and looked all round. The sky, suspended in the heights, was light, fresh, pale, and sarcastic; the tree, the sturdy oak in the middle of the playground, had turned its back, and the old porter near the gate smiled under his moustache and went away.

'A stable-lad,' Mientus muttered. 'A stable-lad. Suppose a stable-lad overheard the rot we talk!'

And suddenly, terrified by his own idea, he made off; in the diaphanous air of autumn he took flight. His friends stopped him.

'Mientus, what's come over you?' they asked him in the diaphanous air. 'You're the leader! What will become of us without you?'

Mientus, caught and held by all these hands, lowered his head and said bitterly:

'Well, what?'

Bobek and Hopek, shaken, said nothing. Bobek, who was in a state of extreme agitation, picked up a bit of wire, mechanically poked it through a hole in the fence, and injured a mother in the eye. He promptly withdrew the bit of wire, and the woman screamed on the other side of the fence. Finally Hopek, not without diffidence, said:

'Well, what are we to do, Mientus?'

Mientus pulled himself together. 'There's no alternative,' he replied. 'We must fight. Fight to the last round!'

'Bravo!' they exclaimed. 'Bravo! Mientus, that's how we like you!'

But their leader made a gesture of discouragement.

'Oh, you and your shouting!' he said. 'All right. If we have to fight, we shall fight. Fight? But we can't fight. Supposing we did beat him up, what should we gain by it? We should only make a martyr of him, a martyr to innocence, and he'd give us martyred innocence by the ton. Swearing, filth, dirt, are useless, useless I tell you, they're nothing but grist to his mill, milk for his adolescence, and that's what he counts on, you take it from me. But luckily for us,' . . . and strange inflexions of anger crept into his voice . . . 'luckily for us, there's something much more effective we can do, we can rid him for ever of his wish to sing.'

'How?' they asked, not unhopefully.

'Like this,' he said in a peremptory tone. 'If Siphon persists in refusing to be told, we'll force him to hear. We'll tie him up. Fortunately we can still get at him through his ears. We'll tie him up, and we'll enlighten him so thoroughly that afterwards even his mother won't recognize him. We'll do him once and for all, the big baby. But mum's the word. Get some rope.'

I was watching these preparations breathlessly and with beating heart when Pimko appeared at the door and called me to take me in to Piorkowski, the head. The pigeons appeared again. With a flutter of wings they came to rest on the fence behind which all the mothers were standing. As we walked down the long school corridor I frantically searched for words with which to explain myself, without finding them, however, for Pimko spat into every spittoon we passed on the way, and ordered me to do the same. The fact that I was spitting made me unable to protest, and it was thus that we arrived at the headmaster's study.

Piorkowski, a giant of a man, received us seated powerfully and transcendentally on his backside. He pinched my cheek with paternal kindness, stroked my chin, and created a sympathetic impression. Instead of protesting I made a slight bow, and he said to Pimko over my head:

'Pretty little backside, pretty little backside! There's no doubt about it, you can rest assured that the grown-ups whom we artificially reduce to childhood offer an even more productive field for our efforts than children in the natural state. No pupils, no school, and with no school where should we schoolmasters be? I count on you not to forget me in future, for my establishment deserves it, our methods of turning out backsides are unsurpassed, and our teaching body is selected for that purpose with the greatest care. Would you like to see the teaching body?'

'With the greatest of pleasure,' Pimko replied. 'It is well known that nothing has a greater effect on the mind than the body.'

Piorkowski half opened the door of the next room, and the two pedagogues discreetly looked inside; I did the same, and was terrified by what I saw. The staff were seated round a table, having tea. I have never set eyes on such a pathetic collection of little old men. They were all eating noisily. The first was chewing his food, the second bolting it, the third masticating, the fourth munching, the fifth gulping it down, and the sixth looked like a moron.

'There's no doubt about it, professor,' the headmaster said with pride. 'The body is well chosen. Not one of them is agreeable, pleasant, normal, or human, they are no more than pedagogic bodies, as you see. If I am ever faced with the necessity of engaging a new assistant, I take the most scrupulous care to ensure that he is perfectly and completely boring, sterile, docile and abstracted.'

'All the same, the French mistress looks pretty wide awake,' Pimko remarked.

'What an idea! I've never managed to talk to her for a minute without yawning at least twice.'

'Oh, that's different, then. I assume nevertheless that they are all fully experienced people, well aware of their pedagogic mission?'

'They are the best brains in the capital,' the headmaster replied. 'Not one of them has an idea of his own in his head. If such a thing ever happened, I should make it my business immediately to throw out either the originator of the idea or the idea itself. All the members of my staff are perfect pupils, and they teach nothing that they have not been taught. Not a single one has an idea of his own in his head.'

'Backsidikins!' said Pimko. 'I see that I shall be leaving my Johnnie in good hands. Only real teachers are capable of instilling into their pupils that delightful immaturity, that pleasing and ineffectual apathy towards life that will have to prevail, if we, God's own pedagogues, are to have a suitably wide field of action. Only with well-trained staff shall we succeed in reducing everyone to a state of childhood.'

'Sh!' said Piorkowski, taking him by the sleeve. 'Sh! You are perfectly right, but be careful, it's not a thing we want over-heard.'

At that moment one body turned towards another body, and said:

'Well, and how are you?'

'How am I?' the second body replied. 'Prices are going up.'

'Going up?' said the first. 'I thought they were going down.'

'Going down?' said the other peevishly. 'My impression is that they are going up.'

'Biscuits are going up,' the first body grumbled, and wrapped the rest of his biscuits in his pocket-handkerchief.

'I keep them on short commons,' said Piorkowski, 'because that is the only way of making them anaemic enough. As you know, there's nothing like anaemia for bringing out the spots and pimples and snuffles of the awkward age.'

Suddenly the English teacher noticed the headmaster at the door, accompanied by a learned and impressive-looking stranger. He gulped his tea down the wrong way, and exclaimed:

'The inspector!'

At this all the bodies rose and huddled tremblingly together like partridges; and the headmaster closed the door in order not to startle them further. Pimko kissed me on the brow and said solemnly:

'Well, Johnnie, run along to the classroom, lessons are about to begin. Meanwhile I'll find you lodgings, and I'll come back and fetch you after school.'

I tried to answer, but the sight of the implacable master suddenly so overmastered me that I was unable to utter a word. I bowed slightly, and made for the classroom, my head humming with unspoken protests. The classroom was humming too. The boys were sitting at their desks and yelling, as if they were about to be silenced for ever.

In this hubbub it was impossible to say exactly when the master appeared on his dais. He was the sad, anaemic body who had maintained in the staff-room that biscuits were going down. He took his seat, opened his book, brushed the crumbs from his waistcoat, closed his mouth, pulled down his cuffs to prevent his sleeves from wearing at the elbows, repressed something in himself, and crossed his legs. Then he sighed, and tried to say something. The din redoubled; everyone yelled, with the possible exception of Siphon, who adopted a positive attitude. The master looked at his class, pursed his lips, opened them, and then closed them again. The boys went on yelling. The master frowned and made a gesture of annoyance, adjusted his sleeves, drummed on his desk, thought about something a long, long way away, took out his watch, put it on the desk, sighed, again suppressed something in himself or swallowed something, and devoted a long moment to collecting his energy. Finally he banged the top of his desk with his book and called out:

'That'll do! Silence! The lesson is about to begin!'

At this the whole class like one man (again with the exception of Siphon) expressed the imperious necessity of immediately leaving the room.

The master, who was known to his pupils as Droopy because of his worn and frail appearance, smiled bitterly.

'That'll do!' he said in the acid tone that came naturally to him. 'So you would like to go to the lavatory! So would the soul like to go to paradise, wouldn't it? And why can't I leave the room? Sit down, all of you! Nobody may leave the room!'

No fewer than seven boys thereupon produced certificates testifying to various complaints which had prevented them from doing their homework. Four others complained of violent headache, another had a rash, and yet another convulsions.

'Gracious heavens!' Droopy exclaimed. 'Why doesn't anyone give me a certificate explaining that through no fault of my own it is impossible for me to do my work? Why can't I have convulsions? What I want you to tell me is why I should have to come here every day, except Sundays and public holidays, instead of having convulsions. Quiet! The certificates are faked, and you are nothing but a lot of malingerers. Sit down, I know you!'

Three boys went up to his desk and started telling him a good story about Jews and birds, but he stopped his ears.

'No, no!' he groaned, 'spare me, I mustn't listen to you, spare me, we must get on with the lesson. Supposing the headmaster walked in!'

At this he started trembling, looked towards the door, and paled with fright.

'And supposing the inspector caught us? I warn you, gentlemen, that the inspector is paying a visit to the school at this very moment. It is a fact. I warn you. Enough of this folly, let us be ready in case the inspector walks in. Let me see. Which of you know his lessons best? Tell me, so that I may shine by letting him shine. . . . Well? Doesn't anybody know anything? You'll be the ruin of me! Come, come, somebody must know a little about something, speak up and tell me frankly. Ah! Pylaszczkiewicz! Pylaszczkiewicz, speak up! Thank you, Pylaszczkiewicz,

I've always thought you a boy I could rely on. But what are you good at, Pylaszczkiewicz? Which of our glorious poets do you know best?'

Siphon rose and replied:

'Excuse me, sir! If you ask me in front of the inspector, I shall answer, but in the meantime I cannot tell you what I know best, because that would mean betraying myself and my principles.'

'Very well, then,' said the master. 'Pylaszczkiewicz's feelings in the matter are most praiseworthy, and I was only joking. Principles above everything, of course! Let me see, then,' he went on severely, looking at the syllabus, 'what are we in for today? Oh, yes, explain and demonstrate why the great poet Slowacki awakens our love, admiration, and ecstasy. Well, then, gentlemen, first I shall say my piece and then you shall say yours. Quiet!' he called out, and all the boys bent over their desks, holding their heads in their hands, while Droopy surreptitiously opened his text-book, shut his mouth, sighed, suppressed something in himself, and began:

'Hm! Hm! Hm! Well, then, why does Slowacki arouse our admiration, love and ecstasy? Why do we weep with the poet when we read that angelic poem *In Switzerland*? Why does exaltation swell our breasts when we listen to the superb and heroic stanzas of *The Spirit King*? Why is there no escaping the magic and seduction of the *Balladina*? Why do the sorrows of *Lilla Weneda* rend our hearts? Hm! Why? Because, gentlemen, Slowacki was a great poet. Walkiewicz, tell me why! Tell me, Walkiewicz. Why the enchantment, the love, the tears, the exaltation, the magic? Why are our hearts rent? Tell me, Walkiewicz!'

It was like listening to another, but lesser, Pimko, a Pimko of narrower horizons.

'Because he was a great poet, sir,' said Walkiewicz.

The boys were carving up the desk-tops with their pen-knives and screwing up little bails of paper and putting them in the ink-wells. The master sighed, choked, looked at his watch, and continued as follows:

'He was a great poet, don't forget that he was a great poet. Why do we feel love, admiration, delight? Because he was a great poet, a great poet. You ignorant dunderheads, get this firmly fixed in your heads and repeat after me: Julius Slowacki was a great poet, a great poet, we love Julius Slowacki, and his poems delight us because he was a great poet—and because his verses are of an immortal beauty which arouses our deepest admiration.'

This level of exposition got on one boy's nerves and he had an acute attack of the fidgets. When he could stand it no longer he burst out:

'But if he has no effect on me whatever, if he simply doesn't interest me, if I can't read two verses of his without falling asleep . . . Heaven help me, sir, but how am I to be sent into transports of delight if I am not sent into transports of delight?'

His eyes were nearly popping out of his head. He sat down again, as if overwhelmed by what he had said. His naïve confession took the master's breath away.

'For heaven's sake hold your tongue, Kotecki,' he said. 'Kotecki, you're trying to ruin me. No marks for Kotecki. He doesn't realize what he is saying.'

Kotecki: 'But I don't understand, sir. I don't understand how I can be sent into transports of delight if I am not sent into transports of delight.'

The master: 'But Kotecki, how can you not be sent into transports of delight if I have already explained to you a thousand times that you are sent into transports of delight?'

Kotecki: 'You have explained it, sir, but I am not sent into transports of delight.'

The master: 'In that case it's a personal peculiarity. Kotecki seems not to be intelligent. Other people are sent into transports of delight.'

Kotecki: 'No! No! On my word of honour they're not, sir! Nobody can be sent into transports of delight by Slowacki's poetry, because nobody reads him, except at school, when they're forced to.'

The master: 'Kotecki, for heaven's sake sit down and keep quiet. The explanation is that only a limited number of intelligent and cultivated people are capable of appreciating him.'

Kotecki: 'Nothing of the sort, sir, even cultivated people don't read him. Nobody reads him, sir, nobody at all!'

The master: 'Kotecki, I have a wife and a young child. At least have pity on the child, Kotecki. Kotecki, it is a well-known and established fact that great poetry necessarily arouses our admiration. Now, Julius Slowacki was a great poet. . . . It may be that Slowacki doesn't move you, my dear Kotecki, but don't tell me, don't tell me that you're not profoundly moved by Mickiewicz, Byron, Pushkin, Shelley, Goethe . . .'

Kotecki: 'He doesn't move anyone, everyone thinks him ridiculous. No one can read more than two verses of him. Heavens, I can't!'

The master: 'Come, come, Kotecki, but that's impossible, absurd. Great poetry, being beautiful, profound, inspired, and great, is bound to move us to the very depths of our souls.'

Kotecki: 'I can't read him. Nobody can.'

The master's brow was wet with perspiration. In an attempt to move Kotecki he produced from his wallet some photographs of his wife and child, but Kotecki's relentless, piercing repetition of *I can't, I can't*, grew, multiplied, and became infectious. It started as a murmur here and there; and it turned out that nearly all of us suffered from the same disability as Kotecki, and the master found himself threatened with it from all sides. He was in a terrible fix; at any moment he might find himself encompassed by a universal disability, the unrestrained proclamation of which might reach the ears of the headmaster and the inspector; at any moment the whole educational edifice might come tumbling about his ears, engulfing his child in the wreckage; and Kotecki obstinately persisted with his *I can't, I can't*. Poor Droopy felt the general inability and helplessness spreading to himself.

'Pylaszczkiewicz!' he exclaimed: 'Pylaszczkiewicz, will you please show me, and Kotecki, and the rest of us, the beauties of

46

a selected passage. Be quick, for delay is dangerous. We must be able to be moved, because otherwise my child is done for.'

Pylaszczkiewicz rose and promptly started declaiming a glorious passage from a great poem, the glorious work of one of the greatest poets.

And Siphon went on declaiming. He had been left totally unaffected by the sudden general helplessness and inability. There was no question of *can't* for him. On the contrary, because of his pure and vigorous principles, he always *could*; and this was due less to his native talents than to the strength of his principles. So he declaimed, with emotion in his voice, meticulous elocution, spiritual fervour, and emphasis. He put into it all the beauty of which he was capable, and the beauty of his recitation multiplied by the beauty of the poem and the greatness of genius and the majesty of art was imperceptibly transformed into a monument of all beauty and all greatness. Moreover, he recited with piety and mystery, inspiration and strength; and he sang the poet's sublime song as the poet's sublime song ought to be sung. Oh, what beauty, what greatness, what genius, what poetry! Fly, wall, finger-nails, roof, blackboard, windows, the threat of impotence were spirited away, wife and child were out of danger, everyone started proclaiming that of course he was fully able to appreciate great poetry, and the only thing that everyone now wanted was that it should stop. At that moment I noticed that my neighbour was smearing my hands with ink —his own were completely smeared with it, and his reason for smearing mine was that his toes were covered by his shoes and socks, and other people's hands are, after all, more or less the same as one's own, so why not? What else was there to do? What could one do with one's legs? Move them; and then what? After a quarter of an hour of this even Kotecki groaned that he had had enough, confessed his appreciation and admiration, apologized, and admitted that he *could*.

'So you see, Kotecki, there's nothing like school for inculcating a love of art. Which of us would have been capable of admiring the great geniuses if the knowledge that they were great geniuses had not been hammered into our heads at school?'

The audience, however, was presenting some very queer symptoms. Everyone's back was bent beneath the weight of the poet, the bard, the master, his child, and the general torpor. The bare partition walls and the bare schoolroom desks with their ink-wells offered not a glimmer of distraction; through the window a small area of wall was visible on which someone had written the simple words: 'He's gone.' So there was nothing for it but to busy oneself either with the pedagogic body or one's own body, and that was why those who did not occupy themselves by counting Droopy's hairs or trying to plumb the mystery of his long nails, tried such things as counting their own hair or unscrewing their necks. Bobek was twisting about, Hopek was grumbling to himself—trying painfully to disarticulate himself, so to speak—some seemed completely immersed in themselves, others had given in to the fatal device of talking to themselves, others were tearing off their buttons and ruining their clothes —in other words, all round there was arising a jungle of absurd reflexes, a desert of senseless actions. The only one to flourish in the midst of this general aridity was Siphon, who was more and more firmly rooted in his principles. The master, who kept remembering his wife and child, endlessly repeated: 'Poet, bard, messianic spirit, the Christ of the nations, the torch of beauty, sacrifice and redemption, hero and symbol.'

The words came in through ears and tormented minds, while faces twitched convulsively, and ceased to be human; fatigued, battered, exhausted, reduced to nullity, they were ready to assume almost any shape—what an exercise for the imagination! And reality, battered and exhausted too, became a world of dreams—oh! escape into dream. . . .

I realized that I must get out of this. Pimko, Droopy, the poetry, school and my school-fellows, in short all my adventures of the morning whirled in my head like a roulette wheel, and the number that came up was that I must escape. How or where I had not the slightest idea, but it was clear that I must get out of this if I were not to be ground to pieces in the fantastic adventures that were befalling me. But instead of running away I put my finger in my shoe, which obviously made it impossible to run away, because you cannot run with one finger at floor-level. It was imperative to escape from Droopy, the boredom, the pretence, the disgust, but, having in my head the poet inserted into it by Droopy and in my shoe the moving finger inserted by myself, I could not run away, and this inability was even more overpowering than that which had affected Kotecki.

In theory nothing could have been easier. All that was needed was to walk out and never come back. Pimko would not have sent for the police, his pedagogic tentacles did not extend as far as that. But I could not make up my mind. Running away presupposes the will to run away, and where are you to get the will from if you are moving your toes with your finger and have lost your face in a grimace of disgust? It was only then that I realized why not one of the boys at the school was able to run away; it was because their faces and their whole personality eliminated the slightest possibility of flight; all of them were the slaves of the faces they were making and, though they should have run away, they did not, because they had ceased to be what they ought to have been. Running away involved more than just running away from the school; it also involved running away from themselves. Oh! to escape, to shake off the callow stripling into which Pimko had turned me, to return to my former adult self! But how can one escape from what one is, where is the leverage to come from? Our shape penetrates and confines us, as much from without as from within. If reality had established its rights for only one single moment, the incredible absurdity of my position would (I felt sure) have been so obvious that everyone would have exclaimed: What on earth is that grown-up doing here? But, against the general extravagance, the extravagance of my own position disappeared. Oh, if I could have seen just one undistorted face to enable me to feel the distortion of my own! But alas! around me were nothing but battered, laundered and ironed faces which reflected my own as in a distorting mirror

49

—and I was held captive by this facial mirage. Is it dream or is it reality? I said to myself. Suddenly my eyes fell on Kopeida, the boy in flannel trousers, who had smiled aloofly in the playground when the others had talked about girls.

He was sitting at his ease, as indifferent to the schoolmaster as he had been to the row between Mientus and Siphon. His hands were in his pockets, and he looked healthy, clean, normal, pleasant, and self-possessed. He was sitting there aloof from his surroundings, with his legs crossed, and he looked at his legs as if so doing enabled him to escape from school.

Was I dreaming or was this reality? How could this be possible? I said to myself. Neither *boy* nor *adolescent*, but a perfectly ordinary, normal boy at last? Perhaps with his aid I might be able to overcome my impotence.

★ 3 ★

The Duel

THE master started looking more and more often at his watch; and the boys started looking at their watches more and more often too. At last the bell rang, bringing release. Droopy stopped short in the middle of a sentence and vanished, and his audience awoke and let loose a terrible roar. Only Siphon remained in silent concentration, completely absorbed in himself.

During the lesson the problem of innocence had been stifled by the monotony of the poet, but with Droopy's disappearance it flared up again; and from the aberrations of the official education system the boys plunged headlong into the turbid waters of Boyhood and Adolescence; and reality gradually faded into a dream-world—oh, escape into dream!

And blood once more mounted to cheeks in the heavy and stifling air, for the clash of opinions became colossal; doctrines, views, and systems sallied forth to battle; and theories clashed over the boys' fevered heads. Communism. Fascism. Catholic Youth Movement. Patriotic Youth Movement. Youth Morality Movement. Boy Scouts. Civic Youth Movement. Heroic Youth Movement. More and more far-fetched words and phrases were launched into the fray. It was obvious that each political party stuffed these boys' heads with a different idea of boyhood, that every thinker stuffed them with his own particular tastes and ideals, and that over and above all that their heads were stuffed with films, popular novels, and newspapers. Hence the furious clash of Adolescent, Young Man, Boy, Young Communist, Young Athlete, High-Minded Churchgoer, Juvenile Delinquent, Young Aesthete, Young Philosopher, Young Sceptic, and Young Cynic of every description, who fell upon each other, insulted and expressed bitter contempt for each other, while groans rose from the wounded lying on the ground, and cries were exchanged of: 'How naïve you are!' 'No, how naïve *you* are!' For all the various ideals without exception, far from being made to their protagonists' measure, sat upon them incredibly awkwardly and gauchely, like ill-fitting clothes. Boys flung them into the fray and then retreated, afraid of what they had done, as if they had shot pellets from a catapult which, once launched, were irrecoverable.

Imprisoned as they were in falsehood, having lost all contact with life and reality, having been battered by all the ideologies and all the schools, their concert was a concert of discord, and all they said was foolish. Their pathos was false, their lyricism phoney, their emotionalism hair-raising, their sentimentalism ghastly, their irony and leg-pulling disastrous, their flights of fancy pretentious and their descents to earth disgusting. And that was the way the world was; the world was exactly like this. They were treated artificially, so how could they be anything but artificial? And, being artificial, how could they be expected to express themselves in other than degrading fashion? That was why impotence floated in the oppressive air and reality gradually gave way to a dream-world, and only Kopeida did not allow himself to be carried away by anything, but kept on tearing up bits of paper and gazing at his legs. . . .

Meanwhile Mientus and Bobek had gone into a huddle, and were preparing ropes and things; Bobek even took off his braces.

A shudder went down my spine. If Mientus was going to carry out his plan of violating Siphon's innocence by way of his ears, reality would indeed be such a nightmare and the world so utterly grotesque that I should no longer be able even to dream of escaping from it. I must prevent it at all costs. But how could I face them single-handed, and with my big toe in my shoe into the bargain? No, I could not do it. Oh, for a single, undistorted face! I went over to Kopeida, who was standing by the window, wearing his flannel trousers, looking out at the playground and quietly whistling between his teeth. He at least seemed not to be harbouring any ideal. How was I to begin?

'They want to violate Siphon,' I said simply. 'We've got to stop them. If they do it, the place will become impossible!'

What would Kopeida say? I waited with trepidation. But, instead of replying, he jumped out of the window on to his two feet, and went on quietly whistling between his teeth.

What did this mean? I was left utterly bewildered. Why had he jumped out of the window instead of answering? Why had he avoided me like this? And why were his legs in the foreground? Why were his legs forelegs? I passed my hand across my brow. Forelegs? Was I dreaming, or was this reality? But there was no time to think, because Mientus came up to me. I realized that he had overheard what I said to Kopeida.

'What are you sticking your nose into our affairs for?' he said. 'Who told you to go sneaking about us to Kopeida? It's no business of his. You'd better not talk to him about me again!'

I stepped back. He let out some disgusting oaths.

'Mientus, you mustn't do that to Siphon,' I muttered.

'Why not?'

'Because you mustn't.'

Hardly had I finished the sentence than he burst out again.

'You know what you can do with your Siphon,' he said. 'You can —— him!'

'You mustn't, Mientus, you mustn't,' I implored him. 'Tell me, Mientus, have you imagined Siphon lying tied up on the ground, and you forcibly violating his innocence through his ears? Have you imagined yourself actua'ly doing that, Mientus?'

He twisted his face in an even more repulsive manner.

'I see that you're another noble adolescent,' he sneered. 'You've been influenced by Siphon, haven't you? Do you know what I'll do with your adolescent? I'll —— him!'

And he kicked my shin.

I sought for words, but once more could not find them.

'Stop it, Mientus,' I said. 'Stop turning yourself into . . . into . . . Siphon's innocence is no reason for you to be indecent.'

He looked at me.

'What do you want of me?' he said.

'I want you not to play the fool.'

'Not to play the fool,' he muttered. A cloud came over his eyes. 'Not to play the fool,' he repeated wistfully. 'Obviously there are boys who don't play the fool. Hall-porters' sons, apprentices, stable-lads. They sweep the streets, or work in the fields. They must laugh at Siphon and me, and all our stuff and nonsense.'

For a moment he dropped his deliberate vulgarity and triviality, plunged into a painful private meditation, and his face relaxed. But then he started, as if he had been burnt with a red-hot poker, and let out a volley of fearsome oaths.

'No, I can't allow us to be taken for a lot of innocents!' he said. 'I've got to violate Siphon's innocence through his ears.' Another volley of oaths followed. Once more he twisted his mouth, and his language was so horrible that I stepped back.

'Mientus,' I muttered mechanically and in terror. 'Let's go away from here. Let's get out of this!'

'Get out of this?'

He stopped swearing, listened, looked at me inquiringly, and became more normal. I clutched at his changed attitude like a drowning man clutching at a straw.

'Let's go,' I murmured. 'Let's drop all this and go.'

He hesitated. His face remained in suspense, hesitating. Seeing that the idea of flight was gaining ground in him, fearing that he might once more relapse into monstrosity, I searched for a way of encouraging him.

'Let's get out of this,' I said. 'We might join up with the stable-lads.'

I knew about his passion for the life of the wage-earner and thought he would fall for the stable-lad bait. I no longer cared very much what he said; all I wanted was to keep him from the horrors that made him twist his mouth. His eyes shone; and he gave me a fraternal dig in the ribs with his elbow.

'You'd like that?' he said, softly, in a friendly voice.

He laughed, a low, pure laugh. I laughed in the same way.

'Ah! to get right away from here,' he said. 'To join up with the stable-lads . . . real lads who take the horses down to the river and bathe . . .'

Then I noticed something dreadful. Something new appeared on his face—a kind of wistfulness—a special kind of beauty appropriate to an educated boy on the point of running away in order to take refuge with stable-lads. His brutality was giving way to charm. He felt on terms of trust with me, and dropped his mask; he set his lyricism free.

'Ah!' he said in a low, sing-song voice. 'Ah! to eat black bread with stable-lads, and gallop across the fields . . .'

His lips half-opened in a strange, bitter smile, his body became more supple and more agile, something like a yoke of slavery appeared on his neck and shoulders. He was now a schoolboy yearning for the freedom of the country, and he openly and unreservedly showed me his teeth. I stepped back. I was in a dreadful fix. Ought I to show him my teeth? If I did not, he was capable of letting out another volley of oaths, but if I did, the consequences might be worse. For was not this new beauty that he would offer me in these moments of confidence even more grotesque than his previous hideousness? Why had I tempted him with his stable-lads? What a thing to have done! I ended by not showing him my teeth, but I rounded my lips and whistled; and thus we stood facing each other, one showing his teeth and the other whistling or laughing silently; and the world seemed to be organizing itself on the basis of boy about to leave baring his teeth. But suddenly, from right on top of us, there was a loud, sardonic yell. A general yell. I stepped back. Siphon, Gabek, and a crowd of others were standing there holding their sides with laughter and yelling, with mocking and jeering faces.

'What is it?' said Mientus, startled out of his life.

'Yah! Yah! Yah!' jeered Gabek.

And Siphon said:

'Mientus, let me congratulate you! Now at last we know your

secret. We've caught you out! Your ideal is a stable-lad. You dream about galloping through the fields with a stable-lad. You pretend to be hard and cynical, but at bottom you're nothing but a dreamer, a sentimentalist, a stable-boy worshipper!'

'Shut your bloody mouths, you bastards!' Bobek shouted with all the vulgarity of which he was capable, but it was too late. Mientus, caught in the middle of his private dream, was not to be saved by the most fearful oaths. He went scarlet, as if he were on fire, and Siphon went on triumphantly:

'Did you see the fine faces he was making?'

At this Mientus might have been expected to let fly at Siphon, but he didn't; he might have been expected to annihilate him with some piece of super-vulgarity, but he didn't. Having been caught *flagrante delicto*, he could do neither; instead he withdrew behind a tone of cold and caustic friendliness.

'Tell me, Siphon,' he said, assuming an air of apparent casualness in order to gain time. 'So you think I make faces? Tell me, don't you make faces?'

'What, me?' said Siphon. 'No!'

'Oh? . . . Well then, I suggest that you look me straight in the eye for a bit. I suggest, if you wouldn't mind, that we just look each other straight in the eye, like this!'

'Why?' asked Siphon, with a trace of anxiety. He took out his handkerchief, but Mientus snatched it from him and flung it on the ground.

'Why? Because I've had enough of the look of your face, I've had enough of it, I tell you! Stop making that face, will you, or I'll show you a face that . . . you'll see . . . I'll show you . . .'

'What will you show me?'

'I'll show you! I'll show you!' Mientus yelled like a maniac. 'You show me, and I'll show you! That's enough talk, you show me your Adolescent and I'll show you mine! We'll see who sticks it longest. You just show me! You just show me! No more words, and no more delicate and discreet looks, to hell with them! I challenge you to an all-out duel of face-making. You'll see what I'll show you! No more talk! You show me and I'll show you!'

Could there be a higher degree of lunacy? Here was Mientus challenging Siphon to a duel of grimaces. Nobody spoke, but everyone stared in amazement at Mientus, as if he had gone off his head, while Siphon thought of a sardonic reply. But there was such fury on Mientus's face that he quickly realized the whole dreadful meaning of the challenge. Grimaces! What an appalling, what an agonizing weapon! No quarter would be given in the struggle. Some of us trembled at the thought of Mientus's bringing out into broad daylight the dreadful weapon which no one had yet dared to use, except after taking precautions to ensure solitude and secrecy. Mientus was proposing to do in public what we had never dared to do, except alone in front of a mirror when nobody could see. I stepped back, for I realized that Mientus intended to debase with his grimaces not only Siphon, but also his stable-lads, the Boy, himself, me, everyone.

'Well, are you afraid?'

'I'm not ashamed of my ideal,' said Siphon without, however, being able to dissemble a trace of anxiety. 'I'm not ashamed.'

But there was a tremor in his voice.

'Very well, then, then that's settled. Here. After school. Choose your seconds. Mine will be Bobek and Hopek. And as umpire (and here Mientus's voice became still more diabolical), as umpire . . . I propose the new boy who has just arrived. He's neutral!'

'What? Me?'

Umpire? Me? Was I dreaming, or was this reality?

'I won't!' I burst out. 'I won't! I don't want to be there at all, I don't want to see it! No, no, no, I won't!'

I dashed forward to make my objections plain, but the general alarm had yielded to general excitement, everyone started shouting, and my appointment as umpire was taken as settled.

At that moment the bell rang, the classroom door opened, and a little man with a beard walked in and took his place at his raised desk.

It was the body who had announced in the staff-room that prices were going up. . . . He was an extremely cordial little old man, a little white dove with a wart on the end of his nasal nose. A death-like silence prevailed when he opened his book. His clear and friendly eyes lingered at the top of the list, and all those whose names began with A trembled; he lowered his eyes to the bottom of the list, and all those whose name began with Z shuddered with apprehension. For no-one had done his homework; in the heat of the argument everyone had forgotten all about his Latin preparation, and, apart from Siphon, who always could, could at any time, there was no one, no one at all, who could. The little old man, however, in total ignorance of the fear that he was inspiring, went on calmly casting his eyes up and down the list of names. He hesitated, pondered for a moment, and finally, with confidence and conviction, pronounced the name of Mydlak.

It was immediately obvious that Mydlak was incapable of translating the Caesar of the day, and, still worse, was unaware that *animis oblatis* was an ablative absolute.

'Come, come, Mydlak,' the good old man said reproachfully, 'so you don't know what *animis oblatis* means, or even what kind of grammatical construction it is? How can that be, Mydlak?'

Sincerely grieved, he gave him a nought. But his face promptly lit up again, and in a burst of recovered confidence he called on Koperski to construe. . . . It was evident that in so doing he felt himself to be conferring on him the highest of honours; with look, gesture, his whole person, he encouraged Koperski to enjoy the pleasures of emulation. But Koperski no more knew what *animis oblatis* meant than did Kotecki, Kapusta, or even Kolek; and in the face of this black picture everyone stiffened into mute and hostile silence. Each time the little old man signified his momentary disappointment by rapidly entering a nought in his book, and in a burst of recovered faith promptly called on another boy. The man might have just landed from the moon; he confidently expected each boy he called on to be worthy of the honour, and to respond accordingly. But nobody did so, and soon he had entered ten noughts in his book without realizing that the only effect of his misplaced confidence was to spread fright, and that nobody wanted his confidence. What a confident little old man! His confidence was incurable. Even if boys pretended to be suffering from headache he declared himself to be delighted.

'You have a headache, Bobkowski? Excellent! Here before us we have an interesting maxim *de malis capitis* which most aptly fits the situation. What? You feel an imperious need to leave the room? But, my dear Bobkowski, why? For that too we find a precedent among the ancients. I refer you to the famous passage in Book V in which Caesar's whole army, having eaten bad meat, found itself in the same predicament. The whole army, Bobkowski! Why do you wish to do the same when you have at hand such a classic description? These books, gentlemen, are life, life!'

Siphon, Mientus and their quarrel were dead, buried, and forgotten. Everyone tried to disappear from view, to cease to exist. The boys shrank, sought to make themselves indistinct and indistinguishable, contracted their hands, feet, stomachs. But no one was bored; no, there was not a trace or suspicion of boredom, for everyone was sadly fearful of being fastened on by the claw of the puerile confidence which the Latin text inspired in the old man. And under the pressure of fear faces—as happens to faces—turned into shadows, illusions of faces, and it was no longer possible to say which was the more illusory, chimerical and mad, the faces, the incredible infinitive with subject accusative, or the old maniac's sadistical confidence; and reality turned gradually into a dream world, oh! let me dream, dream!

The master, however, having dismissed Bobkowski with a nought, thought of another grammatical problem. What was the third person plural of the passive periphrastic subjunctive of the verb *colleo, colleare, colleavi, colleatum*? The idea excited him greatly.

'Very curious and instructive, very curious and instructive indeed,' he exclaimed, rubbing his hands. 'Come on, boys, a question to test your shrewdness! An admirable opportunity to show your sharpness of wit! Now if the passive periphrastic subjunctive of *olleare* is *ollandus sim*, what is the passive periphrastic subjunctive of *colleare*? Come, gentlemen!'

The said gentlemen, however, had been frightened out of existence.

'Come, come, come! . . . *Collan . . . collan . . .*'

No answer. But the old man still refused to abandon hope. Again he said:

'Come, come! . . . *Collan . . . collan . . .*'

He praised, he blazed, he goaded, he forgave, implored, encouraged, strove to instil and elicit knowledge, tried to lure his pupils into the pleasure of possessing it. But suddenly he felt that nobody could and nobody wanted to. He collapsed, and in a hollow voice, saddened by the universal ill will, groaned:

'*Collandus sim! Collandus sim!*'

And he went on:

'How, gentlemen, is it possible that you derive no pleasure and satisfaction from that? Do you not see that *collandus sim* sharpens the wits, stimulates the intelligence, forms the character, improves us from every point of view, and puts us on terms of familiarity with the thought of the ancients? For—now follow me carefully, gentlemen—if the gerundive of *olleare* is *ollandus*, the gerundive of *colleare* must be *collandus*, because the future passive ending of the third conjugation is *dus*, *dus*, *dus*, with the sole exception of the exceptions when it ends in *us*, *us*, *us*! Do you not feel the germ of perfection contained in that termination?'

At this point Kotecki got up and said in desperation:

'But, heaven help us, sir, how can you say that it improves us when it doesn't improve us? How can you say that it stimulates us when it doesn't stimulate us? How can you say that it forms our character when it doesn't form anything? I don't understand, sir!'

The master: 'What are you saying, Mr Kotecki? Do you maintain the termination in *us* does not improve or enrich our minds? Explain yourself, Kotecki!'

Kotecki: 'It doesn't improve or enrich my mind, sir! It does nothing of the sort to me, sir! Heaven help me, sir, but it doesn't!'

The master: 'It does not enrich your mind, Kotecki? But Kotecki, are you not aware that a knowledge of Latin is the foundation of all mental enrichment? Come, Kotecki, what you are suggesting is that thousands of competent teachers have for generations been teaching something entirely devoid of educational value. But Kotecki, surely the fact that we selflessly and unremittingly devote so much effort to instilling Latin into you demonstrates the necessity of learning it? Kotecki, you can take it from me, if you fail to appreciate Latin as you should, the only possible conclusion is that you are not intelligent enough. An intelligence entirely out of the ordinary is required to appreciate the benefits that flow from it, and years of study and application.'

Kotecki: 'But I can't appreciate it, sir, I can't, heaven help me!'

The master: 'I appeal to you, Kotecki. Did we not last year translate the sixty-three lines of Caesar in which he describes how he deployed his legions on the hill? Were those sixty-three lines, plus a page of vocabulary, not a mystic revelation of ancient times? Were they not a revelation to Kotecki of the style, clarity of thought, and correctness of expression, of that military genius Caesar?'

Kotecki: 'No, sir, to me they were not a revelation of anything at all, and I couldn't see any military genius. I didn't want to get a nought, and that was all. I don't like getting noughts. Oh, I can't, I can't!'

The formidable shadow of general impotence once more hovered ominously over the class; and the master felt that he would succumb himself unless he took prompt counteraction by injecting a double dose of faith and confidence.

'Pylaszczkiewicz!' exclaimed the poor man abandoned by everybody, 'do me the favour of immediately recapitulating what we have studied in the course of the term, bringing out all the profundity of thought and felicity of style; and I have confidence, confidence, confidence, because that is what we must have!'

Siphon, who, as has already been mentioned, always could and never suffered from impotence, rose and started reading with perfect fluency and ease:

'Next day Caesar paraded his troops, and reprimanded them for the rashness and impetuosity which they had shown in judging for themselves how far they were to advance and what they were to do, not halting when the signal for withdrawal was given, and refusing to submit to the control of the tribunes and generals. He explained that an unfavourable position made a serious difference; he had experienced this himself at Avaricum, when, though he had the enemy in his grasp without their general and without their cavalry, he had foregone an assured triumph for fear the unfavourable ground should entail a loss, however slight, in the action. He heartily admired their heroic spirit, which entrenched camp and high mountain and walled fortress were powerless to daunt; but just as heartily he reprobated their contempt for discipline and their presumption in imagining that they knew how to win battles and forecast results better than their general. He required from his soldiers obedience and self-control just as much as courage and heroism. Having achieved his purpose, Caesar ordered the withdrawal to be sounded, and immediately halted the Tenth Legion, which he commanded in person. The men of the other legions did not hear the sound of the trumpet, as a considerable valley intervened; still the tribunes and the generals, in obedience to Caesar's command, tried to keep them in hand. Elated, however, by the expectation of a speedy triumph, by the enemy's flight, and by the recollection of past victories, they fancied that nothing was too difficult for their valour to achieve, and pressed on in pursuit till they got close to the wall and gates of the fortress. Then a cry arose from every part of town; and those who were some way off, panic-stricken by the sudden uproar, and believing that the enemy were inside the gates, rushed pell-mell out of the stronghold.'

'*Collandus sim*, gentlemen! *Collandus sim*! What clarity! What style! What thought, what profundity! *Collandus sim*, what a fountain of knowledge! Ah! I breathe, I breathe again! *Collandus sim* for ever and for all eternity, *collandus sim, collandus sim, collandus sim!*'

Suddenly the bell rang, the boys let out a wild yell, and the little old man frowned and walked out.

Simultaneously everybody emerged from the official dream and plunged back into the private dream of Boy *v.* Adolescent! Oh, let me dream, dream! Mientus had made me umpire on purpose, he had done it deliberately, to force me to look on and see it all. The thing had gone to his head; as he was degrading and debasing himself, he wanted to degrade and debase me too; he could not tolerate my having provoked his momentary exhibition of weakness over the stable-lad. But how could I expose my face to such a spectacle? I knew that if it once assimilated such appalling insanity it would never again return to normal, and escape would be impossible. No! No! let them do what they liked, but don't let me be there to see! Moving my toe in my shoe with extreme nervousness, I took Mientus by the sleeve, looked at him imploringly, and said:

'Mientus!'

He shook me off.

'Oh, no, my little adolescent!' he said. 'Nothing doing! You're the umpire, and that's that!'

'Little adolescent!' he called me. What a revolting epithet! It was cruel of him, and I realized that all was lost, and that we were rapidly approaching what I feared most, the reign of insanity, total and complete. Meanwhile even those who normally kept out of things were seized with wild excitement; their nostrils were distended and their cheeks aflame, and it was obvious that the duel of grimaces was to be no mere battle of words, but a matter of life or death. The two principals were surrounded by a mob shouting:

'Come on! Come on! Let him have it! Let him have it!'

Only Kopeida stretched himself with supreme tranquillity and aloofness, picked up his exercise book, and went off home, with his legs.

Siphon was sitting on his Adolescent, as vindictive and alert as a hen on her eggs; it was obvious in spite of everything that he was rather nervous and would have been glad to have been able to back out. But Gabek had been quick to see the enormous advantage he enjoyed by reason of his lofty ideals and noble concepts.

'Don't be afraid, you've got him,' he whispered in his ear to encourage him. 'Think of your principles. You can think up all the grimaces you like because of your principles, while he'll have to invent all his on his own account, because he has no principles.'

Under the influence of this advice Pylaszczkiewicz's face cheered up somewhat and was soon shining again, for his principles gave him the ability to do what was required of him on any occasion and to any extent required. Seeing this, Bobek, and Hopek took Mientus aside, and implored him not to expose himself to inevitable defeat.

'He'll get you and us too, he's a better grimacer than you are, Mientus, you'd better call it off,' they said. 'Pretend to be ill, or faint, or do something, and that'll get you out of it. We'll straighten things out in one way or another afterwards.'

'No,' Mientus replied. 'The die is cast. Clear out! You want me to deflate myself. Get rid of all these gaping idiots for me. I want nobody here except the seconds and the umpire!'

But his features were drawn, and he was noticeably ill at ease. This was in such striking contrast to Siphon's self-assurance that Bobek muttered: 'Poor chap!' And everyone, feeling that something dreadful was going to happen, filed quickly and quietly out of the room, carefully shutting the door behind them.

Only seven of us stayed behind in the empty, closed room—

Pylaszczkiewicz and Mientus, Bobek, Hopek, and Gabek, a boy named Pyzo, who was Siphon's other second, and myself, the umpire, in the middle. Gabek, looking slightly pale, then read out the rules of combat, in a voice that sounded simultaneously menacing and ironic:

'The two contestants will stand facing each other and will make a series of faces. Each and every constructive and beautiful face made by Siphon will be answered by an ugly and destructive counter-face made by Mientus. The faces made will be as personal and as wounding as possible, and the contestants will continue to make them until a final decision is reached.'

He fell silent. Siphon and Mientus took up their positions. Siphon tapped his cheeks, Mientus rolled his jaw, and Bobek, with his teeth chattering, said:

'You may begin!'

At these words reality burst from its frame, unreality turned into nightmare, the whole improbable adventure became a dream in which I was imprisoned with no possibility of even struggling. It was as if after long training a point had been reached at which one lost one's own face. It would not have been surprising if Mientus and Siphon had taken their faces in their hands and thrown them at each other; nothing would have been surprising. I muttered:

'Take pity on your faces, take pity on my face, for a face is not an object but a subject, a subject, a subject!'

But Siphon had already put his head forward, and he made the first grimace so suddenly that my own face was suddenly as distorted as if it were made of papier mâché.

Siphon blinked, like somebody suddenly emerging from the darkness into broad daylight, looked right and left with an expression of pious astonishment, rolled his eyes, looked up, opened his mouth, made a slight exclamation, as if he had noticed something on the ceiling, assumed an expression of ecstasy, and remained still in that inspired pose; then he put his hand on his heart and sighed.

Mientus collected himself and retorted with an alarming and

derisive counter-grimace. He too rolled his eyes, then raised them to heaven, glared, opened his lips in idiotic fashion, and rotated the face that he had thus composed until a fly fell into his cavernous mouth, whereupon he swallowed it.

Siphon paid no attention to this pantomime, which seemed to make no impact whatever on him (he had the advantage over his opponent of acting for the sake of his principles, not just for his own sake). He burst into tears, pious, bitter tears, floods of tears, that reached the heights of remorse, revelation, and ecstasy. Mientus burst into tears too, and sobbed and sobbed until a tear trickled down to the end of his nose—whereupon he caused it to drop into a spittoon, thus reaching a new level of disgustingness. This assault upon the most sacred feelings was too much for Siphon; it shook him; and, in spite of himself, still sobbing, he looked daggers at his opponent. But this was unwise of him, for it was just what Mientus had been waiting for. Realizing that he had diverted Siphon's attention from the heights, he stuck out his face in such an obscene fashion that Siphon, touched to the quick, groaned. Mientus seemed to be gaining the day, and Bobek and Hopek sighed with relief. But their relief was premature; they sighed too soon.

For Siphon, realizing that he had allowed himself to be excessively distracted by Mientus's face, and that irritation was making him lose control of his own, beat a hasty retreat, recomposed his features, and once more elevated his eyes towards heaven. He advanced one foot slightly, slightly ruffled his hair, caused a lock to droop over his forehead, and froze into a position of unshakeable unity with his principles and ideals; then he raised one hand, and pointed towards the stars. This was a powerful blow.

Mientus thereupon pointed his finger too, spat on it, put it up his nose, scratched himself with it, did everything in his power to debase and ridicule Siphon's noble gesture, thus defending himself by counter-attack. But Siphon went on remorselessly pointing towards the sky. In vain Mientus bit his finger, rubbed his teeth with it, scratched the sole of his foot with it; in vain he did everything he could think of to make his finger odious and contemptible; Siphon stood there remorselessly and impregnably pointing upwards, and yielded not an inch. Mientus's position started becoming untenable; he was using up his stock of insulting gestures, and Siphon's finger still pointed remorselessly towards heaven. The seconds and the umpire were petrified with horror. In a last desperate effort Mientus dipped his finger in the spittoon and waved it at Siphon, covered as it was with sweat and spittle. Not only did Siphon fail to take the slightest notice, but his face became diffused with seven colours, like a rainbow after a storm, and lo! there he stood in seven colours, the Boy Scout, Purity Incarnate, the Innocent Adolescent.

'Victory!' Gabek exclaimed.

Mientus looked dreadful. He retreated to the wall, fuming with rage, took hold of his finger, pulled it as if he were trying to pull it out of its socket, in order to destroy this link that bound him to Siphon, to enable him to recover his independence. But he could not pull out his finger, though he tried with all his strength, in spite of the pain. Impotence hung once more in the air. But there was nothing impotent about Siphon, who stood there as calm as the heavens, with his finger pointing upwards, not for himself, but for the sake of his principles. What a ghastly situation! Here was I, the umpire, between two boys each of whose faces was distorted into a horrible grimace, imprisoned between them no doubt for ever and ever, slave of the faces, the grimaces, of others. My face, the mirror of their faces, was distorted too; terror, disgust, fear, left their ineradicable marks on it. A clown between two other clowns, what could I do except grimace? Sadly my toe accompanied their fingers, and I grimaced and grimaced, well knowing that I was losing myself in my grimaces. Never, never, should I be able to escape from Pimko, never should I be able to return to my old self. What a nightmare! Oh, horror, oh, dreadful silence! For there were moments of dead silence, when the clash of arms was stilled, when there was nothing but silent grimaces and gestures.

Suddenly the silence was broken by a wild yell from Mientus. 'Go for him! Get him!'

What was this? So it wasn't over yet? Mientus dropped his finger, leapt at Siphon and struck him in the face, and Bobek and Hopek did the same to Gabek and Pyzo. A moment later an inextricable heap of bodies was writhing on the floor, with me, the umpire, standing over it.

In a flash Gabek and Pyzo were overpowered and tied up with their braces; and Mientus was sitting on Siphon.

'So, my fine young adolescent, you thought you'd got the better of me, did you?' he boasted. 'So you thought that all you had to do was to stick your finger in the air and the trick was done, did you? So you thought, my fine fellow (here he added some disgusting expressions) that Mientus wouldn't be able to get the better of you, did you? You thought he'd let himself be tied round that little finger of yours, did you? Well, then, for your information, when there's no other way out, fingers have to be brought down by force!'

'Let me go!' Siphon gasped.

'Let you go? I'll let you go! I'll let you go soon, but not in this state! Not till I've dealt with your adolescent in my own way. You'll have cause to remember Mientus. We're going to have a little talk. Come here with your ear. Fortunately it's still possible to get at you through your ears. Come here with your ear, I tell you! Come along, my little innocent, I'm going to tell you some things!'

He bent over and started talking softly. Siphon went green in the face, yelled like a pig in the slaughterhouse, writhed like a fish out of water. Mientus was suffocating him. Siphon turned his head this way and that to move his ears away from Mientus's mouth, and Mientus poured his filth first into one ear and then into the other; and Siphon yelled to prevent himself from hearing Mientus's filth; he yelled gravely, dreadfully, he froze into a quintessential yell. It was difficult to believe that the ideal could yell like this, like a wild beast in the primeval forest. His tormentor started yelling too.

'Gag him! Gag him! What are you waiting for, you fool? Stuff a handkerchief in his mouth!'

I was the fool to whom he referred. It was I who was supposed to stuff a handkerchief into Siphon's mouth, for Bobek and Hopek, each of whom were holding down one of Siphon's seconds, obviously could not move. But I would not, I could not, there I stood, rooted to the spot, disgusted with words, gestures, disgusted with every kind of expression. Alas, poor umpire! Where, oh! where were my thirty years? Vanished . . . But, suddenly there was Pimko standing in the doorway, with his yellow buckskin shoes, his brownish overcoat, and his walking-stick, standing there in a manner as definite and absolute as if he were seated.

★ 4 ★

Introduction to Philifor
Honeycombed with Childishness

BEFORE continuing with these authentic memoirs I desire at this point to interpose by way of digression a story entitled *Philifor Honeycombed with Childishness*. You have seen how the evil and didactic Pimko endowed me with a childish little backside; you have seen the idealistic convulsions of our youth; its inability to live, its calamitous lack of proportion and its cacophony, its tragic artificiality, sad boredom, ridiculous pretences, and agonizing anachronisms; as well as the follies of its backsides, faces, and other parts of its body. You have heard the words it uses, the clash between the lofty and the vulgar, and those other words, equally empty and unsubstantial, inflicted on it by its pedagogues; and you have noted how hollow verbiage ended nastily in absurd facial contortions. Thus is man at the very outset stuffed full of verbiage and grimaces; such is the anvil on which our maturity is forged. You will soon be spectators of other grimaces and another duel—the death-struggle between Professor G. L. Philifor of Leyden and Professor Momsen of Colombo (better known as Anti-Philifor), in which words and parts of the body will similarly appear. But it would be wrong to seek any close connexion between the two parts of my book; it would be equally wrong to suppose that in interposing the story of Philifor I had any intention other than that of covering some paper with ink and reducing to some extent the enormous and intimidating pile of blank pages by which I am confronted.

If, however, the eminent connoisseurs and men of learning, the Pimkos who specialize in providing us with an intellectual rump with the aid of the critical weapon known as 'faults of construction', object that from their point of view the motivation behind this bit of padding is of too private a nature and is therefore indefensible, and that there is no excuse for introducing into a work of art everything that I may have written in the course of my life, I shall reply that in my humble opinion the separate parts of the body suffice to form a solid and artistically constructed whole, and that this applies still more to words; and I shall demonstrate that my construction yields in no way to the best examples of logical and precise construction. For the fundamental part of the body is the rump, from which, like the trunk of a tree, everything else branches off; and that applies to all the separate parts of the body, including fingers, arms, eyes, teeth, and ears; moreover, some parts subtly and imperceptibly change into others; and at the pinnacle of the human trunk from which the separate parts spread out is the face (also known familiarly as mug or phiz); thus the latter closes the cycle opened by the rump. Having reached this pinnacle, what course is left open to me but that of retracing my steps by way of the various parts of the body to my rumpish starting-point? And that is the purpose of the tale of *Philifor*. *Philifor* is a constructive retrogression serving as a transition, or to state it in more precise terms, a coda, trill, or rather, intestinal lapse, without which it would never be possible for me to reach the left ankle. Is this not cast-iron construction? Does it not meet the most highly specialized requirements? And what will you say when you have discovered other and deeper links between all these parts—connecting, for instance, finger and liver—and when the mystic role of certain privileged parts, and the hidden meaning behind certain articulations will have been revealed to you, and finally, when you have seen the whole of all the parts as well as the parts of all the parts? I maintain that this bit of padding represents construction of the highest order, and would point out that penetrating analysis of this kind will enable you to fill a hundred volumes, to fill more and more space, to occupy an ever higher place, and to sit in it more and more at your ease. But ... do you like blowing soap-bubbles at daybreak by the lakeside when the fish are darting about and the angler sitting silently by the water-side is gently reflected in the crystalline water?

Moreover, I recommend to you my method of making greater impact by means of repetition; by systematic repetition of a few words, turns of phrase, situations, and parts, I make the impact greater, and thus intensify the effect of stylistic unity, carrying it to the point of mania. It is by repetition that myths are created. Note, however, that this method of construction out of parts is not just construction, but behind the light and frothy form of a superficial newspaper article actually conceals a whole philosophy. Do you not agree that the reader is able to assimilate only one part at a time? He reads, for instance, one part or one passage before breaking off and reading another part or passage later; and he often begins in the middle, or even at the end, and then works his way backwards. Sometimes he reads two or three passages and never returns to the book; and not, mark you, because he is not interested, but because of some totally extrane-ous circumstance; and, even if he reads the whole thing, do you suppose for one moment that he has a view of it as a whole, appreciates the constructive harmony of the parts, if no specialist gives him the hint? Is it for this that authors spend years cutting, revising, and rearranging, sweating, straining and suffering? All to enable a specialist to tell the reader that the work is well constructed? Let us carry the matter a little further, into the realm of everyday experience. May not a telephone call, or a fly, distract the reader's attention just at the moment when all the parts, themes, threads, are on the point of converging into a supreme unity? Suppose, for instance, that at the critical moment your brother walks in and interrupts? Thus a fly, a telephone call, a brother walking in, can lay an author's noble work in ruins. Cruel flies, why do you persecute a species which has lost its tail and is left with nothing with which to protect itself? Consider, moreover, that that unique and exceptional work of yours on which you have expended so much effort and sweat is just one of the thirty thousand equally unique and exceptional works which will appear during the year. Oh! terrible and accursed parts! So it is for this that we laboriously construct; so that part of a part of a reader may partially assimilate part of a part of a book.

It is difficult not to be frivolous about this. Frivolity is not to be avoided; for we learnt long ago to use humour to evade matters that we find too painful. Will there ever be born a serious genius who will be able to confront the minor contingencies of life without taking refuge in misplaced laughter? Alas! my poor style, my poor, frivolous newspaper style! But (to drain the cup of parts to the lees) let us also note that the laws and principles of construction to which we are so subject are themselves only the product of a part, and an insignificant part into the bargain—a tiny segment of the world, a microcosm scarcely bigger than one's little finger, a minute group of specialists and aesthetes all of whom could be crowded into a teashop, whose relentless pressure on each other results in the distillation of ideas of ever greater subtlety. And the worst of it is that their tastes are not real tastes; your construction can never more than partially please them, for they will always prefer it to their own knowledge of construction. So that if the creative artist tries to excel by his sense of construction, it is only to enable the critic to display his expertise on the subject? . . . Silence . . . hush . . . mystery. Here we have the creative artist kneeling at the altar of art, thinking of a supreme masterpiece, harmony, precision, mind, transcendence; and here the critic, his critical status vouched for by his ability to penetrate to the deepest depths of the creative artist's work; after which the book goes to the reader, and the result of the author's complete and total perspiration is an altogether partial reception between the buzzing of a fly and the ringing of a telephone. The contingencies of life get the better of you. It is you who provoke the monster to a duel, but then a puppy comes along and gives you gooseflesh.

And (to take one more gulp from the cup of parts) I should

also like to ask whether in your opinion a work constructed according to all the canons expresses a whole or only part of a whole. Come, come! Is not form born of elimination, is not construction an impoverishment, can words express more than a part of reality? The rest is silence. In the last resort, is it we who create form, or is it form that creates us? Incidentally, some years ago I knew a writer who at the outset of his literary career gave birth to a book of the purest heroism. With the first few words he put down on paper, quite by chance, he touched the chord of heroism; it might equally well have been that of scepticism or lyricism. But the first sentences that flowed from his pen were heroic, and because of this, and by virtue of the laws of construction, it was impossible for him not to go on concentrating and distilling the spirit of heroism until he got to the end. By painstaking revision, by adjusting the beginning to the end and the end to the beginning, he ended by writing a book that was full of life and stamped with the most profound conviction.

But what about the author's deepest conviction? Could a responsible creative artist confess that heroism had flowed spontaneously from his pen and independently of him, and that his deepest conviction was not his deepest conviction, and that he did not know how it had come from outside and attached itself to him? In vain the unhappy hero of this heroism, feeling ashamed of himself, tried to escape from his part, which, having taken a firm hold on him, refused to let go. He had to adapt himself to the situation; and so thoroughly did he do so that towards the end of his career he had completely identified himself with his part; he was as heroic as it . . . and very much afraid of his heroism. He therefore studiously avoided the friends and companions of his youth, for they never recovered from their surprise at such a thorough adaptation of a whole to a part.

Such are the deep and weighty philosophical reasons which have prompted me to construct the present work on the basis of separate parts—regarding the work as part of a work and man as a conglomeration of physical and mental parts—for humanity as a whole seems to me nothing but a conglomeration of parts.

Now, if anyone objects that a partial concept such as mine is in reality no concept at all, but a joke, a snare and an illusion, and that instead of submitting to the severe rules and canons of art I am making a mock of them by clowning and buffoonery and irresponsible grimaces, I shall reply yes, perfectly true, such indeed is my intention. I am not ashamed to admit it, I have just as strong a desire to escape from your art, gentlemen, as I have to escape from you; and the reason is that I can stand neither you, nor your ideas, nor your aesthetic attitudes, nor your coteries.

For, gentlemen, there exist in the world human groups which are some less, some more, disgraceful, shameful, and humiliating than others—and stupidity is not spread equally everywhere. At first sight, for instance, the world of hairdressers has always seemed to me to be more liable to stupidity than that of shoemakers. But the things that happen in the world's artistic circles beat all records in stupidity and ignominy—to such an extent that it is impossible for a normally constituted and balanced person not to sweat with shame in the presence of their childish and pretentious orgies. Oh! those sublime songs to which nobody listens! Oh! those closed gatherings of initiates, the frenzied excitement of those concerts, those private invitations, those exaltations and arguments, even the faces of those declaiming or listening, celebrating the sacred aesthetic mysteries in a hermetically sealed container! What painful antinomy is it that causes everything you say or do in such an environment to be shameful and ridiculous? If in the course of centuries a social group declines into such convulsions of stupidity, it can be confidently assumed that its ideas are in no sort of correspondence with reality, or simply that the ideas on which it is living are false. For there is no doubt that your ideas are the very pinnacle and summit of conceptional naïveté; and, if you want to know how to change them and in which direction you ought to move, I can tell you straight away. But you must listen.

What in reality is a person aiming at nowadays who feels a vocation for the pen, the paint-brush, or the clarionet? Above all, he wants to be an artist. He wants to create art. He wants to feed on beauty, goodness, and truth, and to feed his fellow-citizens on these things; he wants to be prophet, bard, high priest, to offer himself whole to others, to burn on the altar of the sublime in providing humanity with this so desirable manna. Moreover, he wants to devote his talent to the service of an idea, and perhaps lead mankind or his country towards a better future. What noble aims! What magnificent intentions! Are they not identical with those of Shakespeare, Goethe, Beethoven, or Chopin? But here you run into trouble. The awkward fact is that you are neither Chopin nor Shakespeare, but at most a half-Shakespeare, or a quarter-Chopin (oh! cursed parts!), and consequently the sole result of your attitude is to draw attention to your sad inadequacy and inferiority—and it is as if in the course of your clumsy efforts to leap on to the pedestal you were breaking the most precious parts of your body.

Believe me, there is a big difference between the artist who has fulfilled himself and the infinite multitude of semi-demi-artists and quarter-poets who would desperately like to fulfil themselves—and what is appropriate to genius yields quite a different sound when it comes from you. But you, instead of equipping yourselves with ideas and opinions suited to your measure and in harmony with your situation, adorn yourselves with borrowed plumage—and that is why you transform yourselves into eternal candidates, eternal aspirants to greatness and perfection. Eternally impotent and always mediocre, you become the servants, pupils, and admirers of the art on which you dance attendance. It is indeed dreadful to watch all the efforts you make only to produce a failure, to hear you being told that this time you have not quite managed to pull it off, and to see you nevertheless starting out on yet another work—and to watch you trying to put your works across, and consoling yourselves with poor secondary successes, engaging in mutual congratulations, organizing dinners, always seeking out new lies to justify the suspect reason for your existence; and you have not even the consolation of knowing in your bones that your work has real value; because it is all only imitation, repetition of what you learnt from the masters; and all you do is cling to the coat-tails of genius, repeating after it, and in inferior fashion, complaints of obstacles in an area in which there is no room for obstacles. You are in a false situation which, being false, can yield only bitter fruit—and, sure enough, your coteries are the breeding-ground of backbiting, mutual contempt and low esteem; everyone despises everyone else and himself into the bargain, you constitute a mutual contempt society . . . and end by despising yourselves to death.

What does the second-rate writer's situation consist of other than a huge repudiation? The first repudiation, and it is a cruel and humiliating one, is that inflicted on him by the average reader, who flatly declines to enjoy his work. The second is self-inflicted, inflicted by the writer's own self, which he has been unable to express, since he is only a copyist and an imitator of the masters. But the third repudiation, the supreme kick in the pants and the most humiliating of all, comes from the art in which he sought refuge, the art which, because of his impotence and inadequacy, treats him with contempt; and that fills the cup of ignominy. The sub-writer comes under the barrage of universal repudiation, becomes an object of general ridicule, and is left stranded. What, after all, can be expected of a man who has been repudiated three times, each time with greater ignominy?

When a man is finished to that extent, should he not vanish, hide himself somewhere out of sight? Is not the sight of inadequacy rising in broad daylight greedy of honours enough to give the universe the hiccups?

But, above all, answer me this: Do you prefer the crab-apple to the custard-apple, or the other way about? Ignominy, gentlemen, ignominy, ignominy, ignominy. No, I am neither a philosopher nor a theorist, it is you I am speaking of, it is your life to which I am referring; you must realize that it is only your personal situation which gives me pain. It is impossible to detach oneself from other people; there is a kind of impotence which prevents one from breaking the umbilical cord which connects one with the refuse of humanity. The unwanted—the unsmelt flower, the untasted sweet, the rejected woman—have always caused me almost physical pain; such frustration is intolerable—and when I meet an artist in the street, and see that the basis of his whole existence is vulgar repudiation, when I note that all his words and gestures, all his faith and his enthusiasm, all his commas and all his transgressions, all his ideas and all his illusions, exude the disagreeable odour of commonplace repudiation, I feel ashamed; ashamed not only because I am sorry for him, but also because I co-exist with him, and his chimerical existence offends my human dignity. Believe me, the attitude of the second-rate writer is in urgent need of reform, for otherwise the whole world will suffer from a grave malaise. It is appalling that persons who profess to be dedicated to the perfection of style, and hence presumably are sensitive to form, should tolerate without protest being placed in such a false and pretentious situation. Do they not understand that nothing could be more disastrous from the point of view of form and style? For he who is placed in a false and artificial situation cannot utter a single word that is not false and artificial, and whatever he says, does, or thinks necessarily turns against him and does him harm.

But then—you will ask—what ideas should we adopt in order to be able to express ourselves in a more reasonable, more sovereign manner, more consonant with our reality? Gentlemen, it is not in your power to become mature artists overnight; it is in your power, however, partially to cure these evils and to recover your lost sovereignty by withdrawing from the art which gives you such an embarrassing rump. Above all, break once and for all with the words 'art' and 'artist'. Cease intoxicating yourselves with those words which you repeat with the monotony of eternity. Is not everyone an artist? Does mankind create art only when seated at a desk in front of a sheet of paper? Is not art continually being created in the course of everyday life? When a girl puts a rose in her hair, when we make a good joke in the course of an agreeable conversation, when we exchange confidences at dusk, is not that art? Why, then, this terrible division between art and everyday life? Why do you say: Oh, I am an artist, I create art—when it would be more appropriate to say simply: Perhaps I take a little more interest in art than other people? Moreover, why this cult, this admiration only for the kind of art that results in so-called works of art? Whence this naïve belief that men so hugely admire works of art and that we go into ecstasy and pass away when we listen to a Beethoven symphony? Have you never considered how impure, adulterated, and formidably immature is that area of culture which you wish to circumscribe with your over-simple terminology? Above all, the boring and commonplace mistake that you make is this: you refer man's contact with art almost exclusively to the aesthetic sense, and consider that contact from an excessively remote and special point of view, as if each individual communed with art in total solitude, hermetically sealed off from his fellows; whereas in reality we are confronted with a large number of different senses, complicated, moreover, by the intermingling of a large number of different individuals, who influence and affect each other and give rise to collective states of mind.

When a concert pianist plays Chopin, for instance, you say: The audience was roused and carried away by a brilliant interpretation of the master's music. But it is possible that not a single member of the audience was carried away; it is perfectly possible that, if they had not known that Chopin was a great master and the virtuoso a great pianist, they might have received the performance with less enthusiasm. It is also possible that the reason why everyone applauded so enthusiastically, their faces distraught with emotion, was that everyone else was doing the same. For each one of them, believing that all the rest were experiencing enormous, super-terrestrial, delight and pleasure, would tend for that very reason to display the same delight and pleasure; and thus it is perfectly possible that nobody in the hall was directly and immediately carried away by the experience, though everyone, adapting his attitude to that of his neighbour, showed all the external signs of it; and it is only when the whole audience has been thus carried away, when every member of it has been encouraged by everyone else to clap, shout, grow red in the face with pleasure and enthusiasm, it is only then, I say, that these demonstrations of pleasure and enthusiasm arise; for we have to adjust our feelings to our behaviour. It is also certain that in listening to the music we are performing something in the nature of a religious, ritual act; and that at a Chopin concert we prostrate ourselves before the god of beauty in a spirit similar to that in which we piously kneel at Mass. In the former case, however, we are merely paying official homage; and who can say what part is played in this tribute to beauty by beauty itself and what part is attributable to the historico-sociological process? Bah! Mankind, as we know, has need of myths; and it picks out one or the other of its numerous creative artists (who will throw light on the reason for its choice?) and lo and behold! it elevates him above his fellows, starts learning his work by heart, discovers its magic and mystery, adapts its way of feeling to it. Now, if we set about exalting some other creative artist with the same persistence and indefatigability, I am convinced that we could make a similarly great genius of him. Do you not see, then, how many different and often non-aesthetic factors (the monotonous enumeration of them could be extended indefinitely) have accumulated in the greatness of our masters and our semi-obscure, troubled, and fragmentary coexistence with the art which you naïvely sum up in the formula: Let the inspired poet sing and let the listener be enchanted? That is why it sometimes happens that a poet is considered great, magnificent, and marvellous by everyone, though no one, perhaps, has ever enjoyed his work; or why sometimes everyone swoons away in the presence of a fine canvas, though no one ever thinks of fainting in the presence of a copy which may resemble it like two drops of water.

Have done, then, with your aesthetic transports, stop being artists, for heaven's sake drop your way of talking about art, its syntheses, analysis, subtleties, profundities, the whole inflated apparatus; and, instead of imposing myths, model yourselves on facts. That alone and by itself should bring you noticeable relief, freeing you from your limitations and opening your mind to reality. Moreover, you must cast off the fear that this broad and healthy way of regarding art will deprive you of any riches and greatness, for reality is richer and greater than naïve illusions and petty lies; let me tell you straight away about the riches that await you along this new path.

Art certainly consists of perfection of form. But you—and here we are faced with another of the cardinal errors of yours—you imagine that art consists of creating perfect works. You apply the immense and universal aspiration to the creation of form to the production of poems and symphonies, but you have never managed properly to appreciate, or to make others appreciate, the role, and the important role, of form in your own lives. Even in pyschology you have not given form the place to which it is entitled. Hitherto we have always considered the feelings, instincts, or ideas which govern our conduct, and regarded form as at the most a harmless, ornamental accessory. When a widow weeps behind her husband's hearse, we think she does so because she is suffering because of her loss. When an engineer, doctor, or lawyer murders his wife, his children, or a friend, we think that he was driven to it by violent and bloodthirsty instincts. When a politician in a public speech expresses himself stupidly, deceitfully, or pettily, we say he is stupid because he expresses himself stupidly. But the real situation is this: a human being does not externalize himself directly and immediately in conformity with his own nature; he invariably does so by way of some definite form; and that form, style, way of speaking and responding, do not derive solely from him, but are imposed on him from without—and the same man can express himself sometimes wisely, sometimes foolishly, bloodthirstily or angelically, maturely or immaturely, according to the form, the style presented to him by the outside world, the pressure put upon him by other men. And just as worms and insects creep and fly all day long in search of food, so we, without a moment's respite or relief, perpetually seek form and expression, struggle with other men for style, for our own way of being; and when we travel in a tram, or eat, or enjoy ourselves, or rest, or engage in business, we are perpetually in search of form, and we delight in it, suffer for it or adapt ourselves to it, we break or violate it, or let ourselves be violated by it, amen.

Oh, the power of form! It causes nations to perish, and it leads to wars. It is the reason why things arise among us which do not come from us. Without it you will never succeed in understanding stupidity, or evil, or crime. It governs our smallest reflexes, and lies at the foundation of the whole of our collective life. But for you form and style are ideas restricted to the field of art; and, just as you have reduced the function of art to the production of works of art, so do you debase the idea of style and form; for you, style is only style on paper, the style of your stories. Who, gentleman, will chastise the posterior that you present to mankind when you kneel before the altar of art? For you form is not something alive, human, let me say practical and everyday, but a gaudy attribute of art. Bent over your paper, you even forget your own self—and what matters to you is not perfecting yourself in your own personal and concrete style, but perfecting some sort of abstract and imaginary story. Instead of making art your servant, you make yourselves its slave—and that, I imagine, is why in sheep-like fashion you allow it to hamper your development and cast you into perpetual sloth.

See how different would be the attitude of a man who, instead of saturating himself with the phraseology of a million conceptualist metaphysician-aestheticians, looked at the world with new eyes and allowed himself to feel the enormous influence which form has on human life. If he still wanted to use his fountain-pen, he would do so, not in order to become a great writer and create art, but, let us say, the better to express his own personality and draw a clear picture of himself in the eyes of others; or to organize himself, bring order within himself, and by confession to cure any complexes or immaturities; and also, perhaps, to make his contact with others deeper, more intimate,

82

more creative, more sharply outlined, which could be of great benefit to his mind and his development; or, for instance, he might try to combat customs, prejudices, principles which he found contrary to his nature; or again, he might write simply to earn a living. He certainly would not spare effort to ensure that his work possessed an artistically attractive form, but his principal goal would be, not art, but himself. He would no longer write pretentiously, to educate, to elevate, to guide, to moralize, and to edify his fellow-men; his aim would be his own elevation and his own progress; and he would write, not because he was mature and had found his form, but because he was still immature and in his efforts to attain form was humiliating himself, making a fool of himself, and sweating like a climber still struggling towards the mountain-top, being a man still on the way to self-fulfilment. And if he should happen to write a worthless or silly book, he would say to himself: Well, I have written some rubbish, but I have signed no contract with anyone to write a clever or perfect book. I expressed my stupidity, and I am glad of it, for I am formed and fashioned by the severity of the human judgements which I have called down on my head, and it is as if I were being reborn. You see, then, that an artist equipped with this healthy philosophy is so well rooted in himself that neither stupidity nor immaturity can frighten or harm him; he can externalize himself and hold his head high, in spite of his indolence, while you can externalize nothing, for fear makes you voiceless.

That by itself would be a great alleviation. But, in addition, only a poet who approached things in this fashion would be capable of understanding the issue which has hitherto been your supreme stumbling-block—perhaps the most fundamental, the most intimidating issue of all. Let me state it in imaginary form. Let us imagine an adult, mature poet bent over his paper at grips with his work—and looking over his shoulder an adolescent—a semi-cultivated, semi-educated individual—an average girl perhaps, or any other mediocre and obscure young person—and this person, this adolescent, this girl, this semi-educated or other obscure product of sub-culture, seizes hold of his mind with a pair of forceps, attacks his soul, clasps and hugs it, refreshes and rejuvenates it, makes it green again, adjusts it to his or her own fashion and reduces it to his or her own level, yes, holding it tenderly in her arms. But the creative artist, instead of facing the intruder, pretends to take no notice, and foolishly imagines that he can avoid the violation by pretending not to have been violated. Is it not that which happens to all of you, from the great genius to the choice little poet of the back row of the chorus? Is it not true that every mature, superior, major and perfected human being depends in a thousand different ways on human beings who are at a less advanced stage of development? And does that dependence not attack the mind right to its very essence? It does so in such a way that we can say that the senior is always the creation of the junior. Do we not, when we write, have to adapt ourselves to the reader? When we speak do we not submit ourselves to the mind of the person to whom our words are addressed? Are we not fatally in love with youth? Are we not constantly forced to seek the favours of inferior persons, to adapt ourselves to them, to bend our necks, bow either to their power or to their spell? And is not this painful violation of ourselves carried out by semi-obscure individuals the most penetrating and most fertile of them all? Now, all that you have hitherto been able to do is to bury your heads in the sand in order not to see the violation; in your concentration on the polishing of your boring verses you have had neither the time nor the inclination to take any interest in it. You act as if nothing had happened, while in reality you have been violated without respite or remission. Oh, why do you enjoy yourselves only among yourselves? Why is your maturity so mature that it can cohabit only with maturity?

But, if you were less preoccupied with art and more with yourselves, you would not keep silent in face of this terrible violation of yourselves; and the poet, instead of writing for other poets, would feel himself penetrated and fertilized from below, by forces which he had hitherto neglected. He would

84

recognize that the only way of freeing himself from the pressure was to recognize it; and in his style, his attitude, his tone, his form—that of his art as well as of his everyday life—he would set himself to displaying this link with a lower level. He would no longer think of himself only as father, but as simultaneously father and son, and he would no longer write as a clever, subtle, and mature man, but as a clever man always reduced to stupidity, as a subtle man reduced to crudity, an adult perpetually reduced to childhood. And if, on leaving his study, he chanced on a child, an adolescent, a girl, or a semi-cultivated person, he would cease to find him or her boring, and no longer pat these people protectively, didactically, and pedagogically on the back while talking down to them in a superior manner; on the contrary, in a holy fit of trembling he would start groaning and roaring, and would perhaps even fall on his knees before them. Instead of shunning immaturity and shutting himself off in what are called coteries, he would realize that a truly universal style is a style born slowly and gradually in contact with human beings of different social conditions, age, education, and stages of development. And that would ultimately lead you to a form of creation so palpitating with life and so full of tremendous poetry that you would all be transformed into sublime geniuses.

So you see what perspectives and what hopes would be opened up to you by these purely personal ideas of mine. But, if you want them to be one hundred per cent creative and categorical, there is still one more step that you must take, and this is such a bold and tremendous step, and its possibilities as so unlimited and its consequences so devastating that it is only softly and from afar that my lips shall mention it. Well, then, this is it. The time has come, the hour has struck on the clock of ages. *Try to set yourself against form, try to shake free of it.* Cease to identify yourself with that which defines you. Try to escape from all expression of yourself. Mistrust your opinions. Mistrust your beliefs, and defend yourself against your feelings. Withdraw from what you seem to be from outside, and flee from all externalization just as the bird flees from the snake.

For—but frankly I do not know whether the time has yet come to tell you this—it is a false assumption that man should be definite, that is to say, unshakeable in his ideas, categorical in his statements, clear in his ideologies, rigid in his tastes, responsible in his speech and actions, crystallized and precise in his way of being. Examine more closely the chimerical nature of the assumption. Our element is eternal immaturity. The things that we think, feel, and say today will necessarily seem foolish to our grandchildren; so it would surely be better to forestall this now, and treat them as if they were foolish already; moreover, the force that impels you to premature finality is not, as you believe, an entirely human force. We shall soon realize that henceforward the most important thing is not to die for ideas, styles, theories, or even to attach oneself to and buttress oneself with them; but to take a step backwards and withdraw in the face of all the things that keep on happening inside us.

Let the cry be backwards! I foresee (though I do not know if the time has yet come to admit it) that the general retreat will soon be sounded. The son of man will realize that he is not expressing himself in harmony with his true nature, but in an artificial manner painfully inflicted on him from outside, either by other men or by circumstances. He will then begin to fear this form that is his own, and to be as ashamed of it as he was previously proud of it and sought stability in it. We shall soon begin to be afraid of ourselves and our personalities, because we shall discover that they do not completely belong to us. And instead of bellowing and shouting: I believe this, I feel that, I am this, I stand for that, we shall say more humbly: In me there is a belief, a feeling, a thought, I am the vehicle for such-and-such an action, production, or whatever it may be. . . . The poet will repudiate his song, the commander will tremble at his own orders, the priest will fear his altar, mothers will no longer be satisfied with teaching their children principles, but will also teach them how to evade them, to prevent them from being stifled by them. And, above all, human beings will one day meet other human beings face to face.

It will be a long and painful path. For nowadays individuals, like nations, can organize their mental life almost at will, and are able to change styles, beliefs, principles, ideals, and feelings as their immediate interests dictate. But they do not yet know how to live and preserve their humanity without style; and we are far from being able to preserve our interior warmth, our freshness, and our human kindness against the Mephistopheles of order. Great discoveries will have to be made, great blows will have to be struck with our poor bare hands against the tough armour-plate of form. Unparalleled cunning, great honesty of thought, and intelligence sharpened to a degree, will be required to enable man to escape from his stiff exterior and succeed in better reconciling order with disorder, form with the formless, maturity with eternal and sacred immaturity. In the meantime tell me which you prefer, red peppers or fresh cucumbers? And do you like enjoying them quietly sitting in the shade of a tree while a sweet and gentle breeze cools the parts of your body? I ask you this question with the greatest seriousness, with the most complete sense of responsibility for what I am saying, and with the greatest respect for all your parts without exception, for I know that you are a part of the humanity of which I too am part, and that you partially participate in something which is in turn a part and of which I too am a part, at any rate in part, like all other particles and parts of parts of parts of parts of parts of parts of parts of parts of parts of parts. Help! Oh, accursed parts! Oh, bloodthirsty and horrifying parts, once more you assault and persecute and stifle and suffocate me from every quarter. Enough, enough! There's nothing that can be done, nothing that can be done about it. Oh, parts with whom I wanted to take refuge, you now rise against me! Enough, enough, let us leave this part of the book, and go on to another, and I swear before God that in the next chapter there will be no more parts, no parts whatever, because I am getting rid of parts, showing them the door, and remaining (at any rate for my part) inside, without parts.

* 5 *

Philifor Honeycombed with Childishness

THE prince of synthetists, recognized as the greatest synthetist of all times, was the higher synthetist Dr Philifor, who came from the south of Annam, and was Professor of Synthetisiology in the University of Leyden. He worked according to the pathetic spirit of higher synthesis, generally using the method of adding infinity, though sometimes, when occasion arose, he adopted that of multiplying by infinity. He was a well built, rather corpulent man, with a shaggy beard and the face of a bespectacled prophet. By virtue of Newton's principle of action and equal and opposite reaction, an intellectual phenomenon of such magnitude could not fail to provoke a counter-phenomenon in the bosom of nature; hence the birth at Colombo of an eminent analyst who, after obtaining his doctor's degree and the title of professor of higher analysis at Columbia University, climbed rapidly to the top of the academic tree. He was a dry, slightly built, beardless man, with the face of a bespectacled sceptic, and his sole interior driving force was to pursue and humiliate the distinguished Philifor.

He worked analytically, and his speciality was breaking down individuals into their constituent parts, with the aid of calculation, and more particularly flicks of the finger. With the aid of the latter he was able to invite a nose to enjoy an independent existence of its own and make it move spontaneously this way and that, to the great terror of its owner. When he was bored he used frequently to practise this art on the tram. In response to his deepest vocation he set out in pursuit of Philifor, and in a town somewhere in Spain succeeded in procuring for himself the title of Anti-Philifor, of which he was very proud. Philifor, having discovered that he was being pursued, immediately set out on the heels of his pursuer, and the mutual pursuit of the two men of learning went on for a long time—without result, however, because each was prevented by pride from admitting that he was the pursued as well as the pursuer. Consequently, when Philifor was at Bremen, for instance, Anti-Philifor would hurry there from The Hague, refusing, or perhaps being unable, to take into account the fact that at that very moment Philifor for reasons identical with his own was taking his seat in the Bremen-The Hague express. The collision between the two—a disaster on the scale of the greatest railway accidents—finally took place by pure chance in the first-class restaurant of the Hotel Bristol in Warsaw. Professor Philifor, accompanied by Mrs Philifor, was carefully consulting the indicator when Anti-Philifor, who had just got off the train, entered breathlessly, arm-in-arm with his analytical travelling companion, Fiora Gente of Messina. We who were present, that is to say, Dr Theophilus Poklewski, Dr Theodore Roklewski, and myself, realizing the gravity of the situation, immediately started taking notes.

Anti-Philifor advanced silently and gazed into the eyes of Professor Philifor, who rose to his feet. Each tried to impose the force of his personality on the other. The analyst's eyes travelled coldly from his opponent's feet upwards; those of the stoutly resisting synthetist worked in the opposite direction, from the head downwards. As the outcome of this struggle was a draw, with no advantage accruing to either side, the two contestants resorted to a verbal duel. The doctor and master of analysis said:

'Gnocchi!'

'Gnocchi!' the synthetisiologist retorted.

'Gnocchi, gnocchi, or a mixture of eggs, flour and water,' said Anti-Philifor, and Philifor capped this with:

'Gnocchi means the higher essence, the supreme spirit of gnocchi, the thing-in-itself.'

His eyes flashed fire, he wagged his beard, it was obvious that he had won. The professor of higher analysis recoiled a few paces, seized with impotent rage, but a dreadful idea suddenly flashed into his mind. A sickly and puny man in comparison with Philifor, he decided to attack Mrs Philifor, who was the apple of her worthy professor-husband's eye. The incident, according to the eye-witnesses' report, then developed as follows:

1. Professor Philifor's wife, a stout and majestic woman, was seated, silently absorbed in her thoughts.

2. Professor Anti-Philifor, armed with his cerebral gear, placed himself in front of her, and started undressing her with his eyes, from foot to head. Mrs Philifor trembled with cold and shame. Professor Philifor silently covered her with her travelling rug, casting a look of infinite contempt at the insolent Professor Anti-Philifor, but nevertheless betraying some slight traces of anxiety.

3. Professor Anti-Philifor then calmly said: 'Ear, ear,' and laughed sardonically. At these words the woman's ear appeared in all its nakedness and became indecent, and Professor Philifor ordered her to conceal it beneath her hat. This was not of much use, however, for Anti-Philifor muttered, as if to himself, the words 'two nostrils', thus laying bare in shameful and analytical fashion the nostrils of the professor's highly respectable wife. This aggravated the situation, for there was no way of concealing her nostrils.

4. Professor Philifor threatened to call the police; the tide of battle seemed to be turning distinctly in his opponent's favour. The master of analysis said with intense mental concentration: 'Fingers, the five fingers of each hand.' Mrs Philifor's resistance, unfortunately, was insufficient to conceal a reality which disclosed itself to the eyes of those present in all its stark nakedness, i.e. the five fingers of each of her two hands. There they were, five on each side. Mrs Philifor, utterly profaned, gathered her last strength to try to put on her gloves, but an incredible thing happened. Professor Anti-Philifor fired at her point-blank an

analysis of her urine. With a loud guffaw, he exclaimed victoriously: 'H_2O, C_4, TPS, some leucocytes, and albumen!' Everyone rose, Professor Anti-Philifor withdrew with his mistress, who giggled in a vulgar manner, while Professor Philifor, aided by the undersigned, hurriedly took his wife to hospital. (*Signed*) T. Poklewski, T. Roklewski, Anton Swistak, eye-witnesses.

Next morning Roklewski, Poklewski, and I myself joined the Professor at Mrs Philifor's bedside. Her disintegration, set in train by Anti-Philifor's analytic tooth, was proceeding apace, and she was progressively losing her physiological contexture. From time to time she said with a hollow groan: 'My leg, my eye, my leg, my ear, my finger, my head, my leg,' as if she were bidding farewell to the various parts of her body, which were already moving independently of her. Her personality was in its death-throes. We racked our brains for some way of saving her, but could think of nothing. After further consultations, in which Assistant Professor S. Lopatkin took part—he arrived by the seven-forty plane from Moscow—we were confirmed in our conclusion that the situation called for the application of the most extreme methods of scientific synthetism. But none existed. Philifor thereupon concentrated his mental faculties to such good purpose that we all recoiled a step. He said:

'I've got it! A slap in the face! Only a well-aimed slap in the face can restore my wife's honour and synthesize the scattered elements on a higher level.'

It was no easy task to find the world-famous analyst in the big city; not until nightfall did we succeed in tracking him down to a first-class bar, where he was soberly engaged in drinking. He was emptying bottle after bottle, and the more he drank, the more sober he became; and the same applied to his analytical mistress; the truth of the matter was that both found sobriety more intoxicating than alcohol. When we walked in, the waiters, who had turned as white as their napkins, had timidly taken refuge behind the bar, and the two lovers were silently devoting themselves to an interminable orgy of keeping cool and collected.

We drew up a plan of action. Professor Philifor would first of all feint in the direction of the left cheek and then strike out in earnest at the right, while we witnesses, i.e. Poklewski, Roklewski, and myself, all three holders of doctor's degrees in the University of Warsaw, accompanied by Assistant Professor S. Lopatkin, would proceed forthwith to the drawing up of our report. It was a simple and straightforward plan, calling for no very complicated action, but the professor raised his arm, only to let it drop to his side again. We witnesses were left in a state of stupefaction. The slap in the face did not take place. I repeat, the slap in the face did not take place. All that took place was two little roses and a rough illustration of two doves.

With satanic insight Anti-Philifor had foreseen Philifor's move. The temperate Bacchus had had two little roses tattooed on each cheek, as well as something resembling two doves. Anti-Philifor's cheeks and Philifor's planned blow were thus deprived of meaning; slapping roses and doves would be as idle as casually slapping a piece of painted paper. Thinking it out of the question that our learned and universally respected educator of youth should expose himself to ridicule by striking a piece of painted paper because of his wife's illness, we succeeded in persuading him to abandon a course of action which he might subsequently regret.

'Vile dog!' the professor growled. 'Vile, vile, vile dog!'

'You are an amorphous collection of disparate parts,' the analyst replied, in a burst of analytic pride. 'You are an amorphous collection of disparate parts, and so am I. Kick me in the stomach, if you like; it won't be I whom you kick, but my stomach, and that's all. You wished to provoke my face by slapping it? Well, you can provoke my cheek, but not me. I do not exist! I simply do not exist!'

'I'll provoke your face! As sure as God's in His heaven, I'll provoke your face!'

'My cheeks are impervious to provocation,' Anti-Philifor replied with a sneer.

Fiora Gente, who was sitting by his side, burst out laughing.

The cosmic doctor of double analysis leered sensually at his mistress and walked out. Fiora Gente, however, remained. She was perched on a high stool and looked at us with the relaxed eyes of a completely analysed parrot. A little later, at 8.40 p.m. to be precise, we, that is to say Professor Philifor, the two doctors, Assistant Professor Lopatkin and myself, held a conference. Assistant Professor Lopatkin as usual wielded the fountain-pen. The conference proceeded as follows:

The three doctors of law: 'In view of what has occurred, we see no possibility of settling this quarrel in an honourable manner, and we therefore advise the respected professor to ignore the insult to which he has been subjected, because it came from an individual incapable of giving satisfaction.'

Professor Philifor: 'I propose to ignore it, but my wife is dying.'

Assistant Professor Lopatkin: 'There is no way of saving your wife.'

Professor Philifor: 'Don't say that! Oh, don't say that! A slap in the face is the only hope! But there is no slap in the face, there is no cheek! There is no method of divine synthesis! There is no God! But yes! yes! There are faces! There are slaps! There is a God! Honour! Synthesis!'

Myself: 'I observe that the professor is being illogical. Either there are faces, or there are not.'

Philifor: 'Gentlemen, you forget that I still have my two cheeks. His cheeks do not exist, but mine do. We can still achieve our aim with my two cheeks, which are intact. Gentlemen, what I mean is this: I cannot slap his face, but he can slap mine! It will come to the same thing. A face will have been slapped and synthesis achieved!'

'But how shall we get him to slap the professor's face?'

'How shall we get him to slap the professor's face?'

'How shall we get him to slap the professor?'

'Gentlemen,' the brilliant thinker composedly replied, 'he has cheeks, but I have too. There is an analogy here, and I shall therefore be acting less logically than analogically; that will be much more effective, because nature is governed by the law of analogy. If he is the king of analysis, I am the king of synthesis. If he has cheeks, so have I. If I have a wife, he has a mistress. If he has analysed my wife, I shall synthesize his mistress, and in that fashion I shall get from him the slap that he refuses me.'

Without further delay he beckoned to Fiora Gente. We were left speechless with amazement. She approached, moving all the parts of her body, ogling me with one eye and the professor with the other, smiling with all her teeth at Stephen Lopatkin, projecting her front towards Roklewski and her behind towards Poklewski. The impression she made was such that the assistant professor muttered:

'Are you really proposing to attack those fifty separate parts with your higher synthesis?'

The universal synthetisiologist, however, possessed the virtue of never losing hope. He invited Fiora Gente to sit at the small table, offered her a Cinzano, and by way of preamble, to test the ground, said to her sympathetically:

'Soul, soul.'

She did not reply.

'I!' said the professor imperuously and inquisitorially, desiring to awaken her annihilated ego.

'You? Oh, all right! Five zlotys!'

'Unity!' Philifor exclaimed violently. 'Higher unity! Equality in unity!'

'Boy or old man, it's all the same to me,' she said with the most complete indifference.

We gazed in discouragement at this infernal analyst of the night, whom Anti-Philifor had brought up in his own image, and perhaps trained for himself since earliest childhood.

The father of the synthetic sciences refused, however, to be discouraged. A phase of intense effort and struggle ensued. He read to her the first two cantos of the *Divina Commedia*, for which she charged him ten zlotys. He made her an inspired speech on the higher love which unifies and encompasses everything, and that cost him eleven zlotys. For agreeing to allow him to read to her two superb novels by two well-known women novelists about regeneration by love she asked a hundred and fifty zlotys, and refused to consider a farthing less; and finally, when he got to the point of appealing to her dignity, she insisted on fifty zlotys.

'Fancies have to be paid for, grandpa,' she said. 'For fancies there's no fixed rate.'

Opening and shutting her self-satisfied owl's eyes, she remained entirely untouched by the experience. Her charges kept piling up, and Anti-Philifor, wandering round the town, shook with interior laughter at all these desperate endeavours.

In the course of the subsequent conference, in which Assistant Professor Lopatkin and the three professors took part, the eminent seeker after truth summed up his defeat:

'It has cost me several hundred zlotys already and I really do not see the slightest possibility of any synthesis,' he said. 'In vain I had recourse to the supreme unities such as humanity; she turns everything into money and hands back the change. Meanwhile my wife is steadily losing what remains of her homogeneity. Her leg has already got to the point of walking round the room on its own. When she gets drowsy, she tries to hold it with her hands, but her hands refuse to obey her. It is the most shattering, appalling anarchy.'

Dr T. Poklewski, M.D.: 'And meanwhile Anti-Philifor is spreading the story that the professor is a vicious and depraved old gentleman.'

Assistant Professor Lopatkin: 'But might we not after all be able to catch her with the aid of money? I do not yet see clearly the idea for which I am groping in my mind, but things like that happen in nature. Let me explain. I had a woman patient who suffered from shyness. It was impossible to inject boldness into her, because she was incapable of assimilating it. But I succeeded in injecting into her such an enormous dose of shyness that she could not tolerate it. Finding shyness intolerable, she took courage, and became very bold indeed. The best method is to cure the disease by the disease itself. There must be some way of synthesizing her by means of money, but I confess that I do not . . .'

Professor Philifor: 'Money . . . money . . . but money always adds up to a definite sum, a definite amount, which has nothing in common with unity in the true sense of the word. The only sum of money that is indivisible is a farthing, and nobody is impressed by a farthing. . . . But gentlemen, suppose . . . suppose we offered her such a huge sum that she was thunderstruck by it!'

We were left open-mouthed in astonishment. Philifor rose to his feet, his black beard trembling. He was now in one of those hypermanic states which invariably affect genius at seven-year intervals. He sold two houses and a villa in the neighbourhood of Warsaw, and changed the 850,000 zlotys thus realized into one-zloty pieces. Poklewski looked at him in amazement. A simple country doctor, he had never had any understanding of genius, and that was why he failed to understand it now. The philosopher was now sure of himself, however, and sent Anti-Philifor an ironic invitation. The latter sent a sarcastic reply and turned up punctually at nine-thirty in a private room at the Alcazar restaurant, where the decisive test was to take place. The two scholars did not shake hands. The master of analysis laughed, and his laughter was dry and malicious.

'Carry on, sir,' he said. 'Carry on! My woman friend is obviously less liable to composition than is your wife to decomposition. On that my mind is at rest.'

But he too entered progressively into a more and more hypermanic state. Dr Poklewski's fountain-pen was poised and Assistant Professor Lopatkin held the paper at the ready.

Professor Philifor set about things as follows. First of all he laid on the table one zloty. Fiora Gente did not budge. He put down a second zloty; nothing happened. He put down a third; again nothing happened. But when he put down the fourth, she said:

'Oh! Four zlotys!'

At the fifth she yawned, and at the sixth she remarked with an air of indifference:

'What's up, grandpa? Have you gone crackers again?'

Not until after the ninety-seventh zloty did we observe the first symptoms of surprise. At the 115th her eyes, which had been wandering from Dr Poklewski to Assistant Professor Lopatkin and myself, started tending to synthesize somewhat on the money.

At 100,000 zlotys Philifor was gasping painfully for breath. Anti-Philifor was beginning to show signs of alarm, and the hitherto heterogeneous courtesan acquired a certain concentration. She gazed fascinated at the pile, which, to tell the truth was ceasing to be a pile, and tried to count, but she had lost her head for reckoning. The sum had ceased to be a sum, had turned into something impossible to grasp in its entirety, something so tremendous, so inconceivable, that the mind boggled at it, as it does when it considers the dimensions of space. The patient let out a hollow groan. The analyst tried to dash to her assistance, but the two doctors restrained him. In vain he whispered to her to divide the total into hundreds, or five hundreds, but the total refused to yield to this treatment. When the triumphant high priest of synthesis had spent all he had and crowned the pile, or rather the mountain, the Mount Sinai, of money with the last single and indivisible zloty, it was as if some divinity had taken possession of the courtesan. She rose to her feet, showing every symptom of synthesis—tears, sighs, smiles, thoughtfulness—and said:

'Gentlemen, myself. My higher self!'

Philifor uttered a cry of triumph, and with a frantic yell Anti-Philifor broke loose from the two doctors' hold, dashed at Philifor, and struck him in the face.

This synthetic lightning flash snatched from the analytic entrails dispelled the shadows. The assistant professor and the doctors heartily congratulated the gravely dishonoured professor. His sworn enemy writhed and gesticulated in a frenzy against the wall, but no amount of frenzy could now deprive the victorious march of honour of its momentum, and the whole affair, which had hitherto been not very honourable, was now firmly set on an honourable course.

Professor G. L. Philifor of Leyden appointed as his seconds Dr Lopatkin and myself; Professor P. T. Momsen, known by his honorary title of Anti-Philifor, chose the two doctors present. Philifor's seconds honourably challenged Anti-Philifor's seconds, and these in turn challenged Philifor's. Each of these honourable steps created more and more synthesis, and the professor of Columbia University writhed as if he were standing on hot coals, while the sage of Leyden stroked his beard and smiled. At the municipal hospital Mrs Philifor started regaining her unity; in a barely audible whisper she asked for a glass of milk, and hope revived in the doctors' breasts. Honour had made its appearance among the clouds and was smiling down upon mankind. The duel was fixed for Tuesday at 7 a.m.

It was agreed that the fountain-pen should be entrusted to Dr Roklewski, and the pistols to Assistant Professor Lopatkin; and that Dr Poklewski should hold the paper and I the overcoats. The tireless advocate of the cause of synthesis refused to be affected by doubt, dismay or fear. I recall his saying to me on the eve of the duel: 'Young man, I know that I am just as likely to be left on the field of honour as he, but, whatever happens, my spirit will survive and be victorious, for death is essentially synthetic. If he dies, his end will be a tribute paid to synthesis; if he kills me, he will do so synthetically. Hence in any event victory will be mine!' In this state of exaltation, desiring to celebrate more worthily his moment of glory, he invited the womenfolk—his wife and Fiora Gente—to attend in the capacity of simple spectators. I was filled with grim forebodings, I feared . . . what did I fear? I did not know myself. All night I lay a prey to grim anxiety, and not until I reached the appointed duelling ground did I tumble to the reason, which was symmetry; for the situation was symmetrical; hence its strength, but hence also its weakness.

For every move of Philifor led to a similar move by Anti-

Philifor, and the initiative was Philifor's. If Philifor raised his hat, Anti-Philifor must do the same. If Philifor fired, so must he. Moreover, the whole of the action was confined to an imaginary straight line drawn between the two duellists; and this line was the axis of the whole situation. But suppose Anti-Philifor departed from it? Suppose he treacherously wandered from the straight path, basely evaded the iron laws of symmetry and analogy? What vileness, what intellectual depravity might not be hatching in his brain? I was plunged in these thoughts when Professor Philifor raised his arm, aimed at his opponent's heart, fired, and missed. The analyst likewise raised his arm and aimed at his opponent's heart. It seemed almost inevitable that if the former fired synthetically at the heart, the latter must do the same, there seemed to be no possible alternative; no alternative seemed intellectually conceivable. But the analyst made a supreme effort, uttered a savage yell, deflected the barrel of his pistol from the axis of the situation and fired. Where would the bullet strike? Where? Mrs Philifor, accompanied by Fiora Gente, was standing a little to one side, and it struck her little finger. It was a master-shot; the finger was cut clean off and dropped to the ground. Mrs Philifor in astonishment put her hand to her mouth. For a moment we seconds lost all control of ourselves and let out a cry of admiration.

This was too much for the professor of higher synthesis, and something dreadful happened. Fascinated by his opponent's precision of aim, virtuosity and symmetry, and annoyed at our cry of admiration at his marksmanship, he too diverged from the axis, fired, hit Fiora Gente's little finger, and let forth a short, derisive, guttural laugh.

Then the analyst fired again, severing Mrs Philifor's other little finger and causing her to put her other hand to her mouth. Again we exclaimed with admiration. A fraction of a second later the synthetist fired, and with infallible aim deprived Fiora Gente of her other little finger from a distance of six or seven yards. She put her hand to her mouth, and we could not refrain from another exclamation of admiration. And so events took their course. The firing continued, incessant, angry, and as magnificent as magnificence itself; and fingers, ears, noses, and teeth fell like the leaves of a tree in a high wind. We seconds were left with no time to express our admiration at the accuracy of the hail of fire that ensued. The two ladies were soon deprived of all their extremities and natural protuberances; if they did not fall dead it was simply because of lack of time, and I also suspect that they felt greatly flattered at being the target of such consummate marksmanship. With his last round the master from Leyden holed the upper part of Fiora Gente's right lung. Once more we exclaimed with admiration, then silence fell. Life passed from the two women's bodies, they collapsed to the ground, and the two marksmen looked at each other.

And then? They went on looking at each other, without knowing why. And then? And then? They had both run out of ammunition. The dead bodies lay on the ground. There was no more to be done. It was nearly ten o'clock. Strictly speaking, the analyst had won, but what difference did that make? None whatever. If the synthetist had won, it would have made no difference either. Philifor picked up a stone, threw it at a sparrow, and missed; the sparrow flew away. The sun was getting very hot. Anti-Philifor threw a lump of earth at a tree-trunk, and hit it. Philifor threw a stone at a hen which passed across his line of sight; he hit it, and it went and hid behind a bush. The two men of learning then abandoned their positions and went their separate ways.

At dusk Anti-Philifor was at Jeziorno and Philifor at Wawer. The former was shooting rabbits from under the shadow of a windmill; the latter, when he came upon a gas-lamp in an isolated spot, fired at it from fifty paces.

Thus they wandered about the world, firing at what they could with what they could. They sang popular songs and broke windows when they felt like it; and they also enjoyed spitting from balconies at the hats of passers-by. Philifor actually became so skilled that he was able to spit from the roadway at people on first-floor balconies; and Anti-Philifor could put out candles by throwing matchboxes at the flame. Things that they enjoyed even more were shooting frogs with small-calibre rifles and sparrows with bow and arrow; and sometimes they would stand on bridges and throw grass and paper into the stream below. But their greatest pleasure of all was buying a red balloon and chasing it across country, waiting for the thrilling moment when it burst noisily as if struck by an invisible bullet.

And when someone from the academic world recalled their glorious past, their intellectual jousts, analysis, synthesis, and the fame that had now vanished for ever, they would answer rather dreamily:

'Oh, yes, I remember the duel . . . the shooting was excellent!'

'But professor,' I once exclaimed, simultaneously with Roklewski, who had meanwhile married and settled down in Krucza Street, 'you talk like a child!'

And the puerile old man replied:

'Young man, everything is honeycombed with childishness.'

★ 6 ★

Further Inveiglement into Childhood

THUS at the very moment when the appalling psycho-physical violation of Siphon was approaching its climax the classroom door opened and in walked Pimko, clothed in all his infallibility and his exceptional personality.

'How well you young people play ball!' he exclaimed, though it was exceedingly obvious that we were not playing ball—there was no ball in the room.

'So you boys are playing ball,' he continued. 'See how gracefully one boy throws it, how skilfully another catches it!' A flush came over my face, which was pale and contracted with fear, and Pimko noticed it.

'What a healthy colouring you've got already! School is obviously doing you good, and so is playing ball, Johnnie!' he said.

'Come along, then,' he went on. 'Now I'm taking you to Mrs Youthful's, where I've taken a room for you. That's where you'll be living from now on, at Mrs Youthful's.'

And, still talking, he led me away. On the way he talked to me about Mr Youthful, engineer-architect, and his wife.

'You'll find yourself in a very modern environment,' he said. 'Excessively modern, in fact, the Youthfuls' modern ideas are very different from mine. But I detect in you a certain tendency towards posing and affectation, you create the impression that you are still pretending to be grown up. . . . Never mind, the Youthfuls will soon cure you of that and teach you to be yourself. I forgot to tell you that they have a daughter, named Zutka, a young lady who is still at school,' he went on, holding me by the hand and looking at me under his spectacles. 'And a very modern schoolgirl she is too. H'm, she's not ideal company for you, the danger's obvious enough. On the other hand, there's nothing like a modern schoolgirl to attract you towards youthfulness, she'll certainly succeed in converting you to the religion of your age.'

Trams passed. There were flowers in the windows of some of the houses. Someone aimed a plum-stone at Pimko from a top storey, but missed.

A schoolgirl? What was the meaning of this? I saw through Pimko's little plan. He wanted to use her to set the seal on my imprisonment in youthfulness; he thought that if I fell in love with her I should lose all desire to be grown up. I must be allowed not a moment of respite, either at school or at home, I must be allowed no loophole for escape. There was no time to lose. Quickly I bit his finger and ran away. A grown-up woman was just turning the corner. I dashed towards her, dazed, convulsed, my face bruised, in a desperate effort to escape from Pimko and his appalling schoolgirl. But the great reducer to childhood caught up with me in a flash and seized me by the collar.

'To the schoolgirl!' he exclaimed. 'To the schoolgirl! To youth! To the Youthfuls!'

He put me in a cab and took me to the schoolgirl, through streets that were full of people. The sun shone and the sky was full of birds.

'Forward!' he exclaimed. 'Forward! Why do you keep looking back? There's nothing behind you, and there's only me beside you!'

He took my hand and sputtered:

'To the schoolgirl, the modern schoolgirl! She'll make you fall in love with youth! The Youthfuls will reduce you to littleness. They'll give you a little backside. Backsidikins!' he exclaimed so loudly that the horse started lashing out, and the cabby, after reinstalling himself on his seat, turned his back on him with the utmost contempt.

On the point of entering one of those cheap houses which abound in modern suburbs, Pimko seemed to hesitate and, curiously enough, seemed to lose some of his notorious absolutism.

'Johnnie,' he muttered, shaking his head, 'I am making a great sacrifice for you. I am making it for the sake of your youth; it is for the sake of your youth that I am exposing myself to this encounter. H'm, the schoolgirl, the modern schoolgirl!'

He embraced me as if he wanted to seek my favour—but also as if taking leave of me for ever.

Then he started striking the ground with his stick and, in a state of great excitement, declaiming poetry, making quotations, delivering himself of ideas, opinions, aphorisms, all in the very best and most impressive style; but at the same time he seemed to be ill, with a threat pointing like an arrow straight at his pedagogic heart. He quoted the names of writers who were unknown to me but were friends of his, and quietly repeated the flattering things that they had said about him and the flattering things that he had said about them. Moreover, he produced a pencil and wrote the word 'Pimko' three times on the wall—a new Antaeus drawing fresh strength from the mere sight of his own signature. I looked at the master in astonishment. What was the meaning of this? Did he too fear the modern schoolgirl? Or was he merely pretending? How could such a masterly master be afraid of a mere schoolgirl? But the maid came and opened the door. We went in together. The master entered almost humbly, leaving his notorious superiority on the doorstep, and I with my face cruelly crushed and battered, like a crumpled piece of paper. He tapped the floor with his stick and said: 'Is madam in?' At the same moment the schoolgirl emerged from a door at the end of the hall. The modern schoolgirl.

She was sixteen, wore sweater, skirt, and crêpe-soled shoes, was tall, slim, supple, and looked athletic and insolent. I looked at her, and my spirit and my face both trembled. I saw at once that here was a phenomenon perhaps more powerful than

Pimko, as absolute in its way as he. She reminded me of someone, but of whom? Oh, Kopeida of course. You have not forgotten Kopeida? She was like him, but stronger, of the same type, but more intensely, the perfect schoolgirl looking like a modern schoolgirl, perfect in her modernism. She was young twice over —by reason of her age and by reason of her modernity; that was it, she was young because of her youth.

Consequently I was terrified at being confronted with something stronger than myself, and still more terrified when I saw that it was not she who was afraid of the professor, but the professor who was afraid of her. There was shyness in his voice when he addressed her. 'My compliments, young lady,' he said with forced gaiety and courtesy. 'So you are not on the beach? Not on the banks of the Vistula? Is your mother at home? What is the water in the pool like today? Cold, isn't it? But cold water is best. I always used to take cold baths in my time!'

Could I believe my ears? In Pimko's voice I detected old age obsequiously toadying to athletic youth—and I stepped back. The girl did not answer Pimko, she merely looked at him. She put between her teeth the spanner which she had been holding in her right hand, and held him out her left hand with as much indifference as if he had not been Pimko at all. The professor faltered, did not know what to do with the youthful left hand she held out towards him, and ended by taking it between both his hands. I bowed. The girl took the spanner out of her mouth and said:

'Mother's out, but she'll be back soon. Come in!'

She led us into a modern living-room and remained standing while we sat on a divan-bed.

'I suppose your mother is at the committee meeting,' said Pimko, starting a social conversation.

'I don't know,' the modern girl replied.

The walls were painted light blue, and the curtains were cream. There was a wireless set in the corner. The modern furniture was simple, sober, and spotless. There were two built-in cupboards and a small table. The girl stood looking out of the window as if she were alone in the room, and started removing bits of blistered skin from her sunburnt face. Our presence simply did not count so far as she was concerned, she took no notice whatever of Pimko, and the minutes started ticking away. Pimko crossed his legs and his fingers, and started twiddling his thumbs, like a guest who has not been suitably received. He shifted in his seat, cleared his throat two or three times, coughed, tried to keep up the conversation, but the girl stood there with her back turned towards us and went on picking her face. Pimko ended by falling silent and confined himself to remaining seated, but there was something imperfect and incomplete about his silent posture. I rubbed my eyes. What was happening? For something was happening, that was certain. Pimko's sovereign sitting incomplete? The master? The master inadequate? Incompleteness implies that something is lacking. You know the sensation of discomfort you get when something has finished and nothing else has started yet? A void formed in my head. Suddenly I saw age emanating from the master. I had not realized that he was over fifty, it simply had never occurred to me, as if the absolute master were eternal, exempt from time. Old man or master? What a question! Why not simply old master? No, it wasn't that at all. But what new plot were they hatching against me? For I was perfectly certain that he and the girl were hatching some new plot at my expense.

Why in heaven's name was he sitting there like this? Why was he sitting there next to me opposite the girl? His sitting there was all the more irritating to me because I was sitting next to him. It would not have been so bad if I had been able to get up. But the fact of the matter was that it was impossible for me to get up, there was no reason whatever why I should get up. No, no, it wasn't that at all, but why was he sitting opposite the girl? Have pity on me! There was no pity. Why was he sitting there with the girl? Why was his old age not ordinary old age, but a schoolgirlish old age? Fear suddenly gripped me, but I could not move. Schoolgirlish old age, ancestro-juvenile old age, confused, repulsive, half-formed ideas galloped through my mind.

Suddenly a song re-echoed through the room. I could not believe my ears. The master was singing the girl an aria.

Astonishment brought me back to my senses. No, he wasn't singing, he was humming. In his resentment at the girl's indifference he had started humming some operetta tune, thus drawing attention to her bad manners. The result was that he was singing. She was forcing the little old man to sing! Was this old dodderer sprawling on the divan and forced to sing in the girl's presence, the formidable, the absolute, the forceful, the irresistible Pimko?

I felt very weak. In the course of all my adventures since the morning my face muscles had not been allowed a single moment of relaxation, and my cheeks were burning as if I had spent a whole night in a train. But now it seemed as if the train were about to stop. Pimko was singing. I felt ashamed at having allowed myself to be dominated for so long by a harmless little old man of whom a vulgar little schoolgirl took not the slightest notice. My face started gradually returning to normal, I sat back comfortably, and rapidly started recovering my balance and—oh the joy of it!—my lost thirty years. I got up, intending to walk out quietly, without a word of explanation. But the professor seized my hand. He was different now. He had aged, softened, diminished, and I felt sorry for him.

'Johnnie,' he muttered in my ear, 'don't model yourself on this modern girl, who belongs to the new, post-war generation, the sport-and-jazz age! These barbarous post-war manners! This decay of civilization! The lack of respect! The new generation's passion for enjoying itself, its passion to enjoy life! I am beginning to think that this will not be a healthy environment for you! Give me your word of honour that you will not allow yourself to be influenced by this impudent little hussy! You have something in common with her, you are like her in some ways, I know'—the old man spoke feverishly—'because you are, after all, a modern boy! Oh, what a mistake it was to bring you here, to this modern girl!'

I looked at him as one looks at a lunatic. What had I, a man of thirty, in common with a modern schoolgirl? I decided that

Pimko was raving. But he went on warning me against the modern girl.

'These are new times,' he went on. 'You, the young, the rising generation, scorn your elders, and start calling each other by your Christian names straight away. You have no respect for anything, no respect for the past, dancing, America, *carpe diem*! You young people!'

And he launched into terrible flattery of my alleged youth and modernism, saying more or less that we young people were interested only in legs, and flattering us in other ways, while the girl went on picking her face with the most complete indifference, totally oblivious to what was going on behind her back.

In the end I realized what Pimko was trying to do. He was trying to make me fall in love with the girl; he wanted to hand me straight over to her to prevent me from escaping. He wanted to graft an ideal on me, knowing that if, like Mientus or Siphon, I once succumbed to a definite youthful ideal, I should remain its prisoner for ever. To put it in a nutshell, he cared little what kind of boy I became; all he cared about was preventing my escape from boyhood. If he managed to get me to fall in love straight away, if he got me to succumb to the modern youth ideal, he would be able safely to leave me alone and devote himself to his numerous other activities, which might otherwise prevent him from maintaining me permanently in my diminished state. And the paradox was that Pimko, who evidently set such great store by his own superiority, was, for the sake of pushing me at the girl, actually willing to accept the humiliating role of an antiquated old fossil indignant at the ways of modern youth, thus making me the girl's ally against him and propelling me into modernism and youthfulness. But he also nourished another and no less important design. He did not just want to make me fall in love with her; he wanted to bind me to her in the greatest possible immaturity. He did not want me to fall in love with her in the ordinary way; he wanted to see me consumed by that particularly cheap and nasty kind of modern-ancient passion born of a mixture of pre-war fossil and post-war schoolgirl. All this was very ingenious but really too stupid, and I listened to the old man's clumsy praises feeling completely confident of my total liberation. Too stupid? It was I who was too stupid. I was too stupid, because I did not know that it is only stupid poetry which is really alluring and fascinating.

And out of nothing a terrible whole was born, an appalling poetical constellation. Over there at the window was the modern girl, clothed in complete indifference. Here on the divan was the little old professor. And here was I in between them, assaulted by ancestro-juvenile poetry. Heavens, my thirty years—I must get out of this quickly! But, as if the world had been broken to pieces and put together again on an entirely new basis, my thirty years receded and faded, while the girl at the window grew more and more appetizing. And the accursed Pimko went on.

'Legs!' he said, to stimulate my interest in modernism. 'Legs! I know all about you and your fondness for outdoor games and exercise, I know all about the tastes of the young, Americanized generation. You prefer legs to arms, for you only legs count; and thighs! Outdoor games and exercise! Thighs! Thighs!'—he flattered me terribly—'Thighs! Thighs! Thighs!'

And, just as at school he had injected into us the problem of innocence, which had so dreadfully increased the boys' immaturity, so did he now lure me towards the modern thigh. And it was with pleasure that I heard him associating my thighs with those of the young generation, and sure enough, I started feeling a sense of youthful cruelty towards the thighs of the old. A sort of camaraderie of thighs was established between me and the girl, a kind of secret understanding by way of the thigh, a thigh religion, youthful pride in the thigh, veneration for the thigh. What an infernal part of the body! All this, needless to say, took place in silence behind the girl's back; there she stood at the window, on her thighs, picking her face and taking no notice of anything.

All the same, I should have shaken off this thigh business and fled if the door had not suddenly opened and somebody new appeared. The entry of this new, unknown, person put me off my stroke completely.

The new arrival was Mrs Youthful, a plump but cultivated woman, with the severe and responsible features of a member of the Warsaw Infants Aid Committee or the Society for the Suppression of Juvenile Mendicancy. Pimko rose from the divan, completely oblivious of everything, once more the cordial, distinguished professor of a certain age and with a very nasal nose.

'Ah! my dear lady!' he exclaimed. 'Always busy, always active! No doubt we have come straight from the committee meeting, haven't we? Here is young Johnnie whom I have brought along, Johnnie, of whom you so kindly said that you would take charge. Come along, Johnnie, say good afternoon to the lady!'

What! Pimko had once more assumed his lofty, protective tone. Was I to say good afternoon to this old woman, be polite to her? There was nothing else for it, I did so, and Mrs Youthful held out her short and chubby hand, and looked, not without astonishment, at my face, which was oscillating between the ages of fifteen and thirty.

'How old is the boy?' I heard her ask Pimko in an audible aside.

'Sixteen, my dear lady, sixteen! He was sixteen in April. He looks a little too serious, if such a thing is possible, he is rather inclined to pose in order to appear grown up, but he has a heart of gold.'

'Oh, he's a poseur, is he?'

Instead of protesting, I sat down on the divan and remained glued to it. The incredible stupidity of the suggestion stifled all possibility of explanation. I started suffering the torments of the damned. Pimko and Mrs Youthful moved across towards the window, where the girl was, and started a confidential conversation, glancing in my direction from time to time. Every now and then the famous master raised his voice, and, though it seemed accidental, it was deliberate. An additional torment was that I now heard him allying me with himself against Mrs Youthful, just as previously he had allied me with the girl against himself. But now he allied me with himself. Not content with presenting me as a pretentious poseur who gave himself the airs of a grown-up, he expanded on the depth of my attachment to him, delivered a eulogy of my qualities of heart and mind ('his only failing is his fondness for posing, but that will pass with age'); and he injected into his voice a suggestion of old-worldliness, the typically anachronistic tones of an ageing and old-fashioned schoolmaster, making it appear that I too was old-fashioned and the very reverse of modern. Thus he created a diabolical situation. Here was I sitting on the divan, forced to pretend that I could not hear what was being said; over there by the window was the girl—I could not tell whether she was listening or not; and in the background was Pimko, wagging his head and getting worked up about me, all the time subtly flattering the tastes and inclinations of that progressive female graduate, Mrs Youthful.

Only he who appreciates the full meaning of all that is involved in entering into contact with an unknown person, with all the risks entailed in an enterprise so full of traps and pitfalls, will fully understand my state of utter impotence in the face of Pimko and Mrs Youthful. He was introducing me into the Youthfuls in a deliberately false light, and he was deliberately raising his voice to let me hear his doing so; he was using imposture both in introducing me into the Youthfuls and in introducing the Youthfuls into me.

That was why Mrs Youthful very soon glanced at me with simultaneous pity and impatience.

Pimko's bland conversation obviously got on her nerves. Moreover, the enterprising female graduates of the present day, inflamed by collectivism and emancipation, detest artificiality and pretence in the young, and above all cannot stand their posing to grown-ups. As progressives with their faces turned towards the future, they make a greater cult of youth than it has ever previously enjoyed; and nothing irritates them more than seeing a young person sullying his youth by adopting poses.

And still worse; not only do they dislike it, but they like disliking it, for in disliking it they feel themselves to be modern and progressive; so they are always ready to give rein to this inclination to dislike. So Mrs Youthful—incidentally she was pretty fat—needed no second invitation; she was able to set a seal on her relations with me on the basis of the formula modernism-anachronism. Everything depends on the first chord struck, for that is the only one we are free to choose; all those that follow flow inevitably from the first. But Pimko struck the modern note on his venerable professor's bow, and that immediately set the tone.

'No, I don't like him,' she said irritatedly. 'No, I don't like him. A young, *blasé* old man, obviously with no taste for games or outdoor exercise. I can't stand posing and affectation. Compare him to my Zutka, professor, see how simple, sincere, natural she is, look at what your obsolete methods lead to!'

On hearing this I lost the last shreds of confidence I had left in the effectiveness of any protest I might make. Now it would never be possible to persuade her that I was grown up, because my presence made her appreciate more highly than ever her own charms and those of her daughter. When somebody's presence enhances a mother's pleasure in her daughter, the situation is hopeless, the daughter's charms dictate everything. Could I protest? Who says that I could not protest? At any moment, in spite of all the difficulties, I could have got up and explained that the whole thing was a mistake, that I was not sixteen but thirty. I could have done so, but I could not, because the will was lacking. All I wanted was to show that I was not the fusty youth I was being made out to be. That was all. I was indignant at the idea of the girl's being able to hear all that Pimko was telling her mother about me, and at the pitiful idea she would have of me as a result. This put the question of my thirty years completely out of my head. My true age faded, and this new idea throbbed and burned inside me.

Sitting there on the divan, I could not shout out aloud that Pimko was brazenly lying. So I sat up, tried to pull myself together, to look confident and self-possessed, to sit in a modern manner, in fact, and mutely I shouted with the whole of my body that it wasn't true, that I was not like that, but different. Thigh, thigh, thigh! I leaned forward, put fire into my eyes and, sitting naturally and at ease, denounced Pimko's lies with my whole being. If the girl turned round, she would see. . . . But suddenly I heard Mrs Youthful saying quietly to Pimko:

'It's incredible how affected he is. Look at him, he poses all the time!'

I was petrified. Changing my attitude would have shown that I had heard and plunged me deeper into the artificial; whatever I did was henceforward condemned to artificiality. Meanwhile the girl at the window turned and looked at me, looked me up and down just as I was, sitting there without being able to get rid of my artificially natural attitude . . . and I saw the expression of hostility on her face. This made it still more impossible to escape; and I could feel a sharp, juvenile antipathy arising in the girl, an antipathy as sharp and as clean as a smash on the tennis court. Mrs Youthful interrupted her conversation and asked her daughter, as one friend to another of the same age:

'Why are you looking like that, Zutka?'

The girl, without taking her eyes off me, became—made herself—frank, open and truthful, and said with a pout:

'He's been listening to you the whole time. He has heard everything!'

This was a hard blow. I wanted to protest, but could not, and Mrs Youthful, lowering her voice and enjoying her daughter's sally, said to the professor:

'Nowadays they're terribly sensitive to anything that smacks of slyness and underhandedness; in fact they're crazy about frankness and openness. The new generation. It's the legacy of the Great War. We are all children of the Great War, we and our children.' The woman was visibly exultant. 'The new generation,' she repeated.

'What bright little eye-peeps she has!' the professor said smugly.

'Eye-peeps, professor? Eye-peeps? My daughter hasn't got eye-peeps, but eyes, like the rest of us. Zutka, leave your eyes alone!'

But the girl frowned, and shrugged her shoulders, rejecting her mother. This upset Pimko. He turned to Mrs Youthful and said:

'My dear lady, if you find that way of behaving acceptable . . . In my time a girl would never have dared . . . shrug her shoulders . . . at her mother!'

Mrs Youthful, however, expressed her satisfaction, her delight, her enthusiasm.

'It's the age we live in, professor, the age we live in. You don't know the new generation. Profound transformation, revolution of manners, wind of change, subterranean shocks taking place beneath our feet. It's the age we live in. Everything must be transformed, the old must be swept away and only the new left.'

Meanwhile the girl, who was listening, not without contempt, to what the two old fogeys were saying, chose her moment carefully and gave me a short, sharp, savage, surreptitious kick on the shin, in true gangster fashion, without changing her attitude or her expression. That done, she withdrew her foot and remained impassive and aloof from her mother's and Pimko's conversation. While the mother tried to identify herself with her daughter the latter eluded her . . . as if, being the younger, she was proud . . . of being the younger.

'She kicked him!' the professor exclaimed. 'She kicked him! Did you see? She kicked him, while we were talking she calmly and quietly kicked him! This wild young generation! What barbarism, what impudence, what effrontery! She kicked him!'

'Zutka, keep your legs still. And don't worry about your Johnnie, professor, he won't come to any harm. Far worse things happened at the front during the Great War. I myself, when I was a nurse, often used to get kicks from ordinary soldiers.'

She lit a cigarette.

'In my time,' Pimko said. 'In my time. . . . But what would our great poet Norwid have said?'

'Norwid?' the girl asked. 'Who was he?'

She asked the question perfectly, with the athletic ignorance of the younger generation and the surprise appropriate to the times-we-live-in; she did not engage herself excessively in the question, she just asked it for the sake of making a slight demonstration of her athletic lack of knowledge.

The professor started tearing out his hair.

'She has never heard of Norwid!' he exclaimed.

Mrs Youthful smiled.

'It's the times-we-live-in, professor, it's the times-we-live-in!'

The atmosphere became delightful. The girl, for Pimko's benefit, had never heard of Norwid. Pimko became infuriated at her ignorance, for her benefit. Her mother was in ecstasies about the times-we-live-in. I was the only one left out, and I could not . . . no I could not join in, or understand the change of roles by which the old maniac with his worn-out old thighs allied himself with the girl against me, and why I had to provide the counterpoint to his melody. Oh, diabolical Pimko! But, sitting there like that, silent and nursing my kicked leg, I looked hurt and resentful, and Pimko said benevolently:

'Why are you so quiet, Johnnie? You must speak up for yourself from time to time. . . . Are you angry with the young lady?'

'Of course he is!' the girl said jeeringly.

'Zutka, apologize to the young man,' her mother said firmly. 'You have upset him, but you, young man, must stop being upset, and must show a little less resentment. Of course Zutka will apologize, but on the other hand we must admit that we're a little affected, aren't we? . . . Let's have a little more naturalness, a little more life! Come, come, now, look at Zutka and me! We'll get rid of the young man's affected affairs, you can rely on us, professor. He'll be in good hands with us!'

'From that point of view, I believe that living here will do him a great deal of good,' the professor said. 'Come, come, Johnnie, cheer up!'

Everything they said was definite and final, and seemed to settle matters once and for all. The question of the cost of my board and lodging remained to be disposed of, and when that was over Pimko kissed me on the brow.

'Good-bye, young man,' he said. 'Don't cry, I'll come and see you every Sunday, and I'll keep my eye on you at school. My respects, dear lady, and *au revoir*. Miss Zutka, be kind to Johnnie!'

He took his departure, and could be heard clearing his throat and coughing on the way downstairs, huh! huh! huh! h'm! h'm! h'm! I leapt to my feet to begin my protests and explanations.

But Mrs Youthful took me to a very modern little room just off the hall. The hall (as I subsequently found out) served also as Miss Youthful's bedroom.

'Here you are,' she said. 'The bathroom is next door. Breakfast is at seven o'clock. The maid has brought your things already.'

And before I could say thank-you she was off to the meeting of the Warsaw Committee for the Suppression of Juvenile Mendicancy. I was alone. I sat on the chair. Silence. My head was buzzing. Here I was sitting in my new room, in entirely new conditions. After all the people I had seen that day, I suddenly found myself alone. Only the girl kept moving about outside in the hall. I was not alone, but alone with the girl.

★ 7 ★

Love

ONCE more I started mentally protesting and explaining, I must do something, the situation in which I had been put must not be allowed to consolidate, to become permanent, the longer I put off doing something the harder it would be. I sat stiffly on my chair, not raising a finger to unpack the things the maid had brought at Pimko's orders. Now or never, I said to myself. Pimko had gone, Mrs Youthful was out, the girl was alone. There was not a moment to lose, time bred stiffness, awkwardness, difficulties, I must go now, immediately, this very moment, to explain myself, reveal myself to the girl in my true colours, tomorrow it would be too late.

Reveal myself in my true colours, how violently I wanted to reveal myself to her in my true colours, I was bursting to reveal myself to her in my true colours! But reveal myself as what? As a thirty-year-old adult? Not on your life! I had lost all desire to throw off my youthfulness, to confess to my thirty years, my world was shattered, no world existed other than the fine world of the modern schoolgirl, games, athletics, agility, insolence, thighs, legs, barbarism, boating, canoeing, such was the new heaven of my reality! It was as a modern youth that I wanted to reveal myself. The master, Siphon, Mientus, the duel, all that had previously existed had been pushed aside, and all that I cared about was what the girl thought of me. Had Pimko succeeded in convincing her that I was an anti-modern poseur? The only problem that existed for me was that of walking into her room here and now and making a young, natural, modern appearance before her, making her understand that Pimko had lied, and that in reality I was not like that, but different, a being similar to herself, a companion of her own age and time, related to her by the thigh . . .

But what would my excuse be for walking into her room? How could I explain everything to her if I scarcely knew her? I already existed inside her, but in the social sense I was still a stranger. To reach the depths of her being would be extremely difficult for me, I could only hope to touch the surface, I could hardly do more than knock at the door and ask at what time dinner was served. The kick she had given me favoured my plans in no way whatever; it had been a marginal kick, given by the foot without the slightest collaboration from the face, and what was important to me was the face. Seated in my chair like a caged animal, I wrung my hands. What was my excuse to be, how was I to start the ball rolling between Miss Youthful and myself?

At that moment the telephone rang, and I heard her footsteps.

I got up, gingerly half-opened the door, and looked out. There was nobody there, it was beginning to get dark, and she was making an appointment on the telephone with a girl friend, seven o'clock in a bar with Wladys and Wladek (they had their own nicknames and their own private language). You'll come, sure, smashing, yes, no, my leg hurts, I knocked it, idiot, photo, come, you come, I'm coming, O.K., cheerio, bye-bye! These words, softly confided to the mouthpiece by one modern girl to another while nobody else was there, moved me profoundly. Her own language, I said to myself, her own modern, private language! And it seemed to me that the girl, rooted to the spot by the telephone, her mouth glued to the mouthpiece while her eyes were left at liberty, became thereby more accessible, better adapted to my designs. I should be able to reveal myself to her without explanation, make my appearance . . . without comment.

Quickly I straightened my tie, wetted my hair, and combed it to show the parting, for I felt that a straight line across the skull was not without importance in the circumstances; heaven knows why, but it was modern. On my way through the dining-room I helped myself to a tooth-pick, and I made my appearance (the telephone was in the anteroom). I stood in the doorway, cool and impassive, leaning against the embrasure. Silently I presented myself in my entirety, the tooth-pick between my teeth. The tooth-pick was a modern touch. Do not for one moment believe that it was easy to stand there with a tooth-pick in one's mouth pretending complete liberty of movement while inside one felt fatally passive.

Meanwhile the girl was saying to her friend:

'No, you're crazy, the dog, all right then, get on with it, don't go with him, go with her, photo, six, three minutes, wait and see.'

She put down the receiver for a moment and said:

'Do you want to use the telephone?'

She asked the question in a cold, social voice, as if it had not been I whom she had kicked. I shook my head. I wanted her to realize that I was there for no reason whatever except pure companionship, and that I had a perfect right to stand in the doorway while she telephoned, as I was her companion in modernism and her equal in age. Schoolgirl, you must appreciate that between us explanations are superfluous, and that I am perfectly entitled to join you without ado and without formality. I was taking a gigantic risk because, if she asked me for an explanation, I should be unable to supply it, and artificiality, that appalling artificiality, would cause me to beat a hasty retreat. But if she accepted my attitude, tacitly accepted it, I should be able to be modern with her. Mientus, Mientus, I said to myself in alarm, remembering the atrocious grimaces into which he had twisted his face after our first smiles. But with the female sex things were easier. Physical differences helped; they eliminated impotence.

Meanwhile the girl, her ear glued to the receiver, went on talking for a long time without looking at me. Once more the weight of time ominously made itself felt. At last she said:

'O.K., good, the flicks, bye-bye!'

And she put back the receiver.

She went back to her room. I removed the tooth-pick from my mouth, and went back to mine. There was a chair against the wall next to the wardrobe, a chair not meant for sitting but for putting one's clothes on, and I sat on it stiffly and wrung my hands. She had ignored me, she had not even deigned to laugh at me. Never mind, once you have started out on something you must keep on with it, you must settle the matter while her mother is out, you must try again, because otherwise, after that unhappy piece of behaviour, she may once and for all come to the conclusion that you are a poseur, and in any case your pose is taking root, growing, why are you sitting against the wall like this, wringing your hands? Heaven help you, sitting on a chair in your room like this is the very opposite of modernism, it's typically old-fashioned.

I stopped, and listened to what was happening on the other side of the wall.

Miss Youthful was moving about in her room just as all girls move about in their rooms; and while so engaged she was no doubt deciding more definitely than ever that I was an affected poseur. It was a terrible thing to be cast back into my room like this, in isolation, while she moved about next door. But how was I to start, or restart, with her? What was I to do? I had no excuse—even if I had had an excuse, I should have been unable to use it—for the matter was too internal for excuses.

Meanwhile it had grown darker, and the isolation—the illusory isolation of a person who is alone but not alone because mentally he is agonizingly tied to someone on the other side of the wall—and nevertheless sufficiently alone to make the rubbing of hands, the movement of fingers, and other similar phenomena absurd and impossible. The mounting darkness, and the false solitude I was in, went to my head, blinded me, deprived me of my daytime awareness and plunged me into night. How often does night make an irruption into day! Alone in the room in this situation, sitting on my chair, I was deprived of too many senses, it was impossible to remain like this for a moment longer. Things which are not in the least alarming when experienced in company in daylight become intolerable when you are alone. Solitude is aggressive, explosive.

After an endless period of torment I again opened the door and stood in the doorway, still blinded by solitude. I stopped, and realized that I knew no better than before where to start with the girl, how to make contact with her; there was still a barrier all round her, like a closed frontier. What a dreadful thing is that sharp and peremptory demarcation line, form!

She was standing with one foot on a chair, leaning forward, engaged in cleaning her shoe. There was something classic about her position, and I had the impression that she was less interested in making her shoe shine than in privately asserting her type by way of her foot and ankle and maintaining a good modern style. This gave me more courage. I thought that the girl, surprised like this while showing a leg, would be kinder, less stiff.

I went towards her and stood quite close to her, only one or two paces away; I presented myself to her silently, without looking, my eyes withdrawn; I still remember perfectly how I approached her and stopped only a yard away, within the spatial limits in which she began, how I suppressed all my senses in order to approach as close to her as possible, and waited . . . What for? For her to be surprised at nothing. This time I had no tooth-pick and no special attitude. Whether she accepted or rejected me, I tried to be completely passive and neutral. . . .

She removed her foot from the chair and stood upright.

'What do you want?' she asked me without turning her head, hesitantly, like a person who has been approached too closely without good reason. As soon as she stood upright the tension between us increased. I felt that she would have liked to move away, but that I was too close to her for her to be able to do so.

'What do you want?'

'Nothing,' I murmured.

She lowered her hands and looked at me out of the corner of one eye. She was on the defensive.

'Are you trying to be funny?' she said.

'No,' I murmured. 'No.'

Beside me was the table. Farther away there was the stove. On the table were a brush and a penknife. It had grown still darker, everything was a little blurred in the half-light, including the terrible demarcation line. Behind the curtain of darkness I was sincere, sincere with all my strength, propitious to the girl, ready.

I was not pretending. If she accepted the fact that I was not pretending, she would see through the artificiality of my previous behaviour, for which Pimko had been responsible. Did I imagine that a girl could not reject a man who demanded acceptance by her? Did I believe that there, in the dark, the girl would succumb to the temptation of making of me something that suited her? Why should she not like having within her reach someone who was sympathetic and suitable? She would certainly prefer having an American boy-friend in the house to a miserable, old-fashioned, grudge-bearing poseur. So why did she not play her evening tune on me if I lent myself to it? Play, play your tune on me, the modern tune that everyone hums in the big cafés, in the dance halls, and on the beaches, the pure tune of world youth in tennis shorts. Play on me the modernism of white tennis shorts. Won't you?

Miss Youthful, surprised at having me beside her, sat on the table, and put her chin between her hands, not without a trace of physical humour; her face stood out in the dusk, poised between surprise and playfulness . . . and she seemed to have sat down in order to play her tune. . . . That was how American girls sat on the sides of their motor-boats. And the mere fact of her sitting thus established a tacit agreement to prolong the situation. One might have said that she had made herself more comfortable in order to savour . . . with beating heart I noticed that she was setting some of her charms to work. She bent her little head; she moved her leg impatiently; capriciously she pursed her lips, and at the same time turned her big, modern eyes cautiously in the direction of the dining-room, to see if by any chance the maid were spying on us. What would the maid have said if she had discovered us in such a strange situation? Would she have taxed us with an excess of artifice? Or an excess of nature?

But that is just the kind of risk that appeals to these dark young things who can show all that they know only in the dark. I felt that I had conquered the girl by the barbarous naturalness of my artifice. I put my hands in my jacket pockets. Straining towards her, I accompanied her in silence, fervently, with all my strength, putting myself in sympathy with her, putting the whole of my being in sympathy with her. On this occasion time worked in my favour. With each second that passed the artifice grew deeper, but so did the naturalness. I was expecting her suddenly to make some perfectly ordinary remark to me, as if we had known each other for ages, to say something about her leg, for instance, to tell me that it hurt because she had strained a tendon, or to offer me a drink. Martini, whisky, gin?

And she was going to say something of the sort, her lips were actually moving—when the idea suddenly came into her head to say something entirely different. Without wanting to, she said severely:

'What can I do for you?'

I stepped back. She was nettled by what she had said, but did not lose one iota of the attractive, thoroughbred air of a modern girl sitting on a table and swinging her legs; on the contrary, she became more attractive and thoroughbred than ever: and she repeated, with ever greater coldness and severity:

'What can I do for you?'

I turned and walked away, but the back view of myself which I presented to her as I did so nettled her even more, and from the other side of the door I heard her exclaim:

'Completely crackers!'

Repulsed and rejected, I sat down again on the chair by the wall. This is the end, I muttered, she has crushed me. Why did she crush me? Something bit her; she preferred trampling on me to walking by my side. Chair by the wall, I greet you, but I must unpack, the suitcase is in the middle of the room, there's no towel. I sat humbly on my chair and started unpacking and putting my things in the drawers, practically in the dark. I must get everything ready, because tomorrow I go to school—but I didn't turn on the light, no, for my sake it wasn't worth it. How wretched and miserable I felt, but all right, all right, if only I could stay like this, sit down and go on sitting without ever moving again or ever again wanting anything.

However, after a few minutes it became evident that in spite of my lethargy and misery I must become active again. Was there to be no respite? I must go to her room for the third time, show myself to her in the guise of a clown and crackpot, give her to understand that all that had happened previously had been deliberate buffoonery on my part, and that it was I who had been taking the rise out of her, and not the other way about. All is lost except honour, as Francis 1 remarked. In spite of my depression and exhaustion, I rose, and once more prepared to make my entrance. The preparations took a long time. Eventually I half-opened the door and put my head round it. The light was dazzling—she had turned on the light. I shut my eyes.

'Please knock at the door before coming in,' she said impatiently.

I answered with my eyes closed, moving my head:

'Your humble and obedient servant.'

I completed my entry into the room, creeping in in a humorous manner—oh, that unhappy man's creep! I decided to make her angry, for anger, according to the adage, is detrimental to beauty. I counted on making her nervous, because, if I kept my head behind my clownish mask, I should then have the advantage of her.

'You've got no manners!' she exclaimed.

Coming from a modern girl, these words surprised me. They surprised me all the more because she spoke them as convincingly as if good manners had been the highest aspiration of the wild post-war generation. The modern generation makes use alternately of good manners and bad with the greatest possible virtuosity. She made me feel a fool. It was too late to retreat—

the world exists only because it is always too late to retreat. I collected myself, and bowed.

'I cast myself at your feet,' I said.

She got up and made towards the door. Disaster threatened. If she walked out and left me to my clowning, all would be lost. I leapt forward and barred the way. She stopped.

'What is it you want?' she said.

She was getting frightened.

And I, being unable to retreat, carried away by my own momentum, started advancing upon her—I, fool, crackpot, clown, impossible poseur, clumsy buffoon, started advancing upon her, a gorilla advancing upon a helpless damsel. She retreated behind the table, but I continued remorselessly to advance upon her, pointing the way with my finger with ape-like imbecility, advancing upon her in a drunken, imbecile, evil, threatening manner while she retreated to the wall. But—curse the girl!—I noticed in the midst of this crazy progress that in the face of my imbecility she lost not one iota of her attractiveness— that while I behaved inhumanly she, standing against the wall, small, stooping, pale, breathless, her arms dangling and slightly bent, her eyes popping out of her head and incredibly silent and tense with the danger, was very beautiful—cinematic, modern, poetic, artistic—and that fear, instead of making her ugly, made her more beautiful. Another moment passed. I stepped closer, and new situations were necessarily about to rise—it flashed through my mind that this was the end, that I must take her face in my hand—I was in love, I was in love! At that moment there was a sudden squeal from the anteroom; Mientus was assaulting the maid. We had not heard the bell. He had come to see me at my new address and, finding himself alone with the maid, had tried to violate her.

For the effect on Mientus of his duel with Siphon was that he could no longer escape from his terrible grimaces and was unable to act in other than a disgusting manner. When he saw the maid he did not fail to be as brutal and down-to-earth as he was able. The girl had made a noise, so he had kicked her in the stomach, and now he walked into the room with a bottle of brandy under his arm.

'Hallo, Johnnie, old man!' he exclaimed. 'I just dropped in to see you. I've brought some booze and some grub. Oh! But what's the matter with your face? You look like death warmed up. Bah! mine's not much better!

> *'Clash of faces is our fate,*
> *Get drunk on your ugly mug!*

'Who's the Siphon that gave you a face like that? That tart standing against the wall? My respects, darling!'

'I'm in love, Mientus, I'm in love!'

Mientus replied with a drunkard's wisdom.

'So that's what's given you that face! Shake on it, old man! But what a face she's given you! If you could only see yourself! Well, well, well, mine's not so bad either, shake on it, old man! Come along, it's time to wet your whistle, let's go to your room, get some bread to go with the sausage, I've got a bottle to help wash your troubles away! Don't take it to heart, old chap, we'll cheer ourselves up with the bottle. My respects to the young lady, *bon jour, au revoir, mademoiselle*, come along!'

Once more I advanced towards the girl, I wanted to say something, explain, find some magic formula to save the situation, but Mientus dragged me away and, staggering and lurching, drunk, not with alcohol but with our faces, we reached my room. I burst into tears and told him the whole story about the girl, omitting nothing. He listened to me benevolently, like a father, and sang:

> *'No disgrace*
> *Like a face*
> *Out of place . . .*

'Come on, why aren't you drinking?' he said. 'Come on, man, drink! Don't make faces at the bottle, the bottle is to give you face!'

His face was still appalling, dreadfully common and vulgar, and he stuffed into the hole in it sausage and grease-paper together.

'Mientus,' I exclaimed. 'I want to free myself . . . I want to free myself!'

'What? From your face?' he said. 'Balls!'

'From the girl,' I said. 'Mientus, I tell you I'm thirty! Thirty!'

He looked at me in amazement, for there was real distress in my voice. Then he burst out laughing.

'Don't rave, man!' he said. 'Thirty? You're bats! You're raving! (He also used other expressions which I shall not repeat.) Thirty? You know (he took a gulp from the bottle, and spat), I don't know where I know her from, but I know that girl. By sight. Kopeida's running after her!'

'Who's he?'

'Kopeida, a chap in our class. He likes her, because she's the same type as he, modern. Come on, man, drink! That's the only thing. D'you think I've freed myself? My face has turned into a rag, but I'm still haunted by the stable-lad.'

'What? Even since you violated Siphon?'

'Yes, but I've still got the same face. Look what a pair we are!' he said in astonishment. 'I and my stable-lad, and you and your schoolgirl! Drink, man, drink!'

He suddenly grew dreamy-eyed.

'Johnnie,' he said, 'if we could only get away to the country, among the stable-lads! If only we could get away to the country, the fields, the open country'—he started becoming incoherent—'country, stable-lads, stable-lads, country!'

But I didn't care a fig for his stable-lads. All that I cared about was the girl. So Kopeida was running after her. How I envied him. But 'running after' was not the same as 'going with'; evidently they did not know each other. But I did not dare ask any questions. And so we remained with our faces, each plunged in his own thoughts and helping himself to a drink every now and then. Mientus rose lurchingly to his feet.

'I must go,' he said quietly. 'The old woman will be coming

back. I'll leave by way of the kitchen (he whispered) and have another look at the maid. . . . She's not a stable-lad, obviously, but she comes from the country. Perhaps she's got a brother who's a stable-lad.'

He went out, and I was left with the girl. The moonlight turned the impalpable dust hanging in the air to silver.

⋆ 8 ⋆

The Fruit Salad

NEXT morning school, Siphon, Mientus, Bobek, Hopek, Kotecki, the infinitive and accusative, Droopy, divine poetry, the daily impotence. Oh, the endless repetition, the excruciating boredom. Oh, the bard and his inspiration, the poet and his muse, the schoolmaster making his living out of the poet, the pupils at their desks suffering from an acute sense of protest, the toe in the shoe, the boredom, boredom, boredom! The gradual transformation of reality under pressure of repulsion, poetry and pedanticism—oh, let me dream—until it became impossible for anyone to distinguish between the real and the unreal, between truth and fiction, between the felt and the unfelt, between the natural and the artificial, the pretentious and the false; until what ought to be inevitably became indistinguishable from what was, each disqualifying the other and depriving it of all object. Oh, the great school of unreality! The result was that I too for five long hours dreamt uninterruptedly about my ideal, and my face swelled like a balloon, for in this fictitious, unreal world there was nothing to bring it back to normal. The result was that I too had my ideal—the modern schoolgirl. I was in love, a lovelorn, melancholy dreamer. Having failed to conquer the girl, having failed to ridicule her, I was plunged in despair. I knew that all was lost.

I was a prisoner. What can I say about the boredom of those days monotonously divided into two? In the morning I went to school, from school I returned to the Youthful household. I had no more thought of escape, of explaining myself or protesting; on the contrary, I took pleasure in being a schoolboy, because that brought me nearer the girl. I almost forgot my thirty years. The masters were very decent to me, Piorkowski, the head, patted me on the back, and during ideological disputes I too grew red in the face and shouted:

'Modernism for ever! Up with the modern boy! Up with the modern girl!'

That made Kopeida laugh. You remember Kopeida, the most modern boy in the whole school?

I tried to strike up a friendship with him, to discover the secret of his relations with Miss Youthful. But he avoided me, was even more contemptuous of me than he was of the others, as if instinctively aware of my rejection by his spiritual sister, the modern schoolgirl.

In general, the rejection of one type of young person by another type was Draconian and complete. The clean abominated the dirty, the modern regarded the old-fashioned as beneath contempt, and so on *ad infinitum*.

What else is there to say? Siphon died. After being violated through his ears he never became himself again, he was never able to expel what had been injected into him. He spent long hours trying vainly to forget the words of initiation to which he had been forced to listen. He felt a profound aversion for his miscarried personality, and ate his heart out. He grew paler and paler, suffered from obstinate hiccups, spat, choked, puffed and blew, coughed, but no, he could not, and in the end, considering himself unfit to live, one afternoon hanged himself from the hatstand. This caused an enormous sensation; there were even echoes of it in the Press. But Mientus failed to benefit in any way; Siphon's death did nothing to improve the state of his face. Siphon was dead, but what difference did that make? The faces that Mientus had made during the duel had stuck. It is not so easy to get rid of a grimace. A face is not made of india-rubber; once distorted, it does not return to its former shape. The result was that he looked so unpleasant that even his friends Bobek and Hopek avoided him whenever they could; and the more grotesque he became, the more obviously did he indulge in his stable-lad dream, and the more he indulged in his stable-lad dream, the more grotesque did he become. However, unhappiness drew us together; he dreamt about his stable-lads and I about my schoolgirl, and thus we both spent our time dreaming. But reality was still as inaccessible to us as if our faces had been covered all over with spots. He told me that he was thinking of seducing the Youthfuls' maid. That first evening, under the influence of the brandy, he had stolen a kiss from her on his way out through the kitchen, but that had not satisfied him at all.

'What's the good of it?' he said. 'What's the good of stealing a kiss from a maid? She's a girl who walks bare foot, of course, she comes straight from the country, and she has a stable-boy brother, so she tells me, but hell and damnation (he also used other words which I shall not repeat), what's the good of that? A sister's not the same as her brother, a town maid isn't a country stable-boy. I go and see her in the afternoon, when your Mrs Youthful is at her committee meetings, I do the best I can with her. I even go about it peasant-style, but still she won't play!'

Such was the fashion in which he formed his universe—stable-lad filling the foreground and maid occupying a secondary position in the background. School dropped out of my universe; the Youthful household filled it almost completely.

Mrs Youthful, with a mother's perceptiveness, soon realized that I was in love with her daughter. There is no need to specify how stimulated she was by this discovery, coming as it did on top of the stimulation provided by Pimko. An old-fashioned, affected, young man who was unable to conceal his admiration for her daughter's modernism was an instrument she used like a tongue, so to speak, to taste and savour her daughter's charms, and even her own. So I became this fat woman's tongue, and the more old-fashioned, false, and artificial I was, the more both of them enjoyed their modernity, sincerity and simplicity. Two puerile realities—modernity and old-fashionedness—when rubbed together produced electricity and set up thousands of the most fantastic circuits, which twined and coiled to form a world that became ever more fragmentary and green—to such an extent that Mrs Youthful started displaying for my benefit a modernism which in her case simply took the place of youth. At meals and other times there was endless talk of Liberty, Customs, the Times We Live In, Revolutionary Movements, the Post-War Period, etc., etc., and the old woman exulted at being younger, thanks to the Times She Lived In, than a young man who was younger than herself. She made a youth of herself and an old man of me. 'How are you, you little old man?' she used to say. 'How are you, you little rotten egg?'

With the subtlety of a modern female graduate, she inflicted on me the torture of her vital energy and experience and knowledge of life, the kicks she had received while nursing during the Great War, her enthusiasms and her broadmindedness, her liberal woman's bold, progressive, active outlook, her modern ways, her daily hygiene, and the ostentation with which she went to the bathroom. Strange! Strange! Pimko came to see me from time to time. The old professor was delighted at my little backside. 'What an incomparable little rump!' he muttered. And he never missed a chance of still further provoking Mrs Youthful, making the greatest possible play with his old-fashioned school-master act and denouncing the modern schoolgirl with might and main. I noted that in other circumstances, when he was with Piorkowski, for instance, he seemed younger by half, and did not flaunt such antediluvian principles; and I could not make up my mind if it was he who stimulated the Youthfuls' modernity, or if the two phenomena were interdependent and complement-ary, like the two lines of a rhyming couplet. Which of them created the other? Did the modern schoolgirl create the little old man or did the latter create her? Futile and useless question.

In any case both enjoyed themselves, he as old-fashioned pedagogue, she as unbridled youth, and gradually his visits started becoming longer, and he took less and less interest in me and paid more and more attention to the girl. Must I confess it? I became jealous of Pimko. I died a thousand deaths at seeing these two human beings harmonizing with and completing each other, improvising a piquant old-young ode together, and it was disgusting to see that this old goat, whose thighs were in a hundred times worse condition than mine, nevertheless got on so much better with the modern girl than I. Norwid in particular became the pretext for a positive intrigue between them. The worthy Pimko found her ignorance unpardonable, it offended his deepest feelings. She, however, preferred pole-jumping to poetry, and he grew indignant and she laughed, he lectured her, and she rebelled, he implored, and she went on pole-jumping. I admired the skill with which the Master, without ceasing to be the Master, without for a moment dropping his role as Master, nevertheless managed to get so much pleasure from the girl by means of the contrast of opposites, how he excited her by being the master and how she excited him by being the schoolgirl. My jealousy was horrible, though I too excited the girl by contrast and was excited by her in the same way. But the last thing I wanted was to seem old-fashioned to her, for in her eyes I wanted to be modern.

Oh, the agony of it! I could not get her out of my system. All my efforts to free myself were vain. The sarcasms with which I mentally defended myself against her were useless; what is the good of a cheap, sarcastic remark behind a person's back? The truth of the matter was that my sarcasms were nothing but a tribute to the girl, for they concealed a sad desire to please her. If I used irony, it was only to adorn myself, like a peacock, with the feathers of my irony, and that only because I had been rejected. But my irony turned against me, and gave me a still more horrid and repulsive face. I did not dare give rein to it in her presence; she would have only shrugged her shoulders. For a girl—and in that a girl resembles all other human beings—is never afraid of the irony of someone she has rejected. . . . And the sole consequence of the clownish offensive I had conducted in her room was that henceforward she mistrusted and ignored me—in the fashion which only modern girls know how to ignore a person—though she was perfectly well aware that I was taken with her modern attractions. So with subtle, childish

cruelty she increased the latter, carefully avoiding any coquettish-
ness which would have made her dependent on me. It was not
for my sake but for her own that she became more and more
wild, insolent, bold, shrill, supple, sporting, and thighy. After
dinner she would remain seated—oh! how self-assured and
mature in her immaturity—impassive and alone for her own sake,
while I sat there for her sake, unable even for a single moment
not to sit there for her sake, and she absorbed and swallowed me
whole, irony included, and her tastes and inclinations were all-
important for me and I was able to please myself only to the
extent that I pleased her. The agony of it! To be swallowed whole
by a modern schoolgirl, and never to be able to find a single
fault with her style or detect the slightest chink or cranny which
held out the prospect or possibility of flight, liberation, escape.

It was just this which held me under her spell—that maturity
and sovereignty of her youthfulness, the assurance of her style.
While we at school suffered from acne, were everlastingly
plagued with spots and ideals of various kinds, while apathy
pursued us in our movements and gaucheness haunted us at every
step, her exterior was magnificently finished. Youth for her was
not an age of transition; on the contrary, it was the only acceptable phase in human life, the only phase that had value or
importance. *She despised maturity or, rather, for her immaturity
was maturity.* Beards, moustaches, nurses, mothers with children,
were all alike dismissed by her, and it was from that that she
derived her magic power. Her youth needed no ideal, because it
was an ideal in itself. That I, tormented by idealist youth, should
thirst so greatly for this ideal youth should surprise nobody. But
she did not like me. She gave me a horrible face, and every day
it grew a little more horrible.

Heavens! the aesthetic torment and humiliation she inflicted
on me! I know nothing crueller than a person's giving another a
new face. Whatever such a person does is enough to make the
victim act under false colours, foolishly, ridiculously, grotesquely,
for his ugliness nourishes that person's beauty. Believe me, giving
somebody a backside is nothing in comparison with giving him

a face. In the end I actually reached the state of dreaming of the girl's physical destruction, of disfiguring her pretty little face, injuring her, cutting off her nose. But the example of Mientus and Siphon showed that brute force was not of much use; the mind can free itself only by its own efforts. But what could my mind do, since she contained me within herself? Can you escape from inside a person if you have no point of support, no leverage, nothing whatever to cling to outside that person, if you are completely dominated by that person's style? No, with your own strength it is hopeless, impossible—unless a third party comes to your aid, holds you out at least a little finger. But who was there to come to my aid? Mientus, who was not on visiting terms with the Youthfuls (apart from the kitchen, where he went secretly) and was never present at my struggles with the girl? Mr Youthful, Mrs Youthful, or Pimko, all of whom were the girl's accomplices? Or the maid—a hireling, a person without a voice? Meanwhile my face became more and more horrible; and the more horrible it became, the more mother and daughter entrenched themselves in their modernism, and the more face they manufactured and inflicted on me. Oh, what an instrument of tyranny is style! Hell and damnation! But the two witches were deceiving themselves, for the time came when, by accident, because of Mr Youthful (yes, Mr Youthful) the thraldom of style was relaxed and I recovered a little of my power of action. Thereupon I went over completely to the offensive. Up and at them! Tally ho! Tally ho! After her! After the style and beauty of the modern schoolgirl!

It was strange that I should owe my salvation to the engineer-architect. Without him I should have remained a prisoner for ever. It was he who unwittingly provoked a minor transformation, and brought it about that suddenly it was the girl who was inside me instead of my being inside her; yes, the engineer introduced his daughter into me, and for that I shall be grateful to him till the day of my death. I remember how it started; I remember every detail. I came back from school at lunch-time to find the Youthfuls already at table. The maid served potato soup. The girl was sitting there with her usual perfection, with a tremendous amount of physical culture and in crêpe-soled shoes. She took only a very small helping of soup. However, she drank a glass of water and ate a slice of bread; she avoided that tepid, watery, too easy substance, soup, which must certainly have been detrimental to her style; and it is legitimate also to assume that she wished to preserve her appetite until the meat course, for a hungry modern girl cuts a much more dashing figure than a modern girl replete. Mrs Youthful similarly took very little soup; and she did not ask me what school had been like that morning. Why not? Because she disliked asking such maternal questions. Indeed, she disliked the maternal style in general; she had rather be a sister.

'Victor,' she said in the tone of a loyal comrade and reader of H. G. Wells, passing her husband the salt. Then, looking half into the future and half into space and changing to a tone of humanitarian revolt against social abuses and injustices, she added:

'The death penalty is an anachronism.'

Mr Youthful, that responsible engineer and town-planner who had studied in Paris, from which he had brought back the sun-tanned European style, an easy, informal, way of dressing, yellow suède shoes which were always very conspicuous on him, open-necked shirts, horn-rimmed spectacles, an unprejudiced outlook, a virile pacifism, an admiration for the rational organization of labour, and a stock of scientific anecdotes and cabaret jokes, thereupon took the salt-cellar from his wife and said:

'Thank you, Mary.'

Then, in the accents of a well-informed pacifist tinged with a slight suggestion of those of a graduate of the École Poly-technique, he added:

'In Brazil they are throwing barrels of salt into the sea while here it costs six groschen a gramme. The politicians. We technicians. The world must be reorganized. The League of Nations.'

Mrs Youthful sighed deeply, and, simultaneously glimpsing

a better future, participating in Poland's past struggles and dreaming of the Poland of tomorrow, added intelligently:

'Zutka, who was that boy who brought you home? You needn't tell me if you don't want to, you know we don't want to pry into your affairs!'

Miss Youthful indifferently swallowed a piece of bread.

'I don't know,' she said.

'You don't know?' her mother exclaimed delightedly.

'He picked me up in the street,' the girl explained.

'He picked you up in the street?' said her father.

Actually he asked the question mechanically, but it came out rather ponderously, and might have been interpreted as an old-fashioned paternal rebuke. This caused Mrs Youthful to burst out with a (perhaps) slightly exaggerated matter-of-factness:

'And what is there peculiar about that? He picked her up, and what of it? At most he'll have made a date with you, won't he, Zutka? Splendid! Or perhaps you're planning a whole day's canoeing with him. Or going away with him for the weekend, and spending the night with him. Well, what of it?' she said abjectly, 'spend the night with him, and think no more of it. And perhaps you're thinking of taking no money with you and letting him pay for everything, or perhaps it'll be the other way about, so that you'll have to pay for him; in that case I'll give you the money. But I expect you'll manage without any money between you, won't you?' she exclaimed audaciously, with a movement of her whole body.

She was completely carried away by her excitement, but the daughter neatly eluded her mother, who so obviously wanted to enjoy herself by way of her.

'Of course, Mummy, of course!' she said by way of reply, without taking a second helping or rissoles, because mincemeat was no good to her, I suppose because it was too soft and easy. The girl was very careful of her parents; she never allowed them to get too close to her.

The engineer, however, now took up the subject on which his wife had embarked. As she had implied that he was shocked by his daughter's behaviour, he wanted to demonstrate the opposite.

'Of course there's nothing wrong in all that!' he said. 'Zutka, if you want to have a natural child, go ahead! What's wrong about it? The cult of virginity is dead. We, the engineer-architects of the new social order, refuse to subscribe to the outworn cult of virginity, which is good enough for yokels.'

He took a gulp of water and fell silent, fearing that perhaps he might have gone a little too far. Mrs Youthful then took up the cudgels, and impersonally and indirectly set herself to plant a natural child in her daughter's head. She gave free rein to her liberalism, emphasized the extraordinary freedom that prevailed among young people nowadays, etc., etc. This was the Youthfuls' war-horse. When one of them dismounted, fearing to have gone too far, the other got into the saddle and set off at the gallop. This gallop was the more remarkable in that, as has already been mentioned, neither (not even Mr Youthful) liked mothers or children. But it must be appreciated that they bestrode the theme, not from the mother's point of view, but from the girl's, not from a legitimate child's angle, but from a natural child's. Above all, Mrs Youthful desired by means of her daughter's natural child to place herself in the very forefront of the age, and she would have liked it to be begotten casually, accidentally, insolently, on the grass in the course of a sporting day's outing, by a comrade of the same age, as occurs in modern novels, etc. Moreover, the mere fact of talking about it, of encouraging their daughter in this way, partly satisfied her parents' desire; and they were emboldened in their enjoyment of the idea by their aware-ness of my impotence in the face of it. The truth was that I did not yet know how to protect myself against the spell of a sixteen-year-old on the grass.

But what they did not realize was that that day I was in too wretched a state even for jealousy. They had now been ceaselessly and uninterruptedly making and inflicting a face on me for a whole fortnight, with the result that my face was now so pitiful that I could not manage even to be jealous. I realized that the boy of whom the girl had spoken could be no other than Kopeida, but it made no difference—dejection and depression, depression and dejection, wretchedness, immense fatigue, and resignation. So, instead of tackling the subject from its proud, fresh, greeny-blue angle, I tackled it in miserable fashion. A baby is a baby, I said to myself, imagining the delivery, the nurse, the childish complaints, the nappies, the expense; and also imagining that the baby's warmth and the milk would soon do away with Miss Youthful's girlishness and turn her into a heavy, commonplace mother. That was why I turned to the girl and said, pitifully, cerebrally, as if for myself:

'Mamma!'

I said it with great sadness and poverty, and not without the soft, warm motherliness which they refused to admit into their sharp, fresh, youthful vision of the world. Why did I say it? It just came out, that was all. The girl, like all girls, was primarily an aesthete, beauty was her principal blemish, and I, in applying to her type the warm, sentimental and somewhat untidy epithet of 'mamma', had conjured up a grossly maternal and anti-beautiful idea, and I thought that perhaps she would explode. But at heart I knew well enough that she would slip away, leaving the anti-beautiful in me—for the relations between us were such that whatever I did came back and hit me on the nose —it was like spitting into the wind.

But suddenly and without warning an uproarious burst of laughter came from Mr Youthful.

He laughed involuntarily, gutturally, surprised at and ashamed of himself; he held his napkin to his face, his eyes nearly popped out of his head, he choked into his napkin, he laughed convulsively, mechanically, against his will, to such an extent that I was taken utterly aback. What was tickling his nervous system? The word 'mamma'? He was laughing at the contrast between his daughter and the word 'mamma', perhaps he associated some cabaret memory with it, perhaps my sad, plaintive voice brought him back to the outskirts of humanity. Like all engineers, he was an habitué of cabarets, and no doubt the word I used was not entirely unknown in cabarets. And he laughed all the more because he had just been singing the praises of having a natural child. His spectacles fell from his nose.

'Victor!' Mrs Youthful exclaimed.

I poured oil on the flames.

'Mamma!' I said. 'Mamma!'

'I'm sorry,' said Mr Youthful, still convulsed with laughter. 'I'm sorry, I can't help it! I'm sorry!'

The girl stuck her nose in her plate, and I felt almost physically that across her father's laughter what I said had struck home—and that, unless I were greatly mistaken, her father's laughter was changing the situation, causing me to emerge from the girl. I was at last able to get at her and strike home. I said no more.

Her parents realized it too, and hurried to her rescue.

'I'm surprised at you, Victor,' Mrs Youthful said. 'Our young old man's remarks are not at all amusing. They're nothing but a pose, that's all!'

The engineer at last recovered himself.

'What? Did you think I was laughing at him? I wasn't doing anything of the sort, I didn't even properly hear what he said, I just remembered something.'

However, his efforts aggravated his daughter's situation. Though I could not manage fully to understand all that was happening, I said 'Mamma! Mamma!' once or twice more in the same apathetic fashion, and repetition must have given additional force to the word, for the engineer once more broke into a short, guttural, broken, strangled, laugh; and this laugh obviously made him laugh again, for he suddenly guffawed unrestrainedly, again holding his napkin to his mouth.

The she-graduate was by now very upset.

'Have the kindness not to intervene in the conversation,' she snapped at me, but her annoyance only plunged her daughter deeper in the mire. In the end the girl shrugged her shoulders.

'Leave him alone, Mummy,' she said with apparent indifference, but this only plunged her deeper still.

Strangely enough, the situation between us was now so altered that everything they said made matters worse for them. Actually I was enjoying the situation; I felt that I was regaining power in relation to the girl. But at heart I was indifferent; and it was precisely because of my indifference that I was regaining power; and I was aware that, if I exchanged depression and apathy, wretchedness and poverty, for success, my power would vanish, for the truth was that it consisted of a magic super-power based on an avowed and acknowledged lack of it. So, to consolidate myself in my pitiful condition and to demonstrate the extent of my utter indifference to everything, my total unworthiness, I started putting breadcrumbs, scraps of lettuce, and so on into my fruit salad, and stirring the mixture with my finger. My face . . . But no matter, it was all the same to me. What does it matter? I said to myself sleepily, adding a little salt, pepper, and two tooth-picks to my fruit salad. It was all the same to me, I didn't mind what I ate—and I felt as if I were lying in my grave while birds circled overhead. I felt at peace.

'What on earth are you doing? What on earth are you doing? What are you putting all that filth in your fruit salad for?' Mrs Youthful asked quietly, but with nervousness in her voice.

Lethargically I raised my eyes from my plate. 'I like it like this. What does it matter?' I murmured dejectedly. I started eating my fruit salad, and in fact failed to find it in any way offensive. The effect on the Youthfuls is difficult to describe; I had not expected such a definite success.

For the third time the engineer burst into a crude, night-clubbish, kitchen sort of laugh. The girl, bent over her plate, ate her fruit salad in a silent, correct, disciplined, even heroic manner. Her graduate mother grew pale—and looked at me as if hypnotized and in evident fear. Fear!

'It's a pose,' she muttered. 'It's a pose! Don't eat it! I won't allow it! Zutka! Victor! Zutka! Victor! Zutka, Zutka, Victor, stop him! Don't allow it! Oh!'

I went on eating, and why shouldn't I? I'd eat anything, a dead rat if you like, it was all the same to me. Bravo Mientus! I said to myself. Bravo! It's all the same, I'd eat anything, what does it matter? It's all the same to me!

'Zutka!' Mrs Youthful exclaimed. She could not bear seeing her daughter's admirer eating with such a total lack of discrimination. At this point the girl, having finished her fruit salad, rose and walked out of the room. Mrs Youthful walked out behind her, and so did Mr Youthful, hiccuping convulsively and holding his handkerchief to his mouth. There was nothing to show whether they had just finished their lunch or were running away. But I knew; they were running away. I bounded behind them in mental pursuit. Victory! Forward, advance, pursue, harry, strike, kill, capture, dominate, surround, crush, strangle, let no quarter be given! Were they frightened? Then frighten them more! Did they flee? Pursue them! But calm, take it easy, keep your head, don't change from beggar to victor, for it was as beggar that you gained the day. Did they fear that I should introduce anarchy into their daughter as I had into the fruit salad? Ah! Now I knew how to smash the schoolgirl's style! I could stuff her mind with anything I liked, mix, stir, mince, scramble, with complete and absolute freedom. But calm, calm!

Who would have believed that Youthful's explosion of subterranean laughter would restore my capacity for resistance? My thoughts and actions recovered their claws. No, the battle was not yet won, but at least I had recovered the power to act. Just as I had made a mess of the fruit salad, reduced it to anarchy and disorder, so could I wreck the schoolgirl's modernism, stuff her with strange and heterogeneous things, and corrupt her by them. Forward against the modern style, against the beauty of the modern schoolgirl! But softly, softly . . .

* 9 *

Through the Keyhole

I WENT quietly to my room and lay on the divan. I must prepare my plan of action. I was trembling and sweating, for I knew that my pilgrimage was on the point of taking me to the depths of hell. For nothing which is in good taste can be really dreadful (as the word 'taste' indicates); only its opposite, which is 'disgusting', really makes us puke. How delightful, how romantic or classic, are the murders, rapes, blindings, with which prose and poetry abound! Chocolate with garlic is disgusting, but not Shakespeare's magnificent, fascinating crimes. Don't talk to me about your rhymed and mimed sufferings which never offend good taste and go down as easily as oysters. Don't talk to me about the delectable crimes, the atrocities you lap up like strawberries and cream, the appetizing details of poverty, suffering and despair. And why is it that women novelists who do not shrink from heroically dipping their fingers into the most flagrant social abuses, who have no hesitation in describing the agonies of six or a dozen members of a working-class family starving to death, would never dare use those same fingers to pick their noses in public? The answer is that the latter would be much more horrifying. A famine, or the death of a million men in wartime, we can swallow, and even take pleasure in, but that does not alter the fact that some things, in conjunction with each other, are uneatable, disgusting, vomitable, revolting, and intolerable to human sensibilities. The fact of the matter is that our primary duty is to be pleasing to others; our primary duty is to please, to please; you may lose your wife, your husband, your children, your heart may be broken, but it must be broken in accordance with the canons of taste. Now, the operation on which I was about to embark, in the name of maturity, and in order to escape the schoolgirl's spell, was anti-gastronomic, hostile to the stomach and revolting to the palate.

Besides, I nourished no illusions—my success at lunch had been pretty dubious after all; it had been scored principally in relation to the girl's parents; she had extricated herself little the worse for it, she remained remote and inaccessible. How was I to get at her in her modernism? How could I bring her into my operational orbit in spite of the distance between us? For, apart from the mental distance which separated us, there was also the physical distance—we saw each other only at lunch and dinner. How could I spoil her beauty, work on her mind from a distance, when I was not with her, when she was alone? Only, I decided, by keeping a watch on her, by spying on her. This was a task which to a certain extent they had made easier for me, for from my first appearance in the household they had taken me for an eavesdropper and a peeping Tom. Who knows? I said to myself, still apathetically, but with a glimmer of hope. Who knows? If I put my eye to the keyhole, I may see something which will repel me straight away, for many a beauty, alone in her room, behaves in a fantastically revolting manner. On the other hand, I was also taking a grave risk, for some girls who have subjected themselves to the discipline of charm keep just as careful a watch themselves in private as in public, with the result that instead of ugliness I might see beauty—and beauty in solitude is even more shattering. I remembered that when I had suddenly entered her room I had found the girl polishing her shoe in very stylish fashion. As against this, however, the mere fact of spying on her would serve to a certain extent to detract from her beauty, to diminish her; for when we look at beauty in ugly fashion something sticks.

Such were the thoughts which raced feverishly through my mind. Eventually I rose heavily from the divan and went over towards the keyhole. But, before looking through it, I glanced out of the window; outside in the street, illuminated by the autumn light, it was a magnificent, cool, autumn day. Mientus was just creeping in by the back door, no doubt to see the maid. Pigeons were flying in the clear sky over the house next door, a motor-horn sounded in the distance, a nurse was playing with a child, and the window-panes shone in the light of the declining sun. A beggar was standing outside the house, a bearded and hairy old man, unhappy and desperate. He gave me an idea; heavily and awkwardly I went out into the street and cut a green twig from a tree.

'Here are fifty groschen,' I said to the man. 'If you put this twig in your mouth and keep it there until it gets dark, I'll give you a zloty.'

He put the twig in his mouth and, I don't know why, the sight of the fresh green in his aged mouth gave me a feeling of relief. I went back into the house, thanking heaven for the existence of money, which makes it possible to buy oneself accomplices, and put my eye to the keyhole. The girl was moving about the room in the way in which all girls move about their rooms. She put something away in a drawer, took out an exercise book, put it on the table—and I caught sight of her profile, the profile of a typical schoolgirl bent over her exercise book.

I spied on her miserably and without respite from four o'clock to six (the beggar kept the twig in his mouth the whole time). I waited for her to give herself away, to betray by some nervous movement that the lunch-time defeat had left some trace; I thought that she might bite her lips, for instance, or rub her eyebrows. But I waited in vain. It was as if nothing had happened, as if I did not exist, as if I had never appeared on the scene to disturb her schoolgirlishness. As the time passed the latter grew colder, crueller, more and more aloof and inaccessible, and it seemed possible to doubt the possibility of doing any damage to this girl, who behaved in private exactly as she did in public. One almost got to the point of doubting whether anything whatever had happened at lunch-time. Towards six o'clock the door suddenly opened and the she-graduate walked in.

'Are you working?' she asked with relief in her voice, scrutinizing her daughter closely. 'Are you working?'

'I'm doing my German prep,' the girl replied.

Her mother sighed deeply, several times.

'You're working, good! Good! Work! Work!'

Reassured, she gave the girl a kiss. She too suspected that something in her might have cracked. Zutka moved her little head away. Her mother tried to say something; she opened her mouth, but shut it again without saying it.

'Work!' she said nervously. 'Work! Work! Work! Be active, intense! Go to the dance hall this evening, go dancing! Come back late and sleep like lead . . .'

'Leave my head alone, Mummy!' the girl said unkindly. 'Can't you see I'm busy?'

Her mother looked at her with concealed admiration. Her daughter's hardness reassured her completely; she realized that lunch had left no dent in her armour. But the girl's hardness left me with a lump in my throat; it was directed against herself, and nothing is so moving as to see our beloved behaving hardly and cruelly, not only in our presence but in our absence as well, as if to be ready for any eventuality. Moreover, the girl's cruelty painfully accentuated her poetry. When the mother left the room she bent over her exercise book and, remote and cruel, went on with her homework with supreme composure.

I realized that, if I went on much longer allowing the girl to be poetical in solitude and did not immediately establish contact between her and myself, matters might end disastrously. Instead of making her ugly, I was increasing her attractiveness, instead of my seizing her by the throat, it was she who had a grip on mine. To let her know that I was watching her, I noisily swallowed behind the door. She started, but did not turn her head—which showed that she had realized, and she buried her little head in her shoulders, *touchée*. Simultaneously her profile ceased to exist by itself and for itself alone, with the result that it suddenly and manifestly lost all its poetry. The girl, with me gazing at her profile, went on struggling silently and obstinately for a long

146

time, and the struggle consisted in her not moving even her eyelids. She went on writing, and behaved just as if no one were spying on her.

However, after several minutes the keyhole which was looking at her with my eyes started getting on her nerves. To demonstrate her independence and consolidate her impassivity she deliberately sniffed, a noisy, vulgar, ugly sniff, as if to say: Look at me as much as you like, it's all the same to me! This is how a girl shows her supreme contempt. But her sniff was a tactical error, and I was ready for it. As soon as she sniffed, I sniffed too, quietly but quite distinctly, as if sniffing were contagious and I couldn't help it. She went still and silent like a little bird—a nasal dialogue of this kind was totally unacceptable to her—but her nose, having once started, would not leave her alone. After a moment's hesitation she had to take out her handkerchief and blow it, and after that at long intervals she kept imperceptibly and nervously sniffing again. Every time she sniffed, I sniffed. I congratulated myself on having so easily drawn attention to her nose. Her nose was much less modern than her legs, and much easier to get the better of; accentuating it in this way was a great step forward. If only I had been able to give her a nervous cold, if only it had been possible to give modernism a cold in the head!

After all this sniffing it was impossible for her to get up and block the keyhole, which would have been equivalent to an admission that she had been sniffing nervously and because of me. So let silence and nervous sniffing continue, and let hope be dissembled. However, I underrated the girl's deep cunning; suddenly, with a decisive, energetic gesture, she blew her nose with her hand—with her whole arm—and this daring, primitive, sporting, spontaneous gesture gave charm to the sniffing and changed the situation to her advantage. Once more a lump came into my throat. At that moment—I managed to remove myself from the keyhole only just in time—her mother burst into my room.

'What are you doing?' she exclaimed suspiciously, noting my

indeterminate position in the middle of the room. 'Why . . . are you standing there like that? Why aren't you playing games? You ought to be doing something!' she said angrily. She was afraid because of her daughter; my vague attitude in the middle of the room made her suspect some obscure plot against the girl. I did nothing to explain or enlighten her, but stood my ground, apathetic, unhappy, as if rooted to the spot, until Mrs Youthful could stand it no longer and turned her back on me. Her eyes fell on the beggar standing in front of the house.

'What the . . . What's the matter with him?' she exclaimed. 'Why is he holding that twig in his mouth?'

'Who?'

'The beggar! What does it mean?'

'I don't know. He must have put it in his mouth!'

'You spoke to him. I saw you out of the window.'

'Yes, I spoke to him.'

She looked hard at me. She was swaying like a pendulum. She was obscurely aware that the twig in the man's mouth had some secret implication inimical to her daughter, but she was not to know that for me it was a weapon against modernism. The suspicion that I might have told the beggar to put it in his mouth was too absurd to be put into words. She looked at me with strong suspicion about my state of mind and walked out. At her! After her! Pursue! Strike! Capture! Slave of my imagination, victim of my whim! Quiet! Quiet! I dashed back to the keyhole. The way things were developing made it more and more difficult to preserve my primitive attitude of wretchedness and despair; the struggle was becoming more acute, animal cunning was getting the better of prostration and resignation. However, the girl had disappeared; when she heard voices on the other side of the door, she realized that I was no longer watching her, and this enabled her to emerge from the trap. She had gone out. Had she seen the twig in the beggar's mouth, had she realized for whom he was holding it in his mouth? Even if she had not, the branch grafted on the beard, the green bitterness in the beggar's buccal cavity, must have weakened her, it was in too great a conflict with her modern vision of the world. Night was falling, and the lamps bathed the town in violet. The caretaker's boy came back from the grocer's round the corner. The trees were gradually losing their leaves in the limpid, transparent air. An aircraft hummed in the blue sky. The front-door banged, announcing the departure of Mrs Youthful—anxious, nervous, feeling that there was something evil in the air, she was on the way to her committee meeting, desiring to reassure herself and protect herself against any eventuality by something practical, social, mature.

The lady chairman: 'Ladies, today the first item on the agenda is the terrible social scourge of abandoned children.'

Dr Youthful: 'But where is the money to come from?'

Night was falling, and the beggar was still standing in the street with the bit of fresh verdure in his mouth; a discordant note. I was alone in the house. As I stood there in the darkness, searching in my mind how to continue an operation so auspiciously begun, the atmosphere of some detective novel or other, a whiff of Sherlock Holmes, started percolating into the empty rooms. As both females had fled, I decided to search the house; I might find something which might enable me to get at them. In the Youthfuls' bedroom—it was small, bright, spotless, and austere—there was a lingering odour of soap, the highly cultivated, modern, and civilized post-bath odour, a redolence of nail-files, geysers, and pyjamas. I stood there for a long time, sniffing the atmosphere, analysing its constituent parts, trying to find the clue to the prevalent bad taste, to find a way of fouling the whole environment.

At first sight there was nothing to fasten on. This bedroom, clean, tidy, bright, and austere, was at first sight more pleasing than old-fashioned bedrooms. But I could not tell why the modern engineer's dressing-gown, pyjamas, sponge, shaving cream, slippers, digestive tablets, his wife's gymnastic apparatus, and the bright yellow window curtain on the modern window created such a disagreeable impression. Standardization? Philistinism? Neither provided the answer. Then what was it?

149

I stopped, unable to lay my finger on the key to the bad taste, for lack of the words, gestures, actions which would have enabled me to grasp it, put it in concrete form. My eyes fell on a book on the bedside table. It was Charlie Chaplin's *My Trip Abroad*, lying open at the page where he describes how H. G. Wells danced a solo in his presence. 'Then H. G. Wells did a clog dance and did it very well.' This was the clue I needed; the room was nothing but H. G. Wells dancing a solo in the presence of Charlie Chaplin. What was H. G. Wells when he danced his clog dance? A Utopian. The old modernist believed himself entitled to free expression of his pleasure in dancing. He insisted on his right to joy and harmony, he pirouetted visualizing a future world, a world to come in thousands of years, he danced alone, forestalling the years, he danced in theoretical fashion, believing himself entitled to do so. Now, this bedroom was just as Utopian. Was there room here for the snores and grunts of a sleeping man? Or for his wife's plumpness? Or for his beard, which he removed every morning but nevertheless potentially existed? The engineer undoubtedly had a beard, even if he shaved it off every morning with the aid of his razor and shaving cream—and this room was *shaved*. Once upon a time man's bedroom was the murmuring forest, but where, in this bright bedroom among the towels, was there room for the blackness of the trees? What a poor, constricted thing was this cleanliness, this blue and white paint, incompatible with the colour of the soil and the colour of man! And the Youthfuls in their bedroom seemed to me as dreadful as H. G. Wells dancing a solo jig in the presence of Charlie Chaplin.

But it was only when I started dancing myself that my thoughts took shape and turned into action, ridiculing and deriding my surroundings and throwing the bad taste into relief. I danced, and my dance, partnerless and in silence and solitude, grew so mad-brained that it frightened me. After pirouetting at the Youthfuls' towels, pyjamas, beds, and other hygienic accessories, I quickly walked out, shutting the door behind me. I had injected my dance into their modern interior. Now for the schoolgirl's bedroom, to inject ugliness into that too.

But the room, or rather the entrance hall, in which she slept, was infinitely less well adapted to my distaste. The mere fact that for lack of a proper bedroom she slept in a corner of the hall was sufficient to set off a whole train of fascinating and captivating thoughts. It reflected the contemporary hurry and bustle, the girl's nomadism, a kind of *carpe diem* feeling, connected by secret, underground passages to the free-and-easy, hurrying nature of modern youth in the motor age. You could imagine her dropping off to sleep as soon as she laid her modern head on the pillow, and that again was a reminder of the accelerated rhythm of present-day life. Moreover, the fact that she did not have a proper bedroom inhibited me from carrying out an operation of the kind that I had carried out in her parents' room; for the girl in fact slept, not in private, but in public, she had no real nocturnal life of her own, and that hard state associated her with Europe and America, with work camps, barracks, flags, hotels, and railway stations; it opened vast horizons and ruled out the possibility of a corner of her own. The bedclothes hidden in the divan played a merely marginal role; they did not stand out on their own, they were merely a supplement to sleep. There was no dressing table; to look at herself the girl used the big mirror against the wall. There was no hand mirror. Next to the divan-bed was a little black school-desk, with books and exercise books on it. On top of the exercise books was a nail-file, and on the window-sill a pen-knife, a cheap fountain-pen, an apple, an exam syllabus, a photograph of Fred Astaire and another of Ginger Rogers, a packet of scented cigarettes, a tooth-brush, a tennis shoe, and in the latter a flower, a forgotten carnation. That was all. How little, and yet how much!

I remained silent in the face of the carnation. I could not withhold my admiration from the girl. What subtlety she showed! In dropping the carnation into the shoe she killed two birds with one stone—she spiced love with athleticism and athleticism with love; it was not an ordinary shoe, but a tennis shoe, damp with sweat, for she knew the sweat that comes from playing games is the only kind not damaging to flowers; in associating it with the flower, she made it attractive, added to it something flowery and charming. What a cunning creature!

Ordinary, naïve, old-fashioned girls grew azaleas in pots, but she dropped a flower into a shoe, a sports shoe; what is more, she had certainly done it accidentally, unconsciously, without thinking. What a little virtuoso!

I considered what to do in the face of this. Should I put the flower in the dustbin, or in the bearded beggar's buccal orifice? Any such mechanical, artificial response would merely evade the real difficulty. No, the flower's magic must be neutralized on the spot, and not by physical but by mental means. The beggar, the green twig still projecting from his thick beard, still stood faithfully outside in the street, a fly buzzed against the window-pane, the sound of the monotonous chatter of the maid, whom Mientus was trying to tempt with his stable-boy, floated up from the kitchen, in the distance a tram ground its way round a corner—I stood in the midst of these assorted sounds with a vague smile on my lips. The fly buzzed louder, and I caught it. I tore off its wings and legs, made of it a little ball of terrified, metaphysical suffering, not completely round but certainly pitiful enough, and silently put it in the shoe, next to the flower. The sweat that poured from my brow turned out to be more potent than the flowery tennis sweat; it was as if I had allied myself with the devil against the modern girl. The fly, with its mute, voiceless suffering, soiled and degraded the shoe, the flower, the apple, the cigarettes, the whole of the girl's kingdom, and I, standing there with an evil smile on my lips, listened to what was happening in the room and in myself, sounding the atmosphere as if I had gone mad—and I said to myself that it was not only boys who tortured cats and birds, but that sometimes in the same way grown-up children tortured too—to rid themselves or get their own back on some girl. Did Torquemada torture for such a reason? Who can Torquemada's girl have been? The answer is silence.

The bearded beggar, with the green projecting from his mouth, remained at his post, the fly went on suffering in the shoe, which had now become Chinese, Byzantine, my dance went on in the Youthfuls' bedroom, and I started going through the girl's belongings more thoroughly. I opened the wardrobe, but the contents did not correspond to my expectations. The girl's knickers did not detract from her in any way, they had lost their intimate character, they were more like gym shorts. However, in a drawer which I opened with a knife I found a pile of letters, the girl's accumulated love letters. I pounced on them, while the bearded beggar, the fly, and the dance went ceaselessly on . . .

Oh, the Pandora's box I had hit on, oh, the secrets which that drawer contained! It was only then that I realized the terrible mysteries to which the schoolgirls of today hold the key, and what would happen if one of them betrayed the things confided to her. But these mysteries are swallowed up in them like stones in deep water, they are too pretty, too beautiful, to be able to talk about them—and those who are not gagged by their beauty do not receive such letters. There is something supremely moving in the fact that only human beings bound by their own beauty have access to certain shameful secrets of mankind. Oh, adolescence, that receptacle of shame, locked with the key of beauty! Oh, the things that everyone, young and old, deposited in this temple! Rather than allow them to become public they would unquestionably be willing to die three times in succession, be burnt to death over a slow fire . . . and the face of the century, the face of the twentieth century, the century of the confusion of the ages, appeared as doubtful as that of a Silenus.

There were schoolboys' letters, so unpleasant, infuriating, provocative, gauche, slimy, disgusting and disgraceful, that history had never seen the like, even ancient history, or that of the Middle Ages. The only letters which were tolerable were those which, out of fear, said nothing, such as: 'Zutka, tomorrow at the stadium with Louis and Maritza, confirm, Henry.' Those were the only ones which were not compromising. . . . I found two letters from Bobek and Hopek, vulgar in content and commonplace in form, which tried by excessive crudeness to create an impression of maturity. They allowed themselves to be attracted like moths to a candle, knowing that they would be burnt.

The letters from university students were no less timorous, though this was better concealed. You could tell how frightened each one of them was, how much trouble he took, how he weighed and measured his words, in order to avoid falling into the abyss of his immaturity, his thighs. Their thighs would not leave them in peace. There was an irresoluble conflict between the thigh, unconscious and dormant in its primitive verdure, and all the things that the head dreamt about. But for that very reason there was never any reference to thighs, but a great deal about feelings, social or economic or society events, bridge, racing, and even about changing the structure of the state. The politicians, particularly those who clamoured about 'student life', concealed their thighs with supreme ability, but sent the girl all their programmes, proclamations and ideological statements. 'Zutka, would you like to know what our programme is?' they wrote, but their programmes mentioned thighs no more than their letters did, except occasionally by a slip of the pen, as for instance, when one of them, instead of writing: 'The reputation of our country never stood so high,' wrote: 'The reputation of our country never stood so thigh'; and another, instead of writing: 'The situation can be saved by resolute action, not by sighing over past errors,' wrote: 'The situation can be saved by resolute action, not by thighing over past errors.' Apart from these two instances, thighs were never mentioned. They were similarly carefully concealed in the letters—incidentally distinctly lecherous letters—from the aged aunts who wrote newspaper articles about the jazz age and nudity on the beaches, and tried to enter into spiritual contact with the girl to save her from perdition. Reading them created the impression that the question of thighs never arose at all.

Moreover, at the bottom of the drawer was a pile of books of verse of the kind current today, to the tune of two or three hundred or more, which, it must be confessed, the girl had neither read nor even opened. Each was provided with a dedication written in intimate, sincere, honest language, vigorously exhorting her to read the contents or condemning her in studied and trenchant terms if she should fail to do so, exalting her to the skies for agreeing to read them, or threatening her with expulsion from the *élite* if she did not, or imploring her to read them out of regard for the poet's solitude, or his labour, or his mission, or his status as a pioneer, or his sóul, or his inspiration. Curiously enough, they did not mention thighs either, and, still more curiously, the titles of their works did not do so. These were all about dawns and daybreak, and new dawns, and the age of struggle and the struggle of the age, and the difficult age and the youthful age, and youth on guard and the guardianship of youth, and militant youth and youth on the march, and advancing youth and bitter youth, and youthful eyes and youthful mouths and youthful spring and My Spring and Spring and Me and Spring-Time Rhythms and the Rhythm of Machine-Guns, Semaphore Signals, Aerials and Propellers and My Farewells and My Love and My Longing and My Eyes and My Lips, with not a trace of a thigh anywhere; and all this was written in poetical tones with or without studied assonances and with bold metaphors and an intoxication with words. But there was practically nothing which revealed the slightest trace of thigh. Some of the writers, with great skill and much poetic virtuosity, concealed themselves behind beauty, technical perfection, the interior logic of the work, the logical flow of associations, or behind class consciousness, the struggle, the dawn of history, and other similar objectively anti-thigh elements. It was nevertheless obvious at first sight that all this versifying, with its forced and finicky mannerisms useful for nothing and to nobody, amounted to no more than a complicated cipher, and that there must be some good and sufficient reason behind the compulsion which drove these insignificant dreamers to compose such extravagant charades. After a few moments' thought I succeeded in translating into intelligible language the contents of the following:

THE POEM

The horizon bursts like a bottle
The green stain mounts towards the sky
I return to the shade of the pines
And there
I drink the last unassuaging cup
Of my daily Spring.

MY TRANSLATION

Thighs, thighs, thighs,
Thighs, thighs, thighs, thighs,
Thigh.
Thighs, thighs, thighs.

Besides all this—and it was here that the real pandemonium began—there was a pile of intimate letters from judges, lawyers, public prosecutors, chemists, businessmen, landlords, doctors, etc., i.e. the whole tribe of important, respectable people by whom I had always been so much impressed. I was astounded.

Did these men too, in spite of appearances, maintain relations with the modern girl? Incredible, I said to myself, incredible! So they found their maturity so burdensome that, unknown to their wives and children, they addressed long letters to this modern schoolgirl of the top class but one? In their letters, of course, there was less thigh than ever; on the contrary, each one of them explained in detail why he proposed to engage in an 'exchange of ideas' with her, feeling confident that Zutka would understand, would not take it amiss, etc. Then they went on in tortuous but abject terms to pay tribute to the girl, conjuring her between the lines to condescend to dream about them, secretly of course. And each one of them . . . still, however, without any mention of thighs . . . emphasized to the best of his ability the Modern Boy imprisoned in himself.

Here is an extract from a letter from a public prosecutor:

'Though I wear a gown, in reality I am nothing but an errand boy. I am well behaved and disciplined, I do what I am told. I have no opinions of my own. The president of the court can publicly reprimand me, and I have to get up and ask permission to speak, like a schoolboy.'

This from a politician: 'I am a boy, nothing but a boy dedicated to politics.'

A non-commissioned officer wrote this: 'I have to obey orders blindly. I must be prepared to lay down my life in response to a word of command. I am a slave. Our officers always call us "boys", irrespective of our age. Take no notice of my birth certificate, it's a purely external detail, my wife and children are only external accessories. . . . I'm a military boy, with a boy's blind loyalty, and even the soldiers call me a dog, a dog!'

A landed proprietor wrote: 'Now that I have gone bankrupt, my wife will have to go out and cook, my sons will lead a dog's life, and here am I, not a landlord, but a boy in exile, a boy who has lost his way, and I take a secret pleasure in it.'

But thighs were never explicitly mentioned. All the writers wrote postscripts appealing for the most complete secrecy, for if a single word of these confidences became known their careers would be irretrievably ruined. 'Keep this for yourself alone, and don't breathe a word to anyone.' Incredible! These letters revealed to me in a flash the extent of the power wielded by the modern girl. Who was exempt from her charms? What head was immune from her thighs? Under the influence of these thoughts my legs started moving on their own account, and I was on the point of dancing a jig in honour of the old men of the twentieth century, marshalled under the whip like gangs of slaves, when at the bottom of the drawer I noticed a big envelope from the Ministry of Education. I immediately recognized Pimko's handwriting. The letter was dry enough. It said:

I can no longer tolerate your shocking ignorance of things included in the school curriculum.

I invite you to present yourself at my office in the Ministry on Friday at 4.30 p.m. to enable me to explain, comment on, and instruct you in the poetry of Norwid, and thus fill a gap in your education.

I must point out to you that it is in my official capacity that I am inviting you to call here, and that if you fail to appear I shall make written application to your headmistress to have you expelled.

I must reiterate that I can no longer tolerate the gap in your education, and that by reason of my official position I am within my rights in declining to do so.

T. Pimko, PH.D., Hon. Prof., Warsaw.

So things had got to this pitch between them? So he was threatening her, was he? So this was the state of the game, was it? She had made such play with her ignorance that Pimko had ended by showing his teeth. Being unable to make a date with her as Pimko, he summoned her to his presence by virtue of his role as professor of secondary and higher education. Being no longer satisfied with flirting with her under her parents' eyes, he was taking advantage of his position to impose Norwid on her by legal and official means. Being unable to do anything else, he wished at least to penetrate the girl with his Norwid. In my utter astonishment I held the letter in my hand, not knowing whether it boded me good or evil. But another letter lay in the drawer underneath where Pimko's had been; it consisted of a few brief sentences, scrawled in pencil on a crumpled sheet torn from an exercise book—and I immediately recognized Kopeida's handwriting. Yes, Kopeida's, there was no doubt about it. Feverishly I snatched up his laconic, hastily written, crumpled note. There was every indication that it had been thrown in through the window. It said:

I forgot to give you my address (he gave it). If you want to go with me, O.K. Let me know. H.K.

Kopeida! You remember Kopeida? At once I understood everything. My instinct had not deceived me. The boy who had brought the girl home (as they had said at lunch-time) was Kopeida, and Kopeida had thrown this note in through the window. He had picked her up in the street, and now he was making her a complementary proposition—how modern and direct! 'If you want to go with me, O.K.' He had seen her in the street, been struck by her sex appeal, had spoken to her, and later written her a message, devoid of superfluous formalities, in accordance with the new ways of young people among themselves. He had screwed it up into a ball, and thrown it in through the window. Kopeida! And she certainly didn't know his name, for he had not bothered to introduce himself.

All this gave me a lump in the throat. Pimko on the one hand and Kopeida on the other. Pimko, old Pimko, imposing himself, legally, culturally, officially, and severely, with the aid of his professorial role. You must satisfy me about Norwid, schoolgirl, for I am your master and you are my slave. One claimed her as a brother, a companion of the same age, a modern youth; the other as licensed pedagogue and master of secondary education.

Once more they had me by the throat. What did landlords' confidences, lawyers' laments, or poets' ridiculous acrostics matter in the face of these two letters? They announced disaster, catastrophe. The imminent, fatal danger lay in the girl's readiness to yield to Pimko and Kopeida without a trace of sentiment, simply in obedience to her own law, solely because both had rights over her, the one modern and private, the other ancient and public. But then her attractiveness would increase tremendously . . . and neither the dances, nor the flies of my little enterprise would avail me, for she would suffocate me with her attractiveness. If with modern physical a-sentimentality she gave herself to Kopeida . . . or if she went to see Pimko in obedience to his magisterial order . . . girl going to old man because she was a schoolgirl . . . girl giving herself to boy because she was modern. . . .

Oh, the girl's obedience, her enslavement, to the modern schoolgirl pattern! Kopeida and Pimko knew what they were doing in addressing her so crudely and laconically, they knew that it was for that very reason that she would be ready to succumb. Pimko, a man of experience, did not expect her to be frightened by his threat; his calculations were based on the fact that it is pleasing to yield to an old man under threat—almost as pleasing as to yield to a boy for the sole reason that he expresses himself in modern terms. Oh, slavery carried to the point of self-annihilation, oh, slavery to style! Oh, the girl's *obedience*! Yes, yes, it was inevitable . . . and then what should I do, where should I take refuge in the face of this new tide, in the face of this new upsurge? How strange it was! Both, after all, were about to destroy the girl's modern attractiveness; for Pimko was proposing to abolish her athletic ignorance in matters of poetry, and in regard to Kopeida matters were still worse—for they might end in a maternity ward. But the moment of destruction infinitely multiplied her attractiveness. Blessed is ignorance. Why had I stuck my nose into that drawer? If I had not found out—I could have continued the struggle that I had undertaken against the girl. But, now that I knew, I was dreadfully weakened.

Oh, terrible and moving secrets of the private life of an adolescent, oh, diabolical contents of a schoolgirl's drawer! How could I spoil her beauty, abolish its fascination? Holding the two letters in my hand, I wondered what to do, how to thwart the inevitable and potent growth of charms, magic, beauties, and longings.

Finally, in a deep confusion of the senses, I thought of something, a plan so wild and extravagant that it seemed unreal until I started carrying it out. I tore a page out of an exercise book, and on it I wrote in the girl's big, clear handwriting: 'Tomorrow night, Thursday, tap on my window punctually at twelve o'clock. I'll let you in. Z.'

I put it in an envelope and addressed it to Kopeida. I wrote out another note saying: 'Tomorrow night tap at my window just after midnight and I'll let you in. Z.' This one I addressed to Pimko. My calculation was as follows. Pimko, on receiving such an intimate reply to his ceremoniously official letter . . . would cynically do no more or less than lose his head. It would be a real shock to the old man; he would imagine that the girl wanted a *rendezvous* with him in the strict sense of the term. The modern girl's insolence, cynicism, corruption, anarchy, taking into account her age, social class, and education, would completely turn his head. He would be unable to maintain his professorial role, to keep within the framework of strict legality. Secretly and illegally, he would hurry along and tap at the girl's window. There he would meet Kopeida.

What would happen next? I did not know. But I knew that I would raise pandemonium, wake up the family, bring the whole thing into broad daylight, make Pimko look a fool by means of Kopeida and Kopeida look a fool by means of Pimko—and then we should see what all these love affairs would look like, and what remained of the girl's attractiveness.

* 10 *

Escape and Recapture

AFTER a night of torment, I got up at dawn, but not to go to school. I hid behind the curtain of the little hanging cupboard which separated the kitchen from the bathroom. Drawn inexorably into the developing struggle, it was here, in the bathroom, that I must now launch my psychological offensive against the Youthfuls. I must concentrate and reinforce my mind for the decisive battle against Kopeida and Pimko. I was trembling and covered with sweat, but when life and death are at stake there is no room for scruples, and I could not permit myself the luxury of scorning to take this advantage. Try to surprise the enemy in the bath. See him as he really is. Look at him well, and never forget him. When he drops his clothes like the leaves of autumn, and with them all his distinction and elegance, you will be able to fall on him with your whole spirit, like a roaring lion on a sheep. You must neglect nothing helpful to your mobilization, your dynamism, you must assert your superiority over the enemy, the end justifies the means, you must fight, first, last, and all the time. You must concentrate all your energies, use the most modern methods. Such was the wisdom of the nations of the world. The household was still asleep when I took up my strategic position. No sound came from the girl's room, she was sleeping quietly. Youthful, however, was snoring in his bright blue room, just like a foreman or commercial traveller.

But the maid started moving about in the kitchen, sleepy voices made themselves heard, the family started getting out of bed to perform its ablutions and morning rites. I sharpened my senses—in the brutalized state of mind I was in I was like a civilized wild animal of the *Kulturkampf*. The cock crowed. Mrs Youthful appeared in a light grey dressing-gown and an old pair of slippers, her hair half-combed. She walked calmly, with head erect, and her face seemed to reflect a special wisdom, a sanitary convenience wisdom. Before entering the bathroom she walked, head high, in the direction of the lavatory, into which she disappeared, culturally, conscientiously, and intelligently, as a woman well aware that there was nothing to be ashamed of in these natural functions. *She came out even more proudly than she went in*, freed, fortified, and humanized, as if she were emerging from a Greek temple. I realized that she must certainly enter the place in the same way. Could this, then, be the temple from which the modern wives of engineers and lawyers drew their power? Each day she stepped out of it more perfect and more cultivated, holding high the banner of progress, and it was from here that she derived the intelligence and naturalness with which she tormented me so much. But enough. She went into the bathroom. The cock crowed.

Next Youthful trotted in, in his pyjamas, clearing his throat and spitting noisily—hurrying, in order not to be late at the office, bringing the newspaper with him in order to waste no time, wearing his glasses, with a towel round his neck, cleaning his finger-nails with one of his finger-nails, flapping the heels of his bedroom slippers and hopping about capriciously on his bare heels. When his eyes fell on the lavatory door, he let out a little rump laugh, like that of the day before, and went in like a cultivated, gay, mischievous, and particularly humorous engineer-worker. He stayed there for quite a time, smoked a cigarette, sang *Carioca*, and emerged extremely demoralized, a typical stupid little engineer, with a face so cheerfully asinine, so disgustingly lecherous, so revoltingly stupefied, that it was only by exercising all my strength that I was able to refrain from committing an act of violence against it. It was curious that, while the lavatory seemed to have a favourable effect on the wife, its effect on the husband was disastrous, though he was undoubtedly an engineer-builder.

'Hurry up!' he called out frantically to his wife, who was in the bathroom. 'Hurry up! Vicky's got to get to work!'

Under the influence of the lavatory he referred to himself as Vicky, and he walked off with his towel. Through a chink in the glass I peeped cautiously into the bathroom. The she-graduate, naked, was drying her knee, and her face, looking more elevated, intelligent, and pointed than ever, hovered over her big, white, disillusioned thigh like an eagle over a lamb. There seemed to be a dreadful paradox here; the eagle seemed to be hovering impotently, incapable of seizing and carrying the bleating little lamb up into the sky, though it was the she-graduate contemplating her apathetic, female thigh in a hygienic and intelligent manner. When she had finished drying herself she jumped, landed with heels together, put her hands on her hips, and turned her trunk first right and then left, breathing out and breathing in. She raised her leg—her foot was small and pink. Then she raised her other leg. She started doing double-knee bends. She repeated the exercise a dozen times in front of the mirror, breathing through her nose—until her breasts started ringing hollow and my legs started itching to dance an infernal, cultural jig. I leapt back behind the curtain; the girl's light footsteps were approaching, I concealed myself as if in the jungle, ready for the psychological pounce, an inhumanly, superhumanly, bestialized pounce. It was now or never—in surprising her just after she had awoken, untidy and unkempt, I should destroy her beauty in me, her vulgar, schoolgirl charms. We should see if Kopeida and Pimko were able to save her from such annihilation.

She walked in whistling, amusingly, in her pyjamas, with her towel round her neck—every movement precise and supple, all action. In a flash she was in the bathroom, and I dashed over to look at her. Now or never, while she was weakened and relaxed—but she moved so quickly that no relaxation could really affect her. She jumped into the bath and turned on the cold shower. She shook her hair, and her well-proportioned body shivered and shrank under the cold spray. Oh, it was she who seized me by the throat! Without being forced to by anyone, the girl took a cold shower before breakfast, exposing her shivering body to the chilly water to recover her day-time beauty in a youthful renewal.

I could not help admiring the self-discipline of the girl's beauty. Thanks to her speed, precision and virtuosity, she was able to evade that most delicate moment, the passage from night to day; she flew away like a butterfly on the wings of movement. Moreover, she offered her body to the cold water for a sharp, youthful renewal, for her instinct told her that a sharp dose like that neutralized the relaxation. What could harm youth thus whetted and renewed? When she turned the tap to stop the shower and remained naked, wet, and breathless, it was as if she had started living again. Oh, if she had used hot water and soap instead, it would have been useless; only cold water, by renewing her, could impose forgetfulness.

Abjectly and ignominiously I crawled from my hiding-place and went back to my room, convinced of the uselessness of going on spying on her, convinced that on the contrary, it might lead to my perdition. Hell and damnation! Another defeat—at the bottom-most pit of the modern hell I was still suffering defeats. I bit my fingers till the blood flowed, and swore not to admit that I was beaten, but to continue the mobilization of all my forces; and on the bathroom wall I wrote in pencil the words: *Veni, vidi, vici*. Let them at least know that I had seen them. Let them know that they were being watched. Let them know that the enemy did not sleep. Motorization and mobilization. I went to school. At school there was nothing new; Droopy, poetry, Bobek, Hopek, the infinitive and accusative, Kotecki, faces, backsides, finger in shoe, the usual daily impotence, boredom, boredom, and more boredom. As I foresaw, the effect of my note on Kopeida was imperceptible; perhaps he accentuated his leg a little more than usual, perhaps I only imagined it. On the other hand, my school-mates looked at me in horror, and Mientus actually said to me:

'Christ! What on earth have you been up to to get into that state?'

My face, after the motorization and mobilization, was in such a state of agitation that I did not really know what I was sitting on, but what did it matter? I was on tenterhooks, waiting for the night, for tonight was the night of decision. Tonight perhaps victory would be mine. Would Pimko succumb to the temptation? Would the experienced, masterly, double-barrelled master allow himself to be shaken out of his gravity by a childish-sensual letter? Everything depended on that. I prayed to God that Pimko might succumb. I prayed to God that he might lose his head—and all of a sudden I was seized with panic, at the faces and the backsides and the letter, and Pimko, all that had already happened and all that was going to happen, and I got up in the classroom to run away—and then sat down again, for where was I to run to? Backwards, forwards, left or right—could I run away from my own face and my own backside? Sit still, sit still, there's no way out. Tonight will decide. Tonight!

Nothing of note occurred at lunch. The girl and her mother were very laconic, and did not display their usual modernism. They were obviously uneasy; they felt the mobilization and motorization. I realized that the she-graduate was sitting in her chair stiffly, and not without a trace of discomfort, like someone who knows that her posterior has been spied on. The amusing thing was that this gave her a matronly air; this was an effect I had not foreseen. In any case she must certainly have seen my inscription on the bathroom wall. I tried to look at her with all the perspicacity possible, and I said in a pitiful, abject, and absent-minded way that my eyes were sharp and piercing enough to see right through her face. . . . She pretended not to hear, but the engineer exploded with laughter in spite of himself, and he went on laughing, spasmodically and automatically, for some time. Under the influence of recent events Youthful, if my eyes did not deceive me, was developing a certain taste for dirt—he buttered himself enormous slices of bread, stuffed his cheeks full of them, and masticated noisily.

After lunch I tried to spy on the girl through the keyhole, from four to six, but without success, for she did not once come within my field of vision; no doubt she was on her guard. I realized that her mother was spying on me in her turn. She found excuses to come several times into my room, and even naïvely offered to pay for me to go to the cinema. The quarry were becoming more uneasy, they sensed danger in the air without knowing what it was or what I was after—they sensed it, and it was demoralizing them—uncertainty made them uneasy, and there was nothing for their uneasiness to fasten on; they could not even talk about it, for it was so vague that words would only lead them into a bog. The she-graduate gropingly tried to organize some kind of defence and, as I observed, spent the whole afternoon reading Bertrand Russell, and gave H. G. Wells to her husband to read. But he said he preferred his collection of cabaret songs, and every now and then I heard him bursting into a loud guffaw. They were totally unable to pin down their anxiety to anything. In the end Mrs Youthful buried herself in her kitchen accounts, and the engineer started wandering round the house, sitting on one chair after another and humming some pretty lively songs. Knowing that I was in my room and giving no sign of life was getting on their nerves. It was for this reason that I kept completely silent. Silence, silence, silence; sometimes the silence became very intense indeed; the buzzing of a fly sometimes sounded as loud as a trumpet; the vague, the shadowy, the formless came creeping into the silence, and started forming patches of anxiety. Towards seven o'clock I noticed Mientus creeping furtively towards the kitchen and surreptitiously making signs to the maid.

At dusk the she-graduate also started sitting on one chair after another, and the engineer helped himself to a number of drinks in the pantry. They could find neither suitable form nor suitable place for themselves, they could not keep still; when they sat down they jumped up again as if they had been pinched, they moved about restlessly in all directions, as if they were being undermined, as if there were an enemy—behind them. Reality, having emerged from its bed as the result of the shoves I had given it, now overflowed and blinded them, shrieked or rumbled obscurely, and darkness, absurd element of ugliness, dejection and depression, more palpably beset them and rose like a ferment on their increasing terror. When the she-graduate sat down to dinner she concentrated entirely on her face and the upper parts of her body. Youthful, however, appeared in his shirt-sleeves, tied his napkin under his chin, started buttering himself huge slices of bread, and told cabaret jokes, interrupted by loud bursts of laughter. He knew that I had seen him in the place in question, and that put him in a state of vulgar childishness; he adapted himself completely to what I had seen of him, and became the childish, smart, amusing little engineer, winning, whimsical, and mischievous. He also tried a few winks of connivance and comic signs of complicity on me, but to these I, sitting there pale-faced and neutral, naturally failed to respond. The girl sat in her place indifferent and tight-lipped, and with true childish heroism tried to ignore everything—oh, how I tremblingly admired this heroism, which further enhanced her beauty! But the night would decide, the night would pronounce its verdict and, if Pimko and Kopeida let me down, the modern girl would certainly be the winner, and then there would be no escape from my bondage.

Night came, and with it the hour of decision. The exact course of events could not be foreseen; all I knew was that I must co-operate with every distorting, disturbing, ridiculous, caricaturish and inharmonious thing that happened, with every destructive thing—and a faint and sorry sense of fear overcame me, a faint sense of fear, in comparison with which, however, the great fear of a murderer would have seemed negligible and ridiculous. Soon after eleven o'clock the girl went to bed. As I had previously made a slit in the door with a pair of scissors, I could now see the part of the room which had previously been outside my field of vision. The girl quickly undressed, got into bed, and turned out the light but, instead of going to sleep, kept tossing restlessly on her hard couch. She switched on the light again, took an English detective novel from the table, and forced herself to read. She sounded space with her eyes as if trying to detect the source of the threatening danger, to divine its form, to see the outline of the bogy, to guess the nature of the plot being hatched against her; she did not know that it had neither sense nor form—was non-sense, in fact something devoid of form or law, that a disturbing, styleless thing was threatening her modern style, and that was all.

I could hear voices from her parents' room, and dashed to the door. The engineer, in his pants, very gay and amusing, was still telling what were evidently cabaret stories.

'That's enough, Victor!'

Mrs Youthful, in her dressing-gown, was nervously rubbing her hands.

'That's enough, Victor, that's enough, stop it!'

'Just a minute, honey, just a minute, let me finish this one.'

'I'm not your honey, my name is Mary. Take off your pants or put on your trousers!'

'Pants, panties, pantaloons!'

'Stop it, will you?'

Abruptly she switched off the light.

'Hi! Turn the light on, Ma!'

'I'm not your ma, and I can't stand looking at you. What's the matter with you, what has come over you, what has come over all of us? Pull yourself together, because we march together towards the New Age. We who are the strugglers for, the builders, of the New Age!'

'That's the spirit, duckie, that's the spirit! My big duckie! My big duckie, always plucky, not so lucky! Wuff, wuff! Waiter, bring the pepper! Wuff, wuff!'

He didn't really want her any more, she had lost her freshness.

'Victor, Victor, what are you saying?'

'Vicky's enjoying himself, Vicky's having a good time, Vicky's being funny.'

'Victor, what on earth are you talking about? Remember the death penalty!' she exclaimed. 'The death penalty must be abolished. The Age We Live In. Civilization. Progress. Our hopes and aspirations. I keep telling you that I wish you wouldn't refer to yourself as Vicky! What's the matter with you? Zutka! Oh, what a nightmare. There's something evil, something horrible in the air. Treason . . .'

'Treasonkins!' said Youthful.

'No, Victor, no diminutives, please!'

'Treasonkins, Vicky said.'

'Victor!'

He started fondling her.

'Turn the light on!' the she-graduate exclaimed. 'Victor, turn the light on! Leave me alone!'

'Just wait!' exclaimed the engineer, laughing and out of breath, 'just wait, or I'll give you a slap! A slappikins on the neckikins!'

'You dare! Let go, or I'll bite you!'

'A slappikins, honeykins . . .'

And suddenly he started coming out with the whole of the vocabulary of the alcove that he had in reserve. . . . I recoiled in horror. Though not lacking in disgustingness myself, this was too much for me. The infernal *diminutive* which for some time had so totally oppressed my destiny started extending its sway to them. The engineer's excesses were appalling; oh, how monstrous is the petty bourgeois when he kicks over the traces, takes the bit between his teeth! What times ours were! There was the sound of a loud smack. Had he applied it to her face, her neck, or her behind?

The girl's room was now in darkness. Had she gone to sleep? Not a sound was to be heard, and I imagined her sleeping with her head on her arm, weary and half-covered by the bed-clothes. Suddenly she groaned; it was not the groan of a person asleep. She tossed violently and nervously on her divan-bed. I knew that she was panic-stricken, that her eyes were popping out of her head trying to pierce the darkness. Had her sensibilities become so acute that she knew I was looking at her in the dark through the slit? The groan, welling up from the dark depths, was exceedingly beautiful, as if her very star had moaned and vainly appealed for help.

She groaned again, quietly and desperately. Could she be aware that at this moment her father, depraved by me, was pawing her mother? Had she made out the horrors that were approaching from all sides? In the dark I seemed to see the girl wringing her hands, biting her arm till the blood flowed, as if she wished to penetrate with her teeth to the beauty enclosed within herself. The ugliness outside that was threatening every hole and corner of her drove her inwards towards her own charms. What a wealth of these she possessed! In the first place, she was a young girl. In the second place, she was a schoolgirl. In the third place, she was a modern girl. All this she had inside her like a nut in its shell; but she was unable to enter her own arsenal, though she felt my infamous eye upon her and knew that her rejected admirer was waiting to destroy, degrade, her beauty, mentally turn it into ugliness.

I was not in the least surprised when the girl, threatened with lurking ugliness like this, suddenly allowed a mad fit to carry her away completely. She jumped out of bed, took off her night-gown, and started dancing round the room. She ceased to care whether I were looking at her or not, it was now she who challenged and provoked me to battle. Her legs carried her lightly, her hands fluttered through the air, her head caressed her shoulders. She wound her arms round her head and shook her hair. She lay on the ground and got up again. She burst into tears, then started laughing and humming. She leapt on to the table, and from the table to the divan. It was as if she were frightened of stopping, as if she were being chased by rats and mice; and in taking wing like this she seemed to be trying to raise herself above the Atrocious Thing. She did not know where to take refuge. Finally she took a leather belt and started whipping her back with it, in order to suffer youthfully, painfully. . . . She gave me a lump in the throat. How she made her beauty suffer! How she degraded it, trampled on it, made it writhe in the dust! Standing with my eye to the keyhole, I nearly died, with my disgraceful, abject face, torn between hatred and admiration. Meanwhile, borne aloft again by her beauty, the girl danced more and more passionately. I adored and hated her, my whole being shuddered, my throat contracted and dilated convulsively, like indiarubber. Heavens, where the love of beauty can lead us!

The dining-room clock struck twelve. There were three almost inaudible taps on the window. I froze. It had begun. Kopeida was coming. Kopeida. The girl stopped dancing. Three more peremptory taps on the window. She went over and peeped out through the curtain.

'Is that you?'

The loud whisper floated up towards her in the night.

She drew aside the curtain, and moonlight flooded the room. I saw her standing in her night-gown, tense, expectant.

'Who is it?' she said.

I could not help admiring the virtuosity of this young creature. Kopeida's appearance at the window must obviously have taken her by surprise. Another girl in her place, an old-fashioned girl, would have got involved in conventional exclamations and questions. What on earth is the meaning of this? What are you doing here at this time of night? But the modern girl knew instinctively that showing surprise could only harm her, that it was much better not to show it. What finesse! She leaned out of the window, confidently, like a good friend and comrade.

'What do you want?' she said under her breath, holding her chin in her hands.

As he had used the familiar second person singular to her, she used it to him. I was filled with admiration for the incredible transformations of her style, the ease with which she passed straight from her crazy dance to this conversation. Who would have supposed that a moment before she had been leaping madly round the room? Kopeida, though modern too, was slightly disconcerted by her extraordinary composure, but he quickly attuned himself to it, and said to her with boyish indifference, his hands in his pockets:

'Let me in!'

'Why?'

He whistled and answered crudely.

'You know perfectly well. Let me in!'

He was excited, and there was a slight tremor in his voice, but he concealed it. I was afraid he might mention the letter, but fortunately the modern code forbade them to talk a great deal, or to be surprised at each other; they had to pretend that everything was straightforward and self-evident. Casualness, crudity, brevity and audacity—see how they struck sparks of poetry from themselves instead of the groans, sighs, and serenades of the lovers of former times. He knew that the only way of getting the girl was by jaunty indifference, and that there was no question of getting her without it. All the same, he added a trace of sensual and modern sentimentalism by saying, in a muffled voice and with his face against the virgin vine which was trained up the wall:

'You want it too!'

She made as if to shut the window. But suddenly, as if the gesture had persuaded her to do the very opposite, she stopped and pursed her lips. For a moment she remained motionless, only her eyes moving cautiously right and left. An expression of ultra-modern cynicism appeared on her face and, excited by this and his eyes and lips in the moonlight, she leant out of the window and stroked his hair with one hand in a way which was not playful.

'Come in!' she said.

Kopeida showed not the slightest surprise; he had no right to be surprised, either at her or at himself. The slightest hesitation would spoil everything. He must behave as if the whole thing were natural and normal, and he behaved accordingly. Oh, the virtuoso! He climbed through the window and jumped down on to the floor just as if he were in the habit every night of entering the bedroom of a schoolgirl whom he had met for the first time the day before. Once inside, he laughed silently, just to be on the safe side. But she took him by the hair, turned his head towards herself, and passionately put her lips to his.

Oh, God! Oh, God! If she were a virgin, if she were a virgin, if she were a virgin—and offered herself without compunction to the first man who knocked at her window—oh, God! Oh, God! A lump came into my throat. If she were a tart, a sensualist, it would not matter in the least but, if she were a virgin, it must be confessed that she knew how to strike a wild beauty out of Kopeida and herself. Taking the boy by the hair so impudently, so crudely, and so naturally, and in complete silence—and taking me by the throat. Oh! she knew I was watching through the slit, and that was why she shrank from nothing in order to crush me with her beauty. I shuddered. If only it had been he who had taken her by the hair! But no, it had been she. Oh, you young ladies, you ordinary young ladies who get married with great pomp and ceremony, you commonplace young ladies who sometimes permit us to steal a kiss, see how a modern girl opens herself to love and to herself! She pushed Kopeida on to the bed. Again I shuddered. The frenzy was beginning. The girl was obviously playing the trump card of her beauty. I prayed for Pimko to arrive; if he did not, I was lost, I should never, never, never be able to escape from the girl's wild spell. I, who had dreamed of throttling her, was being throttled by her, I who had dreamed of victory, was going down to defeat.

Meanwhile the girl, in the supreme blossoming of her youth, lay entwined with Kopeida on the divan, preparing, with his aid to reach the summit of her enchantments—quite simply, never mind how, without love, and sensually, with no respect for herself or anything else, for the sole purpose of throttling me by her wild, schoolgirl's poetry. Oh, God! Oh, God! She was winning, winning, winning, all along the line!

At last I heard the sound which was my salvation. There was a tap on the window. At last! Pimko was coming up in support. The decisive moments were approaching. Would Pimko manage to destroy her? Might he not do the reverse, might he not increase her beauty and her spell? That was what I thought to myself behind the door, preparing my face to intervene. Meanwhile Pimko's taps on the window brought some slight relief, because it forced them to interrupt their transports.

'Somebody's tapping,' Kopeida muttered.

The girl leapt briskly from the divan. They listened hard, to see if it were safe to return to their revels. There was another tap on the window.

'Who is it?' the girl said. An ardent, guttural voice came from outside.

'Zutka!'

She drew aside the curtain, signalling to Kopeida to withdraw, but Pimko came tumbling into the room before she had a chance to speak; he was afraid of being seen from the street.

'My little Zutka!' he muttered passionately. 'My little Zutka! My little Zutka!'

My letter had turned his head. The commonplace professor with the double-barrelled nose had had his mouth painfully distorted by poetry.

'My darling little Zutka! Won't anyone see us? Where is your mother?'

He was intoxicated even more by the danger than by my letter.

'Oh!' he exclaimed. 'Such a child, so young, so impudent . . . to say nothing of the difference in age and position. How could you . . . how did you dare . . . to me? So you felt something for me? So you felt something for me? Say something . . . tell me what it is that attracts you in me!'

Oh! Oh! Oh! the dirty old professor!

'What . . . what do you mean?' the girl stammered.

The affair with Kopeida was over, finished.

'There's somebody here!' Pimko exclaimed in the semi-darkness.

Silence answered him. Kopeida kept mum. The girl stood between them, in her night-gown, void of significance, annihilated.

It was at this point that I shouted from behind the door:

'Burglars! Thieves! Burglars!'

Pimko spun round like a top several times and jumped into the wardrobe. Kopeida tried to jump out of the window, but didn't have time, and hid in the other wardrobe. I burst into the room as I was, in trousers and shirt-sleeves. I'd got them! I'd got them! The Youthfuls followed close behind me, he still pawing her, she still pawed by him.

'Burglars?' the engineer, in trousers and bare feet, exclaimed vulgarly, the private property instinct awakening within him.

'Someone came in through the window,' I said. I switched on the light. The girl had gone back to bed and was pretending to be asleep.

'What's the matter, what's happening?' she asked in impeccable style.

'Another intrigue!' exclaimed Mrs Youthful, in her dressing-gown, with red cheeks and dishevelled hair looking at me like a basilisk.

'Intrigue?' I said, picking up Kopeida's braces, which were lying on the ground. 'Intrigue?'

'A pair of braces!' the engineer said with stolid stupidity.

'They're mine!' the girl impudently announced.

Her insolence produced an agreeable effect, though obviously nobody believed her. I kicked open the wardrobe door, exposing to view the lower part of Kopeida's body, that is to say, two legs in a pair of well-creased flannel trousers and two feet in light sports shoes. The rest of him was hidden by the dresses.

'Oh, Zutka!' Mrs Youthful said.

The girl hid her head under the blanket, leaving nothing to be seen but her legs and some of her hair. With what art did she play the game! Another in her place would have started protesting, trying to make excuses. But she merely stretched her bare legs, and in moving them played on the situation as on a flute. Her parents exchanged glances.

'Zutka!' Youthful said.

And he and his wife started laughing. All trace of pawing, vulgarity, disappeared from them, and a strange beauty prevailed.

Her parents, enchanted, delighted, happy, laughed joyously, and looked at the girl, who was still capriciously and wildly hiding her head. Kopeida, seeing that there was nothing to fear from the severe principles of the old days, emerged from the wardrobe, and stood there with a smile on his face, a fair boy with his jacket over his arm, caught by a girl's parents. Youthful looked at me spitefully out of the corner of his eye. He was triumphant. I must still have been under the magic spell; I had wanted to compromise the girl, but the modern boy did not in any way compromise her. To make me feel the full weight of my defeat, Mrs Youthful said:

'What is this young man doing here? It's no affair of his!'

So far I had deliberately refrained from opening the door of Pimko's wardrobe; before I did so I wanted the situation to be consolidated in the plenitude of its modern style. But now I silently opened the wardrobe. Pimko was huddled behind the frocks; only a pair of legs, professorial legs in a pair of crumpled trousers, were standing there, incongruously, improbably, absurdly. The effect was utterly disconcerting. The smile was wiped from the Youthfuls' lips. The whole situation tottered, as if an assassin had stabbed it in the flank. It was ridiculous.

'What's the meaning of this?' exclaimed the girl's mother, growing pale.

From behind the frocks there emerged a slight cough and a forced little laugh, with which Pimko prepared his entrance. Knowing that he must now face ridicule, he forestalled it with a little laugh. The effect of this from behind the dresses was so Rabelaisian that Youthful guffawed and then stopped. . . . Pimko emerged from the wardrobe, outwardly ridiculous, inwardly wretched. I felt wild sadism rising within me, but outwardly I laughed. In that laugh lay my revenge.

The Youthfuls, however, were dumbfounded. Two men in two wardrobes? And one of them an old man into the bargain? Two young men—or even two old men—well, at a pinch. But one young man and one old man? And the old man Pimko of all people? The situation had no axis and no diagonal, and what

possible explanation could there be for it? They glanced mechanically at their daughter, but she lay motionless under the
blanket.

It was then that Pimko, hemming and hah-ing and with an
imploring smile, set about trying to clear up the situation. He
started by talking about the letter—which Miss Zutka had written
him—that for his part he had wished to use Norwid to—but
Miss Zutka had addressed him in the second person singular—
he had wished to do the same to her—and that was all. . . .

Never in my life had I heard anything so lame and stupid; the
private, secret content of the little old man's ramblings became
impossible in a situation clearly illuminated by the electric light
in the centre of the ceiling; nobody wanted to understand him,
and so nobody understood him. Pimko realized this, but his
retreat was cut off. The master, knocked off his perch, was
utterly confounded; it seemed impossible that this was the same
infallible, double-barrelled professor who not so long before
had made me a little backside. His explanation took him deeper
and deeper into the mire, and his softness was pitiable; I could
easily have gone for him, but instead found myself making a
gesture of indifference. His obscure and tangled ramblings drove
the engineer to formality—this impulse put in the shade the mistrust with which he regarded my part in the affair. He exclaimed:

'What I want to know is this. What are you doing here at this
time of night?'

His peremptoriness set the tone for Pimko. For a moment he
recovered his style.

'Please do not raise your voice,' he said.

'What? You permit yourself such observations in my house?'
Youthful replied.

At this point Mrs Youthful, who was looking out of the
window, let out a little shriek. A bearded face, with a green twig
in its mouth, appeared over the railing. I had totally forgotten
the beggar. That day, as on the previous day, I had told him to
put the twig in his mouth, but I had forgotten to give him his
money. He had waited patiently all the evening, and now, seeing

us through the window, he came forward to show us his beflowered, hired face, and to remind us of his existence. He turned up like a new dish at a restaurant.

'What does he want?' the she-graduate exclaimed. She could not have been more frightened by a ghost. Pimko and Youthful fell silent.

The wretched man, on whom general attention was now momentarily concentrated, waggled his twig as if it were a moustache. He did not know what to say, so he said:

'Kind ladies and gentlemen, kind ladies and gentlemen!'

'Give him something!'

The she-graduate dropped her hands to her sides and clenched her fists.

'Give him something and tell him to go away!' she shrieked hysterically.

The engineer searched his trouser-pockets, but they were empty. Pimko, clutching convulsively at any change in the situation, hoping perhaps that if in the mounting confusion Youthful accepted money from him his hostility would thereby be somewhat diminished, quickly held out his purse, but Youthful refused it. The question of finding change irrupted through the window and assaulted mankind. As for me, there I was, with my face, observing the course of events, ready to pounce. But in reality I was already looking at it all as if through a pane of glass. Where was my irruption, my revenge, the crash of shattered reality, the collapse of style, and my triumph over the wreckage? This farce was beginning to bore me. Random ideas and questions started passing through my head, such as: Where does Kopeida buy his ties? Does the she-graduate like cats? How much rent do they pay?

Meanwhile Kopeida remained motionless, with his hands in his pockets. He took no notice of me, treated me like a stranger. He was much too angry at being associated with Pimko (from the point of view of the girl) to have any desire to greet a school-fellow in shirt-sleeves; both associations were supremely distasteful to him. When the Youthfuls and Pimko started looking for change he started moving unhurriedly towards the door. I opened my mouth to call out, but Pimko, who had noticed Kopeida's manœuvre, quickly closed his purse and followed his example. The engineer, however, leapt after them like a cat at a mouse.

'One moment, please!' he exclaimed. 'You are not going to leave like this!'

Kopeida and Pimko stopped. Kopeida, furious at Pimko's companionship, moved away from him; but Pimko closed the gap between them again, and so they remained, standing side by side, like two brothers, one old, one young.

The she-graduate, in a dreadful state of nerves, seized her husband's arm.

'Don't make a scene!' she said. 'Don't make a scene!'

This of course provoked him into making a scene.

'Pardon me!' he shouted. 'Pardon me! I am, I believe, the girl's father! I want to know how, and why, you two entered my daughter's room. What is the meaning of it? What is the meaning of it?'

His eyes suddenly fell on me, and he stopped; fear came over his cheeks, he realized that this was grist for my mill, the mill of scandal—and, if he could, he would have fled, abandoned the field. But the words had been spoken, and he could not withdraw them, so he repeated them, but this time more quietly and simply, and merely for the sake of being consistent, inwardly hoping that no one would take up the question:

'What is the meaning of it?'

Silence reigned. No one was able to reply. Everyone present had a good private and personal explanation of his own, but the sum-total of the situation was totally devoid of meaning. Absurdity suffocated in the silence. Then from under the blankets there came the sound of the girl's desperate, muffled sobbing. Oh, the little virtuoso! She sobbed with her naked calves projecting from the blankets, and the louder she sobbed the more conspicuous her calves became, and her sobs united Pimko, Kopeida, and her parents, enveloped them all in a single, desperate, diabolical note. In a flash the affair ceased to be ridiculous and absurd, recovered its meaning, even a modern meaning, though shadowy, sombre, dramatic, and tragic. Kopeida, Pimko and the Youthfuls felt better—and I felt worse, seized by the throat.

'You depraved her,' her mother muttered. 'Don't cry, darling, don't cry!'

'My compliments, professor!' the engineer said angrily. 'You'll give me satisfaction for this!'

Pimko seemed a trifle relieved; this was better than his previous floundering. So they had 'depraved' her. The situation was turning in the girl's favour.

'The police!' I exclaimed. 'Send for the police!'

This was a pretty risky step on my part, seeing that for centuries the police and under-age girls have formed a harmonious, beautiful, and grim combination—that was why the girl's parents both proudly raised their heads; but my object was to terrorize Pimko. He grew pale, gurgled, and coughed.

'The police!' Mrs Youthful repeated, taking pleasure in the thought of the police in the presence of her daughter's bare calves. 'The police, the police!'

'Believe me,' the professor stammered. 'Believe me, you are making a grave mistake, you are accusing me unjustly . . .'

'That is true,' I chimed in. 'I am a witness. I saw everything out of the window. The professor came into the garden because of a necessity of nature. Just at that moment Miss Zutka happened to look out of the window, and the professor had no alternative but to say good evening to her. They got talking, and he popped into the house for a moment.'

Pimko, abject at the thought of the police, seized on this, without realizing its disgusting and repugnant implications.

'That's perfectly true,' he said, 'that's perfectly true, I was in a hurry, and I came into your garden, forgetting that you lived here—and the young lady saw me out of the window—so I had to pretend to be paying a visit—you will understand—

in such a delicate situation—*quid pro quo, quid pro quo*,' he repeated.

This explanation had a disconcerting and shocking effect on all those present. The girl hid her calves. Kopeida pretended not to have heard it. Mrs Youthful turned her back on Pimko but, realizing that it was her back that she was turning on him, turned and faced him again. Youthful's eyelids were flickering. Once more they found themselves in the grip of that infernal part of the body—vulgarity came flooding in over them, and I observed with curiosity how it submerged and overwhelmed them. Was it the same vulgarity as that in which I had recently been sunk? Yes, it seemed to be, but now it was restricted to them alone. No more sign of life came from the girl under the blanket. Youthful guffawed; it was impossible to say what had tickled him; perhaps he associated Pimko's *quid pro quo* with a Warsaw cabaret which once bore that name. He definitely succumbed to the gruesome, buttocky, second-hand laughter of any second-rate little engineer. But this explosion made him lose his temper with Pimko; he leapt at him, and pettily and arrogantly slapped his face. Having done so, he stopped still, his hand still raised, panting for breath. He stiffened and grew serious. I went to my room to get my jacket and shoes, and started slowly dressing, without losing sight of the situation.

Strange rumblings emerged from Pimko as a result of having his face slapped, and he started trembling, but I felt convinced that inwardly he was grateful for the slap, which in some way put him in his place.

'You will give me satisfaction for this,' he said coldly, but with obvious relief. He bowed slightly to the engineer, and the engineer returned the compliment. Pimko took advantage of this to make hurriedly for the door. Kopeida associated himself with the exchange of courtesies, and hastily tried to smuggle himself out in Pimko's wake. At this Youthful started. What! With a question of honour at stake, with a duel in the air, this young puppy proposed to walk quietly out of the house just as if everything were perfectly normal? He had better have his face slapped too. The engineer moved towards him with raised hand, but at the last moment must have decided that it was beneath his dignity to slap the face of a stripling, a schoolboy. His hand hesitated but, being now unable to withdraw, he took the boy by the chin. This indignity infuriated Kopeida more than a slap in the face would have done, and—after the last long quarter of an hour of total absurdity—unleashed his most primitive instincts. Heaven knows what went on in his head; he must have thought that the engineer had done it on purpose, that if you . . . I'll . . . or something of the sort. In any case, responding to a law that might well be described as that of deviation, he bent down and seized the engineer below the knee. The engineer collapsed, and Kopeida plunged his teeth into his left side and held on like a bull-dog, refusing to let go, glaring round the room with a maniacal look in his eyes.

I was just putting on my jacket and tie, but I stopped, out of sheer curiosity. Never before had I been present at such a scene. The she-graduate hastened to her husband's assistance, seized Kopeida's leg, and pulled with all her might and main. This led to another, more complete, collapse. On top of it all Pimko, who was standing only a foot away from the *mêlée*, did something very curious and almost impossible to describe. Had the master lost all self-confidence? Did he lack the strength to remain on his feet while everyone else was on the floor? Did he think that it could not be worse on the floor than on his feet? Whatever the reason, he deliberately and of his own free will collapsed on to his back and raised his limbs in a gesture of complete subsidence. I was just tying my tie. I did not turn a hair even when the girl, suddenly emerging from under her blanket, started—just like an umpire at a boxing match—jumping round her parents, who were struggling on the ground with Kopeida, and calling out: 'Mummy! Daddy!' between her tears. In the midst of the seething ant-heap the crazed engineer, seeking something to hold on to, grabbed her leg just above the ankle and brought her down too; and there all four of them wallowed—in dead silence, as in church—for shame, after all, had them in its grip. At one point I saw Mrs Youthful biting her daughter, Kopeida clutching Mrs Youthful, the engineer punching Kopeida; a moment later one of the girl's calves appeared over her mother's head.

Meanwhile the professor in his corner started feeling a more and more definite attraction for the fray. Lying on his back with all four hoofs in the air, he imperceptibly but definitely edged towards it. He could not get up, he had no reason to, and he could not go on lying on his back; and the inverted ant-heap had become the only way out for him. When the family, accompanied by Kopeida, brushed against him in the course of the struggle he seized Youthful—I don't know where, but I think not far from the liver—and then he was carried off in the maelstrom. I finished packing my most essential things in an attaché case, and put on my hat. They bored me. Good-bye, modern girl, good-bye, Youthful and Kopeida, good-bye, Pimko—no, you can't say good-bye to something that has ceased to exist. Lightly I took my leave. How delightful to shake the dust from one's feet and go away, leaving nothing behind! Was it really true that that arch-pedagogue Pimko had made me a little behind, that I had been a schoolboy, a modern boy with the modern girl, that I had danced a jig in the room, torn off a fly's wings, spied on them in the bathroom, and all the rest of it? No, it had all vanished, now I was neither young nor old, neither modern nor ancient, nor a schoolboy, neither mature nor immature, I was nothing at all, I was zero. Walking out and taking no memories with me. Oh, sweet indifference, sweet oblivion! When everything is dead inside you and nobody has yet succeeded in begetting you again. Oh, it is worth the agony of having lived for death, just knowing that everything inside you is dead, that nothing exists any longer—emptiness and youth, silence and purity—and as I took my leave it seemed to me that I was not going alone, but with myself, that next to me or inside me or around me—someone the same as myself, someone who was in me and mine was with me—and between us there was neither love nor hate, neither laughter nor parts of the body, nor any feeling nor any mechanism, but nothing, nothing at all—for a millionth of a second. For on making my way through the kitchen, groping in the dark, I heard a voice quietly calling me, coming from the recess where the maïd slept.

'Johnnie! Johnnie!'

It was Mientus, who was sitting on the maid, quickly putting on his shoes.

'It's me!' he said. 'Are you going out? Wait a minute, I'll come with you!'

His whisper struck me broadside on, and I stopped as if I had been hit. I couldn't make out his face in the dark, but it must have been dreadful. The maid was snoring heavily.

'Sh! Quiet! Come along!'

He got down off the maid.

'This way, this way . . . careful, mind that basket!'

We reached the street. Dawn was breaking. The little houses, the railings and the bushes, were all arranged tidily in straight lines, and the air, which was clear at ground level, condensed higher up into a desperate mist. Asphalt. Emptiness. Dew. Nothing. Beside me Mientus adjusted his clothing. I tried not to look at him. Behind the open windows of the house the electric light was in its death throes and the puffing and blowing and panting of the *mêlée* continued. The cool air filtered into my bones, the cold of a sleepless night; I started shivering and my teeth started chattering. When Mientus passed the window he noticed the snorting coming from the Youthfuls.

'What's up?' he remarked. 'Is somebody being given a rub-down?'

I didn't answer. Mientus noticed the attaché case I was carrying and said:

'Are you going away?'

I lowered my head. I knew that he would stick to me, that he would follow me, that he would catch me up, for we were both . . .

'Are you going away?' he repeated. 'Then I'll come with you. We'll go together. I've raped the girl. But that's not the reason

. . . it's the stable-lad, the stable-lad. Let's run away to the country! Together! The stable-lad, Johnnie, the stable-lad!' he repeated obstinately.

I held my head straight and stiff, without looking at him.

'Mientus,' I said. 'What do I care about you and your stable-lad?'

But when I walked off he walked with me, and I walked with him, and we walked together.

★ 11 ★

Introduction to Philimor
Honeycombed with Childishness

ANOTHER preface . . . I must provide a preface, a preface is required of me, without a preface I cannot possibly go on. It is my duty to provide a preface, for the law of symmetry here demands the insertion of *Philimor Honeycombed with Childishness* as balance and counterweight to *Philifor Honeycombed with Childishness*; and similarly the introduction to *Philifor Honeycombed with Childishness* must be balanced by an introduction to *Philimor Honeycombed with Childishness*. Whether I like it or not, I cannot, no I simply cannot, evade the iron laws of symmetry and analogy. Moreover, it is time to interrupt, to make an end of, to emerge, even if only momentarily, from greenness and immaturity, and to look a little more sensibly under the crazy burgeoning of buds and pimples and little leaves, to prevent people from saying that I'm as mad as a hatter, incurable poor chap. And before going farther down the path of inferior, intermediate, sub-human terrors, I must explain, specify, rationalize, classify, bring out the root idea underlying all the other ideas in the book, demonstrate and make plain the essential grief, the great-grandmother of all the other griefs which are here isolated and exposed; and I must establish a hierarchy of griefs and a hierarchy of ideas, comment on the work in an analytic, synthetic and philosophical manner, to enable the reader to find its head, legs, nose, and fingers, and to prevent him from coming and telling me that I don't know what I'm driving at, and that instead of marching forward straight and erect like the great writers of all ages, I am merely revolving ridiculously on my own heels. What, then, shall the fundamental, overriding anguish be? Where art thou, great-grandmother of all griefs? The deeper I dig, the more I explore and analyse, the more clearly do I see that in reality the primary, the fundamental grief is purely and simply, in my opinion, the agony of bad outward form, defective appearance, the agony of phraseology, grimaces, faces . . . yes, that is the origin, the source, the fount from which there flow harmoniously all the other torments, follies, and afflictions without any exceptions whatever. Or perhaps it would be as well to emphasize that the primary and fundamental agony is that born of the constraint of man by man . . . i.e. from the fact that we suffocate and stifle in the narrow and rigid idea of ourselves that others have of us. Or at the basis of the book perhaps there lies the supreme and fatal torment

of sub-human greenness, of spots, pimples, little leaves
or the torment of undeveloped development
or, perhaps, the pain of unformed form
or the burden of being created inside ourselves by others
the agony of physical and psychological violation
the torment of concentrated inter-human tensions
the curving and not yet fully explained torment of psycho-
    logical deviation
the marginal discomfort of psychological dislocation and
    psychological failure
the constant pain of treachery and dishonour
the automatic suffering of mechanization and automatism
the symmetrical torture of analogy and the analogical torture
    of symmetry
the analytic torment of synthesis and the synthetic torment
    of analysis
or, again, the suffering of the parts of the body, and dismay
    about the hierarchy of its various parts
the affliction of benign infantilism
of futile pedagogy and pedanticism

of hopeless innocence and naïveté
of remoteness from reality
of chimaeras, illusions, aberration, pretence
of higher idealism
of lower, crude, petty idealism
second-rate dreams
of being reduced in size, or rather the astonishing torment of
  being reduced in size
the torment of being the eternal candidate
the torment of aspiration
of interminable apprenticeship
or, perhaps, the torment of trying to suppress oneself,
  exceeding one's own strength, and the resulting torment of
  general and particular impotence
the erosion of superiority
the suffering of looking down on people
the suffering of superior and inferior poetry
the dull torment of a psychological *cul-de-sac*
the tortuous torture of the tortuous, of the dirty, underhand
  blow, or, rather the sadness of the age, in the general and
  particular meaning of the word
the torment of anachronism, the torment of modernism
the suffering caused by the formation of new social stratifica-
  tions
the torment of the half-educated
or perhaps simply the torment of micro-educated indecorous-
  ness
the pain of stupidity
wisdom
ugliness
beauties, spells and enchantments
or, perhaps, the deadly pain of logic and consistency in stupidity
the desolation of acting a part
the desperation of imitation
the brutalizing torment of brutalization and of saying the same
  thing over and over again

or, probably, the hypomanic torture of hypomania
the unspeakable sadness of the unspeakable
the sadness of non-sublimation
pain in the finger
nail
tooth
ear

the terrifying torture of mutual interdependence and mutual barriers, of reciprocal interpenetration of all torments and all parts, the pain of one hundred and fifty-six thousand three hundred and twenty-four and a half other pains, not counting women and children (as a sixteenth-century French writer would say). Which torture shall we choose as the great-grandmother of all tortures, which part shall we pick on as our point of departure, where shall we seize hold of the book and which of the tortures and parts in question shall we choose? Oh accursed parts, shall I never get rid of you? What a wealth of parts, and what a multitude of tortures! Where shall we find the great-grandmother who established the guiding lines, which torture shall we take as basic? The metaphysical torture? The physical torture? The sociological torture? Or the psychological torture? Nevertheless I must attempt the task, I must, I have no choice, or people would say that I didn't know what I was aiming at, that I was stupidly revolving on my own heels. Perhaps it would be wiser not to specify and demonstrate the essence of the book in terms of tortures at all, but to discuss it in relation to its subject-matter, show that it was born of

hostility to pedagogues and their charges
the prevalence of besotted scholars
sympathy with devoted and profound minds
involvement with the most prominent figures in our contemporary national literature and the most hallowed and representative critics
dislike of schoolgirls

the patronage of mature and distinguished figures

the patronage of distinguished men, connoisseurs, narcissists, aesthetes, brilliant intellectuals

dislike of connoisseurs

of being tied to the cultural aunts' apron-strings

dislike of urban overcrowding

the background of the country aristocracy

involvement with small provincial doctors, engineers, and clerks with limited horizons

involvement with high officials and leading doctors and lawyers with the broadest horizons

involvement with the aristocracy of birth, and other aristocracies

dislike of the vulgar

Probably, however, the work was to a certain extent born as a result of co-existence with real persons, the exceedingly repulsive Mr X, for instance, or Mr Z, whom I detest, or Mr N, who horrifies and bores me . . . oh, the maddening torment of being in their company! And perhaps the basic aim and purpose of the book is merely to demonstrate to these gentlemen the whole extent of the contempt that I feel for them, to get on their nerves, to irritate and anger them, and to put me out of their reach. In that case the purpose of the book would be definite, concrete, private.

Or, who knows? it might have been written in imitation of masterpieces

or out of inability to write an ordinary book?

or as a result of dreams?

Or complexes?

Or childish memories?

Or, perhaps, I just started, and my pen ran away with me?

Or perhaps it was the result of a fear psychosis?

Or some other psychosis?

Or just a blunder?

Or a pinch?
Or a part?
Or a particle?
Or a finger?

Also the task is to evaluate and to assess, and to decide whether the work is a novel, or a book of memoirs, or a parody, or a lampoon, or a variation on imaginative themes, or a psychological study; and to establish its predominant characteristics; whether the whole thing is a joke, or whether its importance lies in its deeper meaning, or whether it is just irony, sarcasm, ridicule, invective, downright stupidity and nonsense, or a piece of pure leg-pulling; and, moreover, to make sure that it is not just a pose, a piece of mystification, a fraud, or the result of a total lack of humour, a total deficiency of feeling or atrophy of the imagination, a collapse of all sense of order, and a total loss of reason. But the sum-total of all these possibilities, torments, descriptions and parts is so vast, so incommensurable, so inconceivable and, what is more, so inexhaustible, that, with the most profound respect for the Word, and after the most scrupulous analysis, it must be admitted that we are no wiser than when we began, cluck! cluck! cluck! as the chicken said. So I invite those who wish to plunge still deeper and get a still better idea of what it is all about to turn to the next page and read my *Philimor Honeycombed with Childishness*, for its mysterious symbolism contains, the answer to all tormenting questions. Philimor, then, having definitely been constructed on the basis of analogy with Philifor, conceals in this strange relationship the secret and definitive meaning of the whole work. After the reader has successfully fished this up into the light of day, there will be nothing to prevent him from plunging still deeper into the dense jungle of the monotonous separate parts.

* 12 *

Philimor Honeycombed with Childishness

AT the end of the eighteenth century a Paris peasant had a child; this child eventually had a child too, and so did this latter child; and so child followed child, until one fine afternoon the last child, having become champion of the world, was competing in a tennis tournament at the Racing Club in Paris, in a tense atmosphere and to the accompaniment of thunderous applause.

However (oh, what strange mischances life holds in store for us!) a certain colonel of Zouaves who was sitting in one of the side seats started envying the brilliant and impeccable play of the two champions; and suddenly, to show the six thousand spectators what he was capable of—particularly as his girl-friend was seated by his side—he took out his pistol and fired at the ball as it flew between the two rackets. The ball burst, and fell to the ground. For some time the two champions continued making strokes in the void, but then, exasperated by the folly of such pointless activity, they dashed at each other and started fighting. The audience burst into thunderous applause.

There, no doubt, the matter might have ended. But an unforeseen contingency arose. In his excitement the colonel (oh, how careful one must be in life!) had not taken into account the spectators sitting in the stand opposite. He had assumed, heaven knows why, that after piercing the tennis ball the bullet would go no farther. But, unfortunately, it continued its trajectory, and hit a shipowner in the neck. Blood spurted from the severed artery, and the first impulse of the injured man's wife was to fling herself at the colonel and seize his pistol. This was impossible, however, as she was hemmed in by the crowd, so she contented herself with slapping the face of her right-hand neighbour. She did so because there was no other outlet for her indignation and because, in accordance with her essentially feminine logic, she felt (in the innermost depths of her unconscious) that, being a woman, everything was permitted her.

But obviously things did not turn out as she expected. For the man she slapped (oh, how fallible are our calculations and how unpredictable our destinies!) happened to be suffering from latent epilepsy; under the influence of the shock he had a fit, and started foaming like a geyser. The unhappy woman found herself between a man spitting blood and another foaming at the mouth. The crowd burst into thunderous applause.

At this point a gentleman who was sitting quite near panicked, and jumped on to the head of a lady seated below him. She rose to her feet, bounded forward, and landed on the court, carrying the man on her back with her in her mad career. The crowd burst into thunderous applause. And there, to be sure, the whole thing might have ended, but for the fact (which only goes to show that in this world one should always be ready for anything and never take anything for granted) that a few yards away there happened to be sitting a poor devil, an obscure retired dreamer, who for years past, whenever he attended any public spectacle, had always ardently desired to jump down on to the heads of the people seated below him, and had restrained himself from doing so only with the greatest difficulty. Now, stimulated by this example, without a moment's hesitation he jumped down on to the woman seated immediately in front of him. The latter (she was a badly paid clerk who had arrived only recently from Tangier) assumed this behaviour to be normal and correct, in fact, that this was how people behaved in high society . . . so she too staggered on to the court beneath her burden, taking care that her movements did not betray the slightest sign of nervousness or timidity.

The educated section of the audience started tactfully applauding, in order to conceal the scandal from the eyes of the representatives of foreign embassies and legations. But at this point a misunderstanding occurred; other, less well educated, spectators took the applause as signifying approval, and all the gentlemen started mounting the backs of their ladies. The foreigners looked on with growing astonishment. What could the more distinguished spectators do in these circumstances? They had no alternative but to mount the backs of their ladies too.

And that, certainly or almost certainly, is how the whole thing might have ended. But at this point a certain Marquis de Philimor, who was sitting with his wife and members of her family in the distinguished visitors' seats, suddenly felt his noble blood rising within him; and he appeared in the centre of the court, in his light summer suit and looking pale but determined, and asked in icy tones if anyone, and if so who, desired to insult the Marquise de Philimor, his wife; and he flung into the faces of the crowd a handful of visiting cards on which were inscribed the words 'Philippe de Philimor'. (Oh, how difficult and dangerous life is, how careful we must be!) There was a deathly hush.

Suddenly at least thirty-six gentlemen, riding their thin-ankled, thoroughbred women bareback, approached the *marquise* in order to insult her and feel as blue-blooded as the *marquis*, her husband. She, however (oh, how mad, how crazy, is life!) was so terrified that she had a miscarriage, and the wailing of an infant was heard at the *marquis*'s feet, under the shoes of the prancing women.

The *marquis*, thus suddenly honeycombed and riddled with childishness, doubled and completed by a baby just at the very moment when he was behaving in a particularly adult and gentlemanly fashion, suddenly felt ashamed of himself and went off home, while thunderous applause broke out among the spectators.

· 13 ·

Out of the Frying Pan

So off we set, Mientus and I, in search of a stable-boy. We
turned the corner, and the villa, and everything else to do with
the Youthfuls, vanished from sight. In front of us there stretched
the long, shiny ribbon of the Filtrowa road. The sun rose like a
yellow ball, we had breakfast at a hairdresser's, the town woke
up, it was eight o'clock by now, and off we went again, I with
my little attaché case and Mientus with a knotty stick. The birds
chirruped and chirped. Onward! Onward! Mientus strode
cheerfully, borne along by hope, and his hope infected me, his
slave. 'To the outskirts! To the outskirts!' he kept repeating.
'There we'll find a smashing stable-boy, a smashing stable-boy!'
The stable-boy painted the morning in bright and pleasing
colours; how amusing and agreeable it was to cross the city in
search of a stable-boy! Who was I about to become? What
would they make of me? What awaited me? I did not know, but
trotted along bravely behind my master, Mientus, and I could
neither grieve nor suffer, because I was cheerful. The entrances
to the houses, which were not very numerous in this district,
were infested with hall-porters and their families. Mientus glanced
at them all, but what a difference there is between a hall-porter
and a stable-boy! Is not a hall-porter merely a potted peasant?
Every now and then we saw a hall-porter's son, but not one that
satisfied Mientus—is it not also true that a hall-porter's son is a
caged, tamed, stable-boy? 'There's no wind here,' Mientus said.
'Between these houses there are nothing but draughts, and I can't
conceive of a stable-boy in a draught. For me a stable-boy can
exist only in a strong wind.'

We left behind nannies and nursemaids pushing creaky prams. Adorned in finery inherited from their mistresses, and with buckled heels, they cast us coquettish glances. Perfumed, with Greta Garbo hair-dos, two gold teeth, and somebody else's child. We saw managers and clerks on their way to work with briefcases under their arm, all in papier mâché, looking very Slavonic and very clerkish, the husbands of their wives and the boss of the female servants, all cuffs and buttons which they wore as if they were adornments of their ego. Above them was the vastness of the sky. We passed a number of smartly dressed women in fur coats—Warsaw chic—some thin and vivacious, others slower and softer—buried under their hats and so alike that they overtook and passed one another without one's realizing it. Mientus did not think them worthy of a glance, and I was so bored that I started yawning.

'To the outskirts!' he cried. 'To the outskirts! There we shall find the stable-boy. Here's there's nothing, everything's cheap and nasty, nothing but the cows and horses of the petty bourgeoisie, doctors' wives and doctors, like old cart-horses. Trash and pestilence! Cows and mules! Look how educated and dumb they are! Distinguished and vulgar!'

At the corner of Wawelska Street we caught sight of some public buildings conceived in the grand style, the impressive sight of which nourishes vast masses of hungry and anaemic taxpayers. These buildings reminded us of school, so we quickened our pace. In Narutowicz Square, where the Students' Hostel is, we came upon the academic fraternity, with threadbare sleeves, short of sleep and ill-shaven, in a hurry to get to their lectures and waiting for the tram. With their noses stuck in their books, they were all munching hard-boiled eggs, stuffing the shells in their pockets and breathing the town dust.

'Nothing but ex-stable-boys,' Mientus exclaimed. 'Peasants' sons working for degrees! To hell with ex-stable-boys! How I hate them! They still pick their noses and study text-books! Book-learning in a stable-boy! Stable-boy lawyer, stable-boy doctor! See how their minds get stuffed with learned jargon!

Look at their great clumsy fingers! It's as disgusting as if they were becoming monks! Some of them would make fine stable-boys, but what's the good of them now? They're travesties of themselves, they've been murdered, liquidated! To the outskirts, to the outskirts, where the air's fresher and the wind blows!'

We turned into Grojecka Street . . . earth, dust, noise, smell —we had left the big houses behind, here there were nothing but little ones. Small and improbable carts, loaded with Jews with all their worldly goods, vehicles loaded with vegetables, feathers, milk, cabbages, wheat, oats, old iron and refuse, filled the streets with noise, clatter and din. In each cart there was either a peasant or a Jew—urbanized peasant or countrified Jew—one hardly knew which to choose. We plunged deeper and deeper into this secondary layer, the immature outlying area of the city, and we saw more and more bad teeth, ears stuffed with cotton-wool, fingers tied up with rags, we came across more and more wavy hair, hiccups, eczemas, cabbages and general decay. Washing was hung out to dry at the windows. The wireless blared continuously, completing the task of public education, and a number of Pimkos, with rather artificially naïve and sincere voices, sometimes gay or cheerful, were cultivating the minds of bakers, instructing them in their civic duties and the love of Kosciuszko.

Tavern keepers revelled in the luxury of high society as described in popular novels, and their wives scratched their backs, deeply affected by Marlene Dietrich. Operation Peda-gogue continued relentlessly, and innumerable specialists worked on the masses, teaching and instructing, influencing and developing, awakening and civilizing them, with simplified grimaces *ad hoc*. Here members of the association of tramway-men's wives dance a round dance, singing with a smile on their lips, and producing *joie de vivre* under the watchful eye of a member of the permanent committee of the Social Gladness organization. There cabmen sang patriotic songs in chorus, producing a singularly naïve effect; while yonder ex-farm-girls were being instructed in how to perceive the beauty of the setting sun; and dozens of idealists, doctrinaires, demagogues, and agitators formed up and reformed and deformed, disseminating their ideas, opinions, doctrines, views, all specially simplified and adapted for the use of simple people. 'Face, face, nothing but face,' said Mientus, with his usual frivolity, 'it's just like school. It's not surprising that they are ravaged by illnesses and ground down by poverty, it would be impossible for such vermin not to be ravaged and ground down. What demon put them in this state? Because I'm convinced that, if they had not been specially prepared and put in that state by somebody, it would be totally impossible for them to produce so much stupidity and muck. Why does it emerge in such abundance from them and not from the peasants, though the peasants never wash? What I want to know is: who transformed the good and worthy proletariat into such a dung factory? Who taught it all that dirt and make-believe? Sodom and Gomorrah! We shan't find our stable-boy here! Onward! Onward! Onward! When will the wind blow? But there's no wind, there's nothing but stagnation, men bathing in humanity like fish in a pond, the stink rises to high heaven, and there's no stable-boy to be seen.

'Unmarried seamstresses grow thin, second-class hairdressers grow fat in cheap comfort, small businessmen suffer from flatulence, servant-girls with nothing to do on their short fat legs come out with awkward, pretentious turns of phrase and false accents, the chemist's wife gives herself airs and holds herself above the washerwoman, who holds herself on high and buckled heels too. Feet . . . in reality bare though shod—feet not meant for shoes, heads not meant for hats, peasant bodies with petty bourgeois embellishments. Nothing but face,' said Mientus, 'nothing sincere or natural, everything false, imitated, and artificial. And not a stable-boy in sight!'

Eventually we chanced on a quite attractive looking young apprentice, a pleasant, well-built, fair-headed young man, but unfortunately he was the possessor of an elevated social conscience and ill-assimilated ideologies.

'Nothing but face,' said Mientus, 'to hell with philosophy!'

Later we came across a typical young gangster, with a knife between his teeth. Though for a moment we took him to be the stable-boy of our dreams, he turned out to be nothing but a suburban braggart in a bowler-hat. A third young man with whom we struck up a conversation at a street-corner seemed at first suitable in every respect, but what is to be done with a person who uses the word 'notwithstanding'?

'Nothing but face,' Mientus muttered furiously. 'It won't do no, it won't do. Onward! Onward!' he repeated feverishly. 'There's nothing here but shit, like at school. The suburbs learn from the town. Hell! The lower classes are obviously nothing but the bottom class at the primary school, and that's surely the reason why they have such snotty noses. By all the spots, pimples and rashes! Are we never to get away from school? Face, face, face! Onward! Onward!'

We pushed on, past little wooden houses, mothers picking fleas from their daughters' heads, daughters picking fleas from their mothers' heads, children wallowing in the gutter, workers coming home from work. From all sides there resounded one single, remarkable word, a key word. It seemed to invade the whole street, it became the proletarian hymn, it smacked of provocation, was trumpeted furiously into space, created at any rate the illusion of strength and life.

'Listen!' said Mientus in astonishment, 'they're giving themselves courage, just as we did at school. For all that, these young puppies won't save themselves from the huge and classic bummery that has been prepared for them. It's a terrible thing, but nowadays there is no one who is not in the maturing stage. Onward! There's no stable-boy here.'

As he said these words a light breeze caressed our cheeks. We had come to the end of houses, streets, canals, drains, hairdressers, windows, workers, wives, mothers and daughters, cant, cabbages, smells, crowds, dust, bosses and apprentices, shoes, blouses, hats, heels, trams, shops, vegetables, gangsters, advertisements, pavements, stomachs, tools, parts of the body, hiccups, knees, elbows, shop-fronts, talk, spitting, blowing of noses, coughing, shouting, children, bustle and din. We had reached the end of the town. Ahead of us lay fields and woods, and an open, asphalt road. Mientus sang:

> *Oh, oh, oh, the green forest!*
> *Oh, oh, oh, the green forest!*

'Get yourself a stick,' he said, 'cut yourself one from a tree. We'll find our stable-boy in the fields. I can see him already. He's O.K.!'

I too started singing:

> *Oh, oh, oh, the green forest!*
> *Oh, oh, oh, the green forest!*

But I could not put one foot in front of another. The song died on my lips. Space. On the horizon . . . a cow. Earth. A duck waddled along in the distance. The immense sky. Blue patches in the haze. At the edge of the town I stopped, and felt that for me life away from the herd, without anything artificial or manufactured, without the human element, humanity, was impossible, and I grabbed Mientus by the arm.

'Let us go back, Mientus,' I said. 'Don't let us leave the town.'

In the midst of the bushes and the unknown vegetation I trembled like a leaf—eliminated from among men. In their absence the distortions that they had inflicted on me seemed absurd and unnecessary.

Mientus hesitated too, but the prospect of the stable-boy got the better of his fear. 'Forward!' he shouted, brandishing his stick. 'I'm not going alone! You've got to come with me! Come on! Come on!'

The wind rose, the trees swayed, the leaves rustled . . . one of them in particular frightened me, right at the very top of a tree, delivered over entirely to space. A bird flew through the air. A dog emerged from the town and made off across the fields. Mientus set off valiantly along the roadside path, and I followed behind him, like a ship debouching into the open sea. The harbour, the towers and chimney-pots, disappeared from view, we were alone. The silence was such that we could almost hear the cold, wet stones sleeping in the earth. I trudged on, with nothing in my mind and the wind whistling in my ears, kept on my feet by the rhythm of walking. Nature. I don't like it, for me nature is man. Mientus, let us turn back, I prefer a crowded cinema to the country wind. Who was it who said that man feels small in the face of nature? I on the contrary, grow, become gigantic, feel utterly fragile, served up naked, so to speak, on the dish of the enormous field of nature in all my human unnaturalness. Oh, where had *my* forest gone, my dense forest of eyes and mouths and words and looks and faces and smiles and twitches? Another forest drew near, a forest of green, silent, tall trees through which the hare picks its way and the caterpillar creeps. As ill luck would have it, not so much as a hamlet was in sight; nothing but fields and woods. I do not know for how long, for how many hours, we trudged on through the fields, apathetically, stiffly, as if on a tightrope. We had no alternative, because standing still was still more tiring, and we could not sit or lie down on the damp earth.

True, we had passed through one or two hamlets, but they seemed dead; hermetically sealed hovels showed nothing but empty sockets. Traffic on the road had ceased entirely. How much longer should we have to go on tramping through the void?

'What's the meaning of this?' said Mientus. 'Have all the peasants been wiped out by the plague? Are they all dead? If things go on like this, we shall never find the stable-boy.'

At last, when we came to another, similarly depopulated hamlet, we decided to knock at one of the hovel doors. The answer was a concert of furious barks; it was as if we were being pursued by a canine pack, ranging from bloodhounds to pugs, all sharpening their fangs for our benefit.

'What's this?' said Mientus. 'Where do all these dogs come from? Why are there no peasants? Pinch me, I must be dreaming!'

The echo of these words had barely died away in the limpid air when a rustic head appeared behind the neighbouring potato clamp and promptly vanished again. We went towards it, and a chorus of furious barking rose from the ditch.

'Good heavens, more dogs?' said Mientus. 'Where has the gaffer gone to?'

Mientus walked round the clamp one way and I walked round the other (to the accompaniment of deafening, frantic barking from the neighbouring hovels), and we found the peasant, as well as his wife and the quadruplets that she was feeding from one anaemic dug (the other had long since become unserviceable). They barked desperately and furiously and tried to run away, but Mientus chased the peasant and caught him. He was so weak that he collapsed to the ground and moaned:

' 'ave pity on me, sorr, 'ave pity! Leave me be, sorr, leave me be!'

'What's the matter with you, man?' said Mientus. 'What's the matter with you? Why did you run away from us?'

At the word 'man' the barking in the huts and behind the fence redoubled, and the yokel went as white as a sheet.

' 'ave pity, sorr, 'ave pity, oi be no man, sorr, leave me be, sorr, please!'

'Citizens,' Mientus then said in friendly fashion, 'citizens, have you gone mad? Why do you and your wife bark like this? We have nothing but good intentions towards you.'

At the sound of the word 'citizens' the barking trebled in intensity, and the woman burst into tears.

'Please, sorr, 'e be no stitizen, 'e be no stitizen, that's the last thing 'e be!' she pleaded. 'Oh 'ow unlucky we be, 'ow unlucky! Here 'ey be, arter us again wi' 'eir intentions!'

'What *is* this about, friend?' said Mientus. 'We have no wish to harm you. We wish you nothing but good.'

'Ow! Ow!' the peasant howled in terror.

' 'e wish us good!' his wife shrieked. ' 'e wish us good! We not 'umans, we dogs, dogs! Wuff! Wuff!'

Suddenly one of the whelps yelped, and the old woman,

realizing that there were only two of us, barked, and bit me in the stomach. I shook her off. By now the whole village had gathered round the fence, barking and giving tongue.

'At 'em! At 'em! Bite the stitizens! Bite 'em and 'eir intentions!' they growled.

While rousing and egging each other in this fashion they steadily approached us, and the worst of it was that in their fury and resentment, or perhaps to give themselves courage, they brought a lot of real dogs with them, and these, while jumping and bounding about, slavered and barked furiously.

The situation was becoming even more critical from the psychological than from the physical point of view. It was six o'clock in the evening, the sun had vanished behind the clouds, it was starting to drizzle, and there we were, in unfamiliar surroundings, under the fine and freezing rain, facing a large number of yokels who were pretending to be their own dogs in order to evade the omni-rapacious activities of the representatives of urban civilization. Their children had forgotten how to talk, but went about on all fours and yapped, and their parents encouraged them. 'Bark, bark, so 'ey'll leave us be! Bark, bark!' they said. It was the first time in my life that I had had occasion to see a whole troop of human beings hurriedly turning themselves into dogs, as a consequence of the law of imitation, out of fear in the face of over-rapid humanization. But there was no defence against them for, though it is possible to defend yourself against a dog-dog or a peasant-peasant, in the face of men who growl, bark, and try to bite you, you are helpless.

Mientus dropped his stick. I looked gauchely at the damp and mysterious grass on which I was destined shortly to end my life in highly confusing circumstances. Farewell, parts of my body! Farewell, my face, and farewell also my domesticated and tamed posterior! For it seemed certain that we were about to be devoured in an unprecedented manner at this very spot. But suddenly the whole situation changed, a motor-horn sounded, a car drove into the middle of the throng and stopped, and my Aunt Hurlecka, *née* Lin, exclaimed:

'Johnnie, darling! What on earth are you doing here?'

Ignoring the danger, ignoring everything (aunts are like that), she got out of the car, covered in her shawls, and ran forward with outstretched arms to kiss me. My aunt! My aunt! Where could I hide? Better be eaten alive than caught on a main road by an aunt! This aunt had known me since my childhood, the memory of my sailor-suit was engraved in her memory, she had seen me rocked in the cradle. She came up to me and kissed me on the forehead, and the peasants stopped barking and burst out laughing, the whole village split its sides with laughter . . . they realized that I was not an all-powerful clerk, but auntie's little boy. Mientus took off his cap, and my aunt held out her auntish hand for him to kiss.

'Is this your school-friend, Johnnie? Delighted!' she said.

Mientus kissed my aunt's hand. I kissed my aunt's hand. My aunt asked if we weren't cold, where we were going, where we had come from, what for, when, why, and how. I told her that we were on an outing.

'An outing? But children, who let you go in this wet weather? Jump into the car with me. I'll take you home, to Bolimowo. Your uncle will be delighted!'

There was no point in protesting, my aunt put protests out of the question. There we were, with my aunt, on the main road, in the mounting mist under the drizzling drizzly drizzle. We got into the car. The chauffeur sounded his horn and started up; the peasants surreptitiously roared with laughter, and the car, threaded on to the telegraph wires, moved away. We were off.

'Aren't you pleased, Johnnie?' my aunt said. 'I'm your materno-maternal aunt, your mother was the aunt of the aunt of the niece of my aunt on my mother's side. Your poor dead mother! Dear Marie! Let me see, how many years is it since I last saw you? It's four years since Francis's wedding. I still remember how you used to play in the sand—do you remember playing in the sand? What did those people want with you? Oh, what a fright they gave me! I find the people very uninteresting nowadays. There are germs everywhere, don't drink anything but boiled water, and don't eat fruit without peeling it or soaking it in hot water. Please put this shawl round your shoulders if you don't want to upset me, and let your friend put another one round his—please, please, don't be upset with me, there's nothing to be upset about, I could be your mother, your mother must be very worried about you!'

The chauffeur sounded his horn. The car buzzed, the wind buzzed, my aunt buzzed, elms, pines, and oaks, farms and swamps whizzed by; we bumped at speed over the ruts, and bounced in our seats.

'Don't drive so fast, Felix,' my aunt went on. 'Do you remember Uncle Francis? Christine is engaged, Theresa has had the 'flu. Henry is doing his military service. You've grown thinner, if you've got toothache, I've got some aspirin. And how are you getting on at school? Are you doing well? You ought to be good at history, because your poor mother was very good at it, you take after her. You've got your mother's blue eyes, your father's nose, but the real Pifczycki chin. Do you remember how you sobbed when they took the peach-stone away from you, and how you sucked your thumb and cried "Boo! Boo! Boo! Cha! Cha! Cha! Tuff! Tuff! Tuff!" . . . (Oh, accursed aunt!) Let me see, let me see, how many years ago was that? Twenty, twenty-eight, nineteen hundred and . . . of course, of course, I was just leaving for Vichy, I had just bought my green dressing-case, yes, that's it, so you must now be thirty . . . thirty . . . of course, just thirty! Please put the shawl on, darling, you have to be very careful of draughts!'

'Thirty?' said Mientus.

'Thirty!' my aunt said. 'He was thirty on St Peter's and St Paul's day. He's four and a half years younger than Theresa, and Theresa is six weeks older than Sophie, Alfred's daughter. Henry got married in February.'

'But he goes to our school, he's in the second form!'

'Of course! Henry got married in February, five months before I went to Menton—the cold spell—Helen died in June. Thirty—Mother came back from Podolia. Thirty. Just two years

206

after Thomas had the croup. The ball at Modelany—thirty. A sweet? Johnnie, would you like a sweet? (Aunts always have sweets.) Do you remember how you used to hold out your little hands and say: "Sweety, aunty, please! Sweety, aunty, please!" I still have the same sweets, they're very good for coughs, do keep yourself covered, darling!'

The chauffeur sounded his horn. The car sped on. Telegraph poles, trees, huts, bits of fields, bits of forest, and bits of I don't know what parts of the country whizzed by. The open plain. Seven o'clock. Darkness. The chauffeur sent shafts of light ahead of him, my aunt switched on the light in the back of the car and invited us to suck childish sweets. Mientus in astonishment sucked a sweet too, and so did my aunt, holding the bag in her hand. We all sucked sweets. Woman, I'm thirty, I'm thirty, don't you understand? No, she did not understand. She was too good, too kind. Too good and too kind. Goodness and kindness incarnate. I drowned in her goodness, sucking her sticky sweet. To her I was still only two; or, rather, for her did I exist at all? No, I did not. Uncle Edward's hair, my father's nose, my mother's eyes, the Pifczycki chin, parts of the family body. My aunt was drowned in the family, and smothered me with her shawl. A calf leapt on to the roadway and stayed there, stupefied and stubborn. The chauffeur trumpeted like an archangel, but the calf refused to give way. We stopped, and the chauffeur got out and shooed it away, and on we went again, and my aunt described how I used to write big letters on the window with my fingers when I was ten. She remembered things that I did not remember, knew me as I had never known myself, but she was too kind for me to be able to kill her; God, not without good reason, has drowned in kindness all that aunts know about our ridiculous, lamentable, and anonymous past. On we went, we passed through a huge forest. Fragments of trees flashed by illuminated by the headlights, fragments of the past flashed by in our memory, we were in a bad region, a region of ill omen. How far we had gone! Where had we got to? A huge slice of the brutal and obscure provinces surrounded our little box, inside which my aunt went on talking about my fingers, one of which I had once cut—I must still have the scar; while Mientus, with his stable-boy on the brain, sat there dumbfounded at my thirty years. It started raining heavily. The car turned into a secondary road—bumps and ruts—turned again, and dogs, huge mastiffs, dashed furiously at us. A keeper came and chased them away, but they went on growling, barking, and yelping. A flunkey appeared at the gateway, and behind him another flunkey. We got out.

The country. The wind moved the trees and the clouds. The outline of a big house stood out against the night, an outline not unknown to me, obviously because once upon a time I had lived here. My aunt was afraid of the damp, and the servants took her by the arm and deposited her in the antechamber. The chauffeur brought up the rear with the luggage. The side-whiskered old butler helped my aunt off with her wraps. The maid undressed me. The young male servant undressed Mientus. Puppies sniffed at us. I knew all this, without remembering it . . . it was here that I was born and spent the first ten years of my life.

'I've brought some guests!' my aunt exclaimed. 'Edward, this is Stanislas's son. Alfred, your cousin. Isabel, Johnnie, your cousin. This is Johnnie, poor dear Marie's son. Johnnie, your Uncle Edward!'

Handshakes, kisses on the cheek, reciprocal embracing of parts of the body, displays of cheerfulness and hospitality. We were shown into the drawing-room, seated on old Biedermayers, and interrogated about our health, about how we were; and I in turn made inquiries into my interrogators' health; and from health the conversation branched off into illness, caught us, and would not let us go. My aunt had heart trouble, Uncle Edward suffered from rheumatism, Isabel had recently been anaemic and was very subject to colds, the poor girl's tonsils were not in order, but there was no real cure. Alfred was also very liable to colds, and had had serious trouble with his ear, it had swollen a month ago, at the beginning of the damp and windy autumn. Enough—it seemed unhealthy to be acquainted so soon after our arrival with all the family's innumerable complaints but, whenever the conversation showed signs of flagging, my aunt whispered '*Isabelle, parle*,' and Isabel, to revive it, and to the detriment of her own charms, promptly brought up yet another illness. Stiff neck, rheumatism, arthritis, pain in the joints, gout, catarrhs and coughs, sore throats, 'flu, cancer, nettle-rash, toothache, constipation, general anaemia, liver, kidneys, Karlsbad, Professor Kalitowicz and Dr Pistak. It looked as if with Dr Pistak the subject was exhausted, but to keep the conversation going my aunt brought up Dr Wistak, who had a quicker ear than Dr Pistak, and that set them off again—Wistak, Pistak, fevers, nose and throat complaints, affections of the respiratory tract, doctors, stones, chronic indigestion, malaise and red corpuscles. I could not forgive myself for having mentioned the subject of health, though obviously it would have been impossible for me to have done otherwise. It was particularly trying for Isabel, and I realized what it cost her to display her scrofula in public simply to prevent an awkward pause in the conversation; but it was impossible to be silent in the presence of two young people who had just arrived in the house. Did everybody who arrived in the country get caught in this fixed mechanism? Was illness the sole introduction? This was the illness of the country aristocracy: traditional good manners forced them to get into contact with people by way of catarrh, and that, surely was why they looked so pale and seemed to be suffering from such bad colds as they sat there in the lamplight, with their puppies on their knees. The country! The country! Ancient and time-honoured laws! Strange mysteries! What a contrast to urban crowds and streets!

Only my aunt took a really kind and genuine interest in my uncle's fevers and dysentery. The maid, red in her white apron, came in to replenish the lamp. Mientus, who said little, was impressed by the abundance of servants, and by two old sabres hanging on the wall. There was nobility in all this, but I could not tell whether my uncle too remembered all about my childhood. He treated us rather like children, but these people treated themselves rather like children, children with a *Kinderstube* handed down from their ancestors. I dimly remembered playing some sort of game under the broken table, and the fringes of the old sofa standing in the corner came back to me from the past. Had I bitten them or chewed them or plaited them, made them wet or dirty, and if so with what? And when? Or had I stuffed them up my nostrils? My aunt was seated erect on the sofa, in the old school manner, sticking out her chest, her head held a little backwards. Isabel sat with her body bent and sickly from the conversation, with crossed fingers; Alfred, with his elbows on the arms of his easy-chair, gazed at the tips of his shoes, and uncle was teasing the basset-hound and taking interest in an autumn fly which was flying about under the ceiling—the enormous white ceiling. Outside there was a gust of wind, the trees rustled under the burden of their remaining half-dead leaves, the shutters creaked, and a slight draught passed through the room—and I had a sudden premonition of a new and hyper-trophied face. The dogs howled. When was I going to howl? For I was certainly going to. For the ways of these squireens, rather quaint and unreal and somehow pampered, inflated in an incredible void . . . delicacy and idleness, refinement, amiability, finesse, distinction, pride, tenderness, potential absurdity, custom reflected in every word . . . filled me with fear and mistrust. But which was more threatening—the solitary fly on the ceiling which had survived into the autumn, my aunt and my childish past, Mientus and his stable-boy, the family complaints, the fringes of the sofa, or the whole lot together, accumulated and concen-trated on the point of a needle? In the expectation of an inevitable face I sat silently on the old and patriarchal Biedermayer which had come down from my forebears, while my aunt, sitting on hers, groaned to keep the conversation going, and said that draughts at this time of year were bad for the joints. Isabel, an ordinary, commonplace young woman of the kind one meets in thousands on estates in the country, a young woman who differed in no way from her kind, started laughing to maintain the conversation —and everyone else laughed too—a properly amiable and social imitation of a laugh—and then stopped. For whom, against whom, did they laugh?

But Uncle Edward, who was tall, thin, delicate, rather bald, had a long, pointed nose, long thin fingers, delicate lips, a refined and distinguished manner, an extraordinary ease in his way of behaviour and the negligent elegance of a man of the world, sank back in his armchair and put his yellow-chamois-slippered feet on the table.

'What times we live in!' said he. 'What times we live in!'

The fly buzzed.

'Don't fret, Edward, don't fret!' my aunt said kindly. And gave him a sweet. But Edward did fret, and then he yawned. He opened his mouth so wide that you could see his tobacco-stained molars; and he yawned twice with the greatest nonchalance.

'Ta-ra-ra-boom-te-ay!' he grumbled, 'the dog danced ever so lightly and the cat applauded politely.'

He took out his silver cigarette-case, drummed on it with his fingers, and dropped it on the floor. He did not pick it up, but yawned again. Against whom, for whom, did he yawn like this? The family, sitting on their Biedermayers, followed the performance in silence. Francis, the old servant, came in.

'Dinner is served,' he announced.

'Dinner,' said my aunt.

'Dinner,' said Isabel.

'Dinner,' said Alfred.

'The cigarette-case,' said Uncle Edward.

The flunkey picked it up and handed it to him, and we went into the Henry IV style dining-room, with old portraits hanging on the wall; a samovar was boiling in the corner. We were served with *jambon au gratin* and peas. Conversation was resumed.

'Swallow it down, swallow it down,' said Uncle Edward, helping himself to a little mustard and a pinch of pepper (but against whom did he help himself to mustard and pepper?). 'There's nothing better than *jambon au gratin* when it's properly cooked. The only place where you get good ham nowadays is at Simon's restaurant. Ta-ra-ra-boom-te-ay, you can't get it anywhere else!'

'What about a glass of something?' said Alfred. 'Come on, what about it?'

'Do you remember the ham they used to serve at Bidou's before the war?' Uncle Edward asked.

'Ham is very heavy for the digestion,' my aunt said. 'Why have you taken such a small helping, Isabel? No appetite again?'

Isabel answered, but nobody listened, because everybody knew that she was talking only for talking's sake. Uncle Edward ate noisily, but with delicacy and refinement, though, manœuvring delicately over the plate, he picked up a mouthful of ham with his fingers, seasoned it with mustard or gravy, and slipped it into his buccal orifice. To one mouthful he added a little salt and to the next a little pepper. He buttered himself a slice of toast, and actually spat out a bit that he didn't like. The butler hurriedly caused it to vanish. But against whom did he spit? Against whom did he season his ham? My aunt stowed away abundantly but with subtlety, and not without kindness. Isabel ate dutifully. Alfred absorbed apathetically, and the staff served unobtrusively, 'on tiptoe'. Suddenly Mientus froze, with his fork half-way to his mouth. His eyes darkened, his face turned ashen, his lips half-opened, and a marvellous musical-mandoliny smile flowered on his horrible face—a smile of recognition, of meeting and greeting, so there you are, here am I! He put his hands on the table, leaned forward, and his upper lip curled as if he were about to burst into tears. He did not burst into tears, however, but only leaned forward a little more. He had seen his stable-boy. The young man-servant serving peas in the dining-room was his stable-boy. There was no doubt about it. The stable-boy of his dreams.

The stable-boy. He was about Mientus's age, not more than seventeen, neither big nor small, neither handsome nor ugly, neither dark nor fair, and he waited on us assiduously, barefoot, with a napkin over his left forearm, in his shirt-sleeves and collarless, in the Sunday-best trousers that all country stable-boys have. He had a face, but it had nothing in common with Mientus's disastrous face; it was not a fabricated, but a natural, village face, crudely outlined and rustic. It was not a face that had turned into a mug, but a mug that had never attained the dignity of a face. It was a mug like a leg! Oh, lad unworthy of possessing an honourable face, unworthy of being 'fair' or 'handsome'! Stable-boy unworthy of being a valet! Gloveless and barefoot, he changed his masters' plates—unworthy of a livery, but nobody seemed surprised. Oh! stable-boy! What ill-chance to find him here, at my aunt's and uncle's! Now, it's beginning, I said to myself, chewing my ham as if it were india-rubber, now it's beginning. And now, just to keep the conversation going, they started encouraging us to eat; and I had to sample the stewed pears; and then they offered us some little home-made cakes, for which I had to thank them, and I had to eat some, I had to, and I had to eat some stewed prunes, which stuck in my throat, while my aunt, to keep the conversation going, apologized for the poverty of the repast. 'Ta-ra-ra-boom-te-ay!' Uncle Edward, sprawling over his plate, negligently flung into his wide-open maw a succession of prunes which he held between two fingers.

'Eat! Eat! Fill your bellies, my friends!' he said, swallowing and clicking his tongue. And then he said, as if on purpose, with ostentatious self-satisfaction:

'Tomorrow I'm going to sack five men without paying their wages, because I haven't got any money.'

'Edward!' my aunt expostulated kindly.

'The cheese, please!' Uncle Edward went on.

Against whom did he say that? The staff went on serving on tiptoe. Mientus was engrossed; he devoured with his eyes the lad's undistorted, rustic, village face, drained it as if it were some unique drink. Under his heavy, insistent stare the lad lost countenance, and nearly upset the tea-pot over my aunt's head. Old Francis discreetly boxed his ears.

'Francis!' my aunt exclaimed kindly.

'He only need pay attention to what he is doing,' Uncle Edward grumbled, and helped himself to a cigarette. The servant leapt forward, match in hand. My uncle exhaled a cloud of smoke from between his thin lips, Cousin Alfred did the same through his no less thin lips, and we went back to the drawing-room, where each of us once more sat on his priceless Biedermayer. The wind could be heard howling furiously behind the shutters.

'How about a game of bridge?' said Cousin Alfred with a certain briskness.

But Mientus couldn't play, so Alfred remained silent and seated. Isabel said something; she pointed out that it often rained in the autumn, and my aunt asked me for news about Aunt Rosa. The conversation languished, my uncle crossed his legs, leaned back, and contemplated the ceiling, where a fly was desperately flying in all directions; and he yawned, exhibiting his palate and a row of yellow teeth. Alfred silently devoted himself to slowly swinging his leg and contemplating the reflections on his toe-caps. My aunt and Isabel sat with their hands in their laps, the basset-hound, seated on the table, looked at Alfred's foot, and Mientus, sitting in the shadow with his head between his hands, kept desperately silent. My aunt shook herself out of her torpor and ordered the servants to get the guests' room ready, to put hot-water bottles in the beds, and to leave nuts and preserves in the room in case we felt hungry. My uncle thereupon casually remarked that he would like some too, and the menials hastily produced it. We had some too, though we didn't want anything, but we could not refuse the delicacies provided, as there they were on plates all ready to be eaten, and our hosts pressed us to eat them; and they had no alternative but to press us to eat them because there they were on the plates all ready to be eaten. Mientus, however, refused, he absolutely insisted that he didn't want any and I guessed why —the stable-boy was in the room—but my aunt kindly gave him a double portion, and on top of it offered me sweets from the little bag she had. What sweetness, oh what sweetness! I didn't want anything, the helping of preserves was too much, but with the plate in front of me I couldn't say no. Everything came up: my childhood, my aunt, sailor-suit, family, fly, puppy, Mientus, full belly, suffocation, the wind outside, too much to eat, saturation, abuse, shocking wealth, the Biedermayer which was fascinating from underneath. But I couldn't get up and say good-night without any preamble, it was impossible. In the end we tried to do so, but we were asked to stay for just a little longer. Against whom did Uncle Edward put yet one more prune into his tired and sugary mouth? Isabel suddenly sneezed, and this precipitated the good-nights. Farewells, salaams, expressions of gratitude, entwinings of parts of the body. The maid led us to our room by a staircase that awakened vague memories. A valet brought up the rear with the nuts and preserves. It was hot and airless. The preserves came up on me. Mientus had the hiccups too. The country . . .

As soon as the door shut behind the maid, he said:

'Did you see?'

He sat down and hid his face in his hands.

'You mean the young servant?' I said with feigned unconcern.

I drew the curtains. The light from the window shining out on to the dark grounds frightened me.

'I must speak to him! I'll go down. No, better ring for him. He's surely been ordered to attend on us. Ring twice!'

'What for? (I tried to dissuade him.) It may lead to complications. Think of my uncle and aunt, Mientus. Don't ring, first tell me what you expect to do with him.'

He rang.

'Hell!' he said. 'As if the preserves weren't enough, they've given us apples and pears as well. Put them in the cupboard. . . . Hide the hot-water bottles, I don't want him to see them.'

He was in a rage, the kind of rage that conceals fear of what fate has in store for you, the rage of the most intimate human affairs.

'Johnnie,' he muttered, trembling, tenderly, sincerely. 'Johnnie, you saw him, he's got an ordinary, normal, untwisted face. A face with no grimaces. We shall never find a better stable-boy, never! Help me! I can't deal with this alone!'

'Take it easy! What do you want to do?'

'I don't know, I don't know! I want to be his friend, I want to fra-fra-ternize with him,' he confessed shamefacedly. 'I want to fra-fra-ternize with him. Be his friend. I must! Help me!'

The servant came in.

'Sir?' he said.

He stood just inside the doorway, awaiting orders. Mientus told him to pour water into the wash-stand basin. He poured water into the wash-stand basin, and waited. Mientus told him to open the wardrobe. He opened it, and waited again. Mientus told him to hang the towel on the towel-horse. He hung the towel on the towel-horse, and Mientus told him to put his jacket away in the wardrobe. All these orders made Mientus suffer cruelly. He gave orders, and the servant obeyed without batting an eyelid—and the orders grew more and more like an ironical dream. Ordering the stable-boy about instead of fraternizing with him! Spending the night ordering him about in accordance with one's sovereign whim! In the end Mientus ran out of orders and, for lack of anything else, ordered the servant to take the hot-water bottles and apples from the wardrobe in which they were hidden, and whispered to me brokenly:

'You try. I can't go on!'

Unhurriedly I took off my jacket and sat down at the head of the bed, swinging my legs—that seemed the most comfortable position in which to begin with the stable-boy.

'What's your name?' I asked.

'Bert,' he replied, and it was obvious that this was his real name and not just short for Albert, as if he were unworthy of the name of Albert or of a whole name to himself. This made Mientus tremble.

'Have you worked here for long?'

'Let me see, just a month, sir.'

'And where did you work before?'

'Before, sir? With the 'orses.'

216

'Are you happy here?'

'Yes, sir.'

'Bring us some hot water.'

'Very good, sir.'

When he went out Mientus had tears in his eyes. He wept. Tears streamed down his tortured face.

'Did you hear?' he said. 'Did you hear? His name's Bert. He hasn't even got a proper name. How that suits him! Did you see his face? An ordinary face, an ordinary face without a grimace on it! Johnnie, if he won't fra . . . ternize with me, I don't know what I shall do!'

He had bursts of anger, reproached me for having ordered the boy to fetch hot water, could not forgive himself for having told him, for lack of any other ideas, to take the hot-water bottles out of the wardrobe.

'He certainly never uses hot water,' he said. 'No doubt he never washes at all. But in spite of that he isn't dirty. Johnnie, do you realize that though he never washes he isn't dirty? In him dirt is not disgusting, he's not disgusting at all. . . . And just think of our dirt . . . our dirt . . .'

In the guest-room of the old manor house Mientus's passion broke out. He dried his tears. The stable-boy came back with a jug of hot water. This time Mientus conducted the attack, taking up the thread where I had left it.

'How old are you?' he said, looking straight in front of him.

'Good gracious, sir, how should I know?'

This took Mientus's breath away. The stable-boy did not even know his own age; divine stable-boy, free of the absurd contingencies of life! On the pretext of being about to wash his hands he went over towards where the lad was standing and, forcing himself not to tremble, said:

'We must be about the same age.'

This was a statement, not a question; it left it open to the lad to reply or not. Fra . . . ternization was about to begin.

'Yes, sir,' he replied.

Mientus unavoidably went back to questions.

'Did you learn to read and write?'

'Good gracious! And where would I do that, sir?'

'Have you got relatives?'

'I've got a sister, sir.'

'And what does she do?'

'She milks the cows, sir.'

The lad was standing and Mientus walking round the room. There seemed to be no getting away from questions and orders, orders and questions. So Mientus sat down, and said:

'Take off my shoes.'

I sat down too. The room was long and narrow, and there was something perverse about the way we moved about it. The house, which was big and austere, stood in a dark and gloomy park. The wind had dropped, which didn't help; a strong wind might have helped the situation. The stable-lad knelt and held his face over Mientus's proffered foot, and Mientus's face hovered feudally over his; Mientus's face was pale and dreadful, hardened by giving orders, powerless to ask more questions. Suddenly he said:

'Does your master ever slap your face?'

The lad's face lit up, and he exclaimed with rustic delight:

'Slap my face? And 'ow, sir, and 'ow!'

This caused me to leap forward like a jack-in-the-box and hit him with all my strength on the left cheek; the blow resounded in the silence like a revolver-shot. The lad put his hand to his face, dropped it, and rose to his feet.

'You certainly know 'ow to 'it too, sir!' he muttered with respect and admiration.

'Get out!' I shouted at him.

He got out.

'What on earth have you done, what on earth have you done?' groaned Mientus, wringing his hands. 'And I wanted to shake hands with him! I wanted to shake hands with him! Then our faces would have been the same, and everything . . . and everything . . . But you slapped his face! And I put my foot in his hands! He took off my shoes!' He groaned. 'He took off my shoes! Why did you do it?'

I had not the slightest idea. My hand had shot out as if it had been on a spring, and I had told the lad to get out. I had struck him, but why? There was a knock on the door, and Cousin Alfred, carrying a candle, came in, in trousers and slippers.

'Has somebody been shooting?' he said. 'I thought I heard a shot. Has somebody been shooting?'

'I slapped your Bert's face.'

'You slapped Bert?'

'He helped himself to my cigarettes.'

I preferred to get in first with my version of the incident before he heard the servant's version. Alfred was rather surprised, but then started laughing agreeably.

'That's fine!' he said, 'that'll cure him of the habit! . . . So you slapped his face,' he went on, rather incredulously.

I laughed, and Mientus cast me a glance that I shall never forget, the glance of a man who has been betrayed . . . and went off to the lavatory. My cousin followed him with his eyes.

'Your friend looks upset,' he remarked. 'Upset with you. A typical bourgeois!'

'Bourgeois,' I said. What else could I say?

'Bourgeois,' said Cousin Alfred. 'It's by treating Bert like that that he'll learn to respect you. You have to know them. They like it.'

'They like it,' I said.

'They like it, they like it! Ha! Ha! Ha! They like it!'

I no longer recognized my cousin, whose attitude towards me had previously been rather reserved. Now all trace of reserve had vanished. His eyes shone, he liked Bert's having had his face slapped, and he liked me; a young aristocrat had emerged from the chrysalis of the listless, morose schoolboy; it was as if Alfred had sniffed the forest and picked up the scent of the plebs. He put the candle on the window-sill and sat at the foot of the bed, a cigarette between his lips.

'They like it!' he said, 'they like it! You can slap 'em, but you must tip 'em too. No tips, no slaps, that's my belief! My father and Uncle Sigismund once slapped the head porter at the Grand Hotel.'

'And,' I said, 'Uncle Eustace once slapped a hairdresser.'

'And Grandmother Evelyn, she knew how to slap! But that was in the good old days. Some time ago Henry Pac got drunk and bashed his chauffeur's face in. D'you know Henry Pac? Very decent fella! And Bob Pitwicki smashed a window at the Cockatoo with a paint merchant's face. And once I gave an engineer a sock in the eye. D'you know the Pipowskis? She shows off a bit, but she's got her head screwed on. Tomorrow we might go partridge shooting.'

Where was Mientus? Where on earth was Mientus? Why hadn't he come back yet? Meanwhile Cousin Alfred showed no signs of wanting to go to bed. Bert's slapped face had drawn us together like a glass of brandy, and he went on breathing out clouds of cigarette smoke and talking about slapped faces and partridges, Mrs Pipowski, very decent little woman, y'know, cabarets and dancing girls, Henry, Lulu, you know what life is, that damned agricultural science, got to mug it up, you know, the lolly, and when would I finish my studies? I answered more or less the same thing, and he answered more or less the same thing, and I answered more or less the same thing. And then he got back to the subject of slaps, you had to know when and whom and how, and I said that it was better to hit a person on the ear than on the jaw. But I didn't really feel so sure, there was something unreal about it all, for nowadays slapping wasn't so common, manners had grown more civilized. I tried to say so, but couldn't, the conversation had become too attractive, and we were intoxicated by the baronial myth, the baronial fiction, and went on talking like two young lords of the manor.

'There's no harm at all in an occasional slap. On the contrary, there's nothing like it!' he said at last. 'It's getting late, we must see each other in Warsaw. I'll introduce you to Henry. Good gracious, it's midnight, and your friend hasn't come back yet, he must have indigestion! Good night!'

He clasped me in his arms.

'Good night, Johnnie!' he said.

'Good night, Alfred,' I said.

But why didn't Mientus come back? I sponged my perspiring brow. Where had that conversation with my cousin come from? I looked through the shutters; it had stopped raining, you couldn't see more than fifty paces, it was only here and there that you could guess the shape of the trees in the dark mass of the night, but their shapes seemed even darker than the night, and vaguer. In the darkness the park was dripping with humidity, penetrated by the sordid, enigmatic, and unknown expanse of fields beyond. Being unable to guess the shape of what I was looking at, looking but seeing nothing but shapes blacker than the night, I closed the shutters, and retreated to the other end of the room. All this was most inopportune. My striking the stable-lad had been inopportune. My conversation with Alfred had been inopportune. It was obvious that in this house slapping a face was like a glass of brandy; how different from a dry and democratic urban slap! The devil take it! What did a servant's face amount to in this feudal domain? By what mischance had it come about that I had drawn attention to it by slapping it, and actually talking to Alfred about it? But where had Mientus got to?

He came back at about one o'clock. He did not walk straight in, but first peeped round the half-open door to see if I were asleep; then he crept in like someone who has been out on the spree. He undressed quickly, and turned down the lamps. I noticed when he bent that his face had undergone a new and exceedingly crude transformation . . . his left cheek was swollen; it looked like a little apple, a little apple in a dish of stewed fruit, a kind of brew in which everything he had been doing was mixed up in miniature. Damn this miniaturization! Once more it had come into my life, this time on the face of a friend. A crazy clown was interfering with it. What brute force had thus transformed him? When I asked he answered in a sharp, strained voice:

'I've been in the kitchen, fra . . . ternizing with the stable-lad. He hit me in the face.'

'He hit you in the face?' I said, unable to believe my ears.

'Yes,' he said with glee—rather thin and artificial glee. 'We are brothers now. In the end I managed to get on good terms with him.'

But he spoke like a Sunday sportsman boasting about his bag, or a townsman boasting of having got drunk at a country wedding. He was in the grip of a crushing, devastating force, but his attitude to that force was not honest. I plied him with questions, and he ended by confessing reluctantly, with his face buried in his hands:

'I ordered him to hit me.'

'What? (My blood ran cold.) You ordered him to hit you? You actually ordered him to hit you in the face? Now he'll take you for a lunatic. (I felt as if I too had been struck in the face.) I congratulate you. If my uncle and aunt find out . . .'

'It's your fault,' he said gloomily. 'You shouldn't have hit him. You started it. You enjoyed playing lord of the manor. I had to let him hit me, because you hit him. . . . Otherwise we could never have met on equal terms and I shouldn't have been able to fra . . . ter . . .'

He turned out the lamp, and in broken phrases described his desperate efforts to achieve this equality. He had found the lad in the kitchen, cleaning the gentry's shoes, and had sat down beside him, whereupon the lad had got up. Again and again he had tried to make contact with him, to gain his confidence, to make him talk, to force his friendship, but all the words that came to his lips had turned to idyllicism, sentimentality, absurdity. The lad had answered as best he could, but it was obvious that all this was starting to bore him, and he could not imagine what this crazy young gentleman wanted of him. In desperation Mientus had fallen back on the cheap verbiage of the French Revolution, explained that all men were equal, and on this pretext had insisted on shaking hands with the youth, but this the latter had vigorously refused to do.

'My 'and's not for the likes of you, sir,' he had said.

It was then that the fantastic idea had come into Mientus's

head that, if he could get the lad to strike him it would break the ice.

'Hit me in the face!' he had begged him, losing all restraint. 'Hit me in the face!'

He had held his face out to be hit, but the lad remained as obstinate as ever.

'Why should I hit you, sir?' he said.

Mientus went on begging and imploring him, and in the end, infuriated by the lad's stubbornness, yelled at him:

'Hit me because I tell you to, you bastard! Hit me, you bastard! What are you waiting for?'

At that the lad hit out in earnest, and Mientus saw stars, and the room reeled round him.

'Again, you bastard, again!'

Once more Mientus saw stars, and again the room reeled. When he opened his eyes he saw the lad standing there, with his hands, waiting for more orders. But a blow in the face delivered by order was not the real thing—it was like having your shoes cleaned or having water poured into your wash-basin, and there was a flush of shame on the face of the giver of the blows.

'Again! Again!' the martyr muttered, in order to force the lad to fra . . . ternize on his face; and again he saw stars, and the room reeled. Oh, being struck in the face in the empty kitchen, among the washing, over a tub of hot water!

Fortunately these gentlemanly extravagances ended by making the son of the people laugh; no doubt he had come to the conclusion that the young gentleman was not quite right in the head (and nothing makes the vulgar more daring than the eccentricity of their masters); and in his rustic fashion he started treating the whole thing as a joke, and this led to familiarity. The lad quickly got to the point of fraternizing to such an extent that he tried to extract a tip from Mientus while still going on hitting him.

'Give me something to buy tobacco with,' he kept repeating.

This rustic, savage mockery, unfraternal and the reverse of friendly, was still not the real thing, however; it led, not to the fraternization of Mientus's dreams, but in the very opposite direction. But he stood his ground, preferring being maltreated by the stable-lad to crushing him beneath his gentlemanly superiority. The kitchen-maid, Maria, came in from the yard with a damp cloth to wash the kitchen floor, and was astonished at the scene. ' 'eavens, what a row!' she exclaimed. The house was asleep, and she and the stable-boy were able with impunity to have a good time at the expense of the young gentleman who was paying them a visit, mocking him with their great rustic guffaws. Mientus himself encouraged them, and joined in the laughter.

But gradually, while still mocking at Mientus, they started mocking at their masters too.

'That's what gennlefolk be loik!' they said, with the heavy, earthy, irony of the farmyard and the scullery. 'That's what gennlefolk be loik! Does nothing but stuffs 'emselves all day long till 'ey burst. Stuffs 'emselves and stuffs 'emselves, and goes to sleep with 'eir bellies sticking up in the air, 'ey walk about their rooms and talks and talks and talks! The amount 'ey puts away! Oi'm only a poor servant, but oi couldn't manage 'alf of it. Lunch, and tea, and chocolate biscuits, and fried eggs for breakfast! 'ey be great guzzlers, the gentry, 'ey be, 'ey does noth'n all day long, and that's what makes 'un ill. And when the gennleman cloimbed Vincent, the gamekeeper, at the boar-hunt! Vincent was stand'n behind 'un with t'other gun. The gennleman, 'e foired at the boar, and the boar went for 'un, and 'e threw away 'is gun and cloimbed Vincent—be quiet, Maria!—yes, 'e cloimbed Vincent! There weren't no tree around, so 'e cloimbed Vincent! Afterwards 'e gave 'un a zloty to keep 'is mouth shut, and told 'un that if 'e didn't keep 'is mouth shut, e'd get the sack!'

'Good 'eavens, the things you be say'n! Stop it, or you'll give me the belly-ache!'

Maria tightened her girdle.

'And the young lady, she goes out walkin', and she walk and she look, and she walk, and she look. The gennlemen goes walkin' too, and 'ey looks too. Mr Alfred, 'e looks at me, though 'e'd a done better not to! Once 'e even tried layin' 'is 'ands on me, but what a 'ope! 'E keep look'n to see if anyone was com'n, and I ended by laugh'n at 'un and runn'n away. Afterwards, Mr Alfred, 'e give me a zloty to keep mi mouth shut, because 'e said 'e'd 'ad a drop too much.'

'Aye, that's it, a drop too much,' the stable-lad chimed in. 'I knows a lot o' girls who won't go with 'un, because 'e always keeps on looking to see if anyone's com'n. Now 'e's got some'un, old Josephine, the widow, down i' the village, 'e meet 'er i' the bushes down by the pond; and 'e make 'er swear not to tell a living soul, 'e do!'

'Ha! Ha! Ha! Will you stop it, Bert! It's 'cos 'ey be so spoilt, the gennlefolk, 'ey be so delicate!'

'So delicate 'ey even 'as to 'ave 'un's noses wiped for 'un, 'cos 'ey can't do it 'emselves. When I first came 'ere, I couldn't get over it. 'and me this, fetch me that, bring me t'other, you even 'as to 'elp 'un on with 'un's overcoats, 'ey can't do it' emselves. If oi 'ad to be coddled like that, oi'd rather be dead, I would! I 'ave to cream the master all over every night!

'And oi 'as to rub the young lady,' the slut chimed in, 'rub 'er all over with me 'ands, she be so delicate, she be!'

'Gennlefolk be soft, 'ey 'as delicate little 'ands, ha! ha! ha! Sweet Jesus, 'ow 'ey goes for walks, and eats, and talks and talks and talks, and bores 'unselves to death.'

'Stop it, Bert, you know the mistress be very koind!'

'Course she be koind, see'n 'ow she suck the blood of the 'ole village . . . course she be koind! We work for 'un and the master, 'e walk about the fields and watch us. The mistress be 'fraid o' cows! Yes, she be 'fraid o' cows, she be! The gennlefolk talks and talks and goes for walks. Ha! Ha! Ha! 'ey be soft!'

The slut was exclaiming and the stable-lad denouncing when Francis walked in.

'What! Francis the butler?'

'The devil himself must have sent him,' Mientus said in desperation. Maria's cackling must have woken him. He didn't dare say anything to me, of course, but he started giving Maria and the stable-boy a dressing-down, told them not to make such a row at this time of night, and to get out, it was time they had finished their work, as it was past midnight, and they hadn't cleaned the kitchen yet. They went off at once. Devil take the man!'

'Had he heard?'

'Very likely, I don't know. What a loathsome type! Flunkey in side-whiskers and stiff collar. Peasant with side-whiskers. Traitor to the people. Traitor and spy! If he heard, he'll tell! We were having such a wonderful talk!'

'This will probably cause a shocking scandal,' I said.

'You're a traitor too!' Mientus hissed angrily at me. 'You're a traitor too! You're all traitors! Traitors!'

It was a long time before I got to sleep. Rats and mice danced their saraband in the attic overhead, and I listened to their squeals, their sudden leaps, their scuffles and pursuits, the fearful abortive blows exchanged by the savage animals. Water dripped from the roof. The dogs barked automatically, and our hermetically sealed room was a box of darkness. Mientus lay awake on his bed, and I lay awake on mine. We both lay on our backs, with our hands behind our heads, gazing at the ceiling. Both of us were wide awake, as was indicated by our imperceptible breathing. What was he doing under the cloak of darkness? Yes, what was he doing? For if he was awake he must be doing something . . . and the same applied to me. For a person who is awake must be doing something, he has no alternative. So he was doing something, and I was doing something. What was he thinking about, lying there tense and on edge, as if in the grip of a pair of pincers? I prayed that he would go to sleep, for then, perhaps, he would be less silent, more genuine, less baffling, more relaxed.

I spent the night on the rack. What was I to do? Run away at dawn? I was certain that old Francis would report to my uncle the blows that the stable-lad had struck Mientus and the things that he had said about his betters. And then pandemonium would break out, dissonances and deceptions, a veritable witches' sabbath. Face! Face was about to begin all over again—and arse. Was it for this that we had run away from the Youthfuls? We had awakened the monster, we had unchained the audacity of the lackeys. During that dreadful night, lying sleepless on my bed, I hit on the secret of the manor house, the secret of the rural aristocracy, the numerous and disturbing symptoms of which had from the outset given me a premonition of the approach of facial terror, of face. The secret was the servants. The clue to the gentry was the common people. Against whom did my uncle yawn, against whom did he put an extra sugared plum in his mouth? Against the people, against his lackeys! Why did he not pick up his cigarette-case when he dropped it? In order to have it picked up by the servants. Why had he received us with so much hospitality, lavished so much kindness and attention and delicacy on us? To distinguish himself from the servants and maintain his gentlemanly position against them. Whatever these people did was in some way directed at and against their servants, everything could be traced back to their domestic and farm servants.

Moreover, how could it be otherwise? In town, where we all wore the same clothes, used the same language and made the same gestures, we ceased to be aware that we were landed gentry; we were linked to the proletariat by a multitude of infinitesimal gradations, could descend imperceptibly to the gutter by way of the barber, the fruiterer, and the cabby. But here the gentleman stood out like a solitary poplar in a flat land-scape. There was no transition between master and servant, because the bailiff and the village priest each lived in his own house. The roots of my uncle's baronial pride of race plunged straight into the plebeian subsoil; and it was from the plebs that it drew its sap. In towns servitude was of each to all and was exercised indirectly and discreetly, but here the master was in crude and direct control of his people, and held out his foot for them to clean his shoes . . . and my uncle and aunt certainly knew what was said about them below stairs, what they looked like through plebeian eyes. They knew, but the knowledge was unwelcome, they stifled, crushed, repressed it into the deepest depths of their consciousness.

To be waited on by your own plebeian! To be thought of and commented on by him! To be everlastingly refracted in the vulgar prism of the servant who freely enters your rooms, overhears your conversation, looks at your person, and with the breakfast coffee has access to your table and your bed . . . to be the daily subject of below-stairs infra-gossip and never be able to explain oneself, never to meet and talk to these people on a level of equality. True, it is only by way of the domestic servants, the valet and the housemaid, that you can penetrate to the marrow of the rural aristocracy. Without the valet you will never understand the master, without the chambermaid you will never grasp the spiritual essence of the country ladies, the inner meaning of their take-offs and flights . . . and the young man of the house is a consequence of the strapping farm-girl. Oh! at last I understood the reason for the strange constraint and apprehension which afflict the townsman when he arrives in the country; it is that these people are terrorized by the plebs, the plebs has them in its pocket. That is the reason for the continual sense of discomfort; a perpetual death-struggle into which are distilled all the poisons of subterranean secret struggles, a struggle a thousand times worse than any purely economic dispute. The struggle is imposed by the foreign and the exotic—physical foreignness and mental exoticism. Among the plebeians their minds were as if in a huge forest; their delicate, thoroughbred bodies were surrounded by the bodies of the vulgar as in a jungle. Their hands felt revulsion from the great paws of the plebs, their baronial feet detested those of the people, their faces hated the common faces, their eyes loathed the common eyes, the great round, rustic eyes of the people, their delicate fingers were repelled by the great clumsy fingers of the plebs . . . and this was aggravated by being constantly touched . . . 'tended' as the stable-lad put it . . . by them, pampered by them, rubbed with cream by them. To have close to you, under your own roof, different, strange parts of bodies, and to have none other! For many leagues around there were nothing but vulgar limbs and vulgar language; and perhaps there were only the priest and bailiff who resembled them a little. But the bailiff was an employee, and the priest wore skirts. Did not the eager hospitality which they showed in detaining us for so long after dinner derive from their isolation? With us they felt more at ease. But Mientus had betrayed the baronial faces with the stable-lad's village face.

The lad's perverse gesture in striking Mientus in the face —Mientus was, after all, his master's guest and a master himself— was bound to have equally perverse consequences. The traditional hierarchy depended on the domination of the baronial parts of the body, and it was a tense, feudal hierarchy, in which the master's hand was as good as the servant's face and his foot reached to half the height of the whole rustic body. This hierarchy was long-established, sanctified by immemorial usage. A mystic link, hallowed by the passage of centuries, connected baronial and plebeian parts of the body, and it was only within the hierarchy that the masters could make contact with the people. Hence the magic of the slap in the face. Hence Bert's almost religious awe of a box on the ear. Hence Alfred's baronial fantasies. Certainly nowaday they no longer beat their servants (though Bert had admitted that Alfred sometimes struck him), but the slap in the face still held sway among them, and that maintained their position. But now? Had not a gross plebeian paw permitted itself familiarities with a young master's face?

Now the domestic servants would raise their heads. Below-stairs gossip had already begun. Now the vulgar, demoralized and made more insolent by familiarity between parts of the body, were beginning to mock their masters, plebeian criticism was rising like a tide; and what would happen when my uncle and aunt found out, and the baronial countenance was suddenly brought up against the people's crude mug?

* 14 *

Zenith and Culmination

AFTER breakfast next morning my aunt took us aside. It was a fresh, sunny morning, the earth was dark and damp, the bluish foliage of the clumps of trees in the big courtyard rustled in the breeze, and under them the family chickens scratched. In the morning time stood still, and golden rays caressed the smoking-room floor. The family dogs made their way idly from one corner to the other. The family pigeons cooed. My aunt was internally agitated by a wave that came up from the depths.

'Please tell me, Johnnie,' she began. 'Francis told me that . . . it seems that . . . this friend of yours . . . is being familiar with the servants. I hope he's not an agitator.'

'A theorist, mother, nothing but a theorist,' Alfred chimed in. 'Don't take any notice of him, mother, he's a mere theorist who doesn't know the first thing about life. He came to the country with his head stuffed full of theories, he's nothing but a drawing-room democrat!'

He was gay and baronial after the events of the night before.

'But Alfred, the young man doesn't indulge in theories, but in practice. Francis says he saw him shaking hands with Bert!'

Fortunately the old servant had not told everything, and my uncle, as I had occasion to find out, did not know the worst. I pretended to know nothing about anything, and referred vaguely to Mientus's socialist principles. I did so laughingly (how often life imposes laughter on us). Thus the affair was pigeon-holed for the time being. Obviously nobody breathed a word to Mientus. Until lunch-time we played King, because Isabel proposed that fashionable game, and it was impossible to refuse.

So King held us in its net until lunch. Isabel, Alfred, Mientus and I, laughing and bored, threw our cards down on the green felt, big ones on top of little ones, and hearts are trumps, ladies and gentlemen. Alfred played in dry, synthetic, routine fashion; he played his cards dextrously and horizontally, with a cigarette in his mouth, picking them out by the corners with his white fingers. Mientus kept wetting his fingers with saliva, held his cards tight, and I noticed that he was ashamed of playing this game, which was baronial in the extreme; he kept looking towards the door, fearing that the stable-lad would see him; he would have preferred playing cork-penny squatting on the ground. But it was lunch that I was chiefly worried about, because I feared Mientus would not be able to stand the stable-lad's presence; and my fears turned out to be justified.

For lunch there was fish with mayonnaise, tomato soup, *escalopes de veau*, and stewed pears, all prepared by the vulgar fingers of the cook and served on tiptoe by the staff. Francis appeared in white gloves, and the barefooted little lackey with a napkin over his arm. Mientus, pale and with downcast eyes, absorbed the delicate and carefully prepared viands which Bert offered him, and suffered at being fed by the stable-lad on such delicacies. On the other hand my aunt, desiring to give him indirectly to understand the full enormity of the things he had said in the kitchen, spoke to him with exceptional affability and charm, and asked him all about his family and his dead father. Forced to answer in high-flown phrases, he did so, in exasperation and in as low a voice as possible, in order to avoid being overheard by the stable-lad, at whom he did not dare to look. And that is perhaps why it came about, while the sweet was being served, that, instead of answering one of my aunt's questions, oblivious of everything, with his spoon in his hand and a shy and ardent smile on his contracted and grimacing face, he suddenly sank his eyes in those of the stable-lad. I could not jog him with my elbow, as I was sitting on the opposite side of the table. My aunt fell silent, and the little lackey burst into an embarrassed, rustic laugh, as the vulgar do when they are stared at by their masters; then he put his hand over his mouth. The butler tweaked his ear. My uncle lit a cigarette and breathed out a cloud of smoke. Had he seen? It had been so obvious that I feared he was going to order Mientus to leave the table.

Uncle Edward now breathed smoke out through his nose instead of through his mouth.

'Some wine!' he exclaimed. 'Bring a small bottle of wine!'

He was in high spirits. He lolled back in his chair, and drummed on the table with his fingers. 'Wine, Francis,' he said. 'Fetch us a bottle of Dame Thérèse from the cellar. Bert! Coffee and cigars, to hell with cigarettes!'

Raising his glass in honour of Mientus, he embarked on reminiscences. He told us how in his time he had gone pheasant-shooting with Prince Severinus; and, with a special toast for Mientus, ignoring the rest of the company, he went on to talk about the barber at the Hotel Bristol, the best barber he had come across in the whole of his life. He warmed up, grew animated, the servants redoubled their attentions, rapidly refilling the glasses and serving them with their fingers. Mientus, looking cadaverous, drank, not knowing to what to attribute Uncle Edward's unexpected attentions. He died a thousand deaths, but had to swallow the old wine with its delicate bouquet in Bert's presence.

To me too my uncle's reaction was unexpected. After lunch he took me by the arm and led me into the smoking-room.

'Your friend,' he said with aristocratic realism, 'your friend is a queer. Ahem! He's running after Bert. Didn't you notice? Ha! Ha! Ha! Provided the ladies don't notice. Prince Severinus used to like a little of that too sometimes!'

He stretched his long legs. Oh, with what aristocratic virtuosity did he say those words! With what baronial good breeding, acquired in contact with four hundred waiters, seventy barbers, thirty jockeys, and the same number of butlers . . . and with what pleasure did he air his piquant, hotelier's, *bon viveur*'s, *grand seigneur*'s knowledge of life! That is how the genuine aristocracy of birth, when confronted with a case of sexual degeneracy or perversion, displays the virile maturity it has learnt from waiters and barbers. But this highly seasoned wisdom made me suddenly furious with my uncle, like a cat confronted with a dog; his over-facile and lordly interpretation of the situation roused my indignation. I forgot all my fears, and it was I, in order to anger him, who told him the whole truth. May Heaven forgive me! The impact of his hotelier's maturity caused me to relapse into green immaturity, and I decided to give him something to swallow that was less cooked and less elegantly served than the things you get in fashionable restaurants.

'It's not that at all, uncle,' I said naïvely. 'He wants to frater-nize with him, that's all.'

This took Uncle Edward aback.

'He wants to fraternize with him?' he exclaimed in astonish-ment. 'What do you mean, fraternize?'

He looked at me askance.

'He wants to fra . . . ternize.' I said. 'Fra . . . ternize with him.'

'Fra . . . ternize with Bert? Fra . . . ternize? I suppose you mean he's an agitator, stirring up the servants. An agitator, is he? A Bolshevik?'

'No, he wants to fra . . . ternize with him, that's all.'

Uncle Edward rose, and flicked the ash from his cigar. He paused, searching for words.

'So it's fraternizing, is it?' he said. 'Fraternizing with the people, is that it?'

He tried to classify the phenomenon, to find an acceptable formula for it from the worldly and social point of view. Purely boyish fraternization was for him an unassimilable dish, which he knew was not served in good restaurants. What upset him most was that I, in imitation of Mientus, pronounced the word 'fraternize' with a slightly sly and shameful hesitation.

'So he fraternizes with the people,' he said cautiously.

'No, he fraternizes with the boy.'

'What do you mean? Does he want to play ball with him, or what?'

'No, they are simply good friends. They just fra . . . ternize like two schoolboys.'

Uncle Edward blushed, perhaps for the first time since he had started frequenting barbers' saloons. Oh, that reluctant blush of a sophisticated adult in the presence of an *ingénu*! He took out his watch, looked at it, and wound it, searching for scientific, political, economic, or medical terms in which to enclose the indelicate subject as in a box.

'It's a perversion, is it? A complex? He fra . . . ternizes? Fra- . . . ternizes? *Mais qu'est-ce que c'est que ça: il fra . . . ternise? Fraternité, égalité, fraternité?*'

He dropped into French, but unaggressively . . . on the contrary, like someone taking refuge in French. Nevertheless he was defenceless against the Boy. He lit a cigarette, put it out, crossed his legs, tugged his little moustache.

'*Il fraternise. Mais qu'est-ce que c'est, fraternise?* Ye gods! Prince Severinus!'

With quiet obstinacy I kept repeating the word 'fraternize', and not for anything in the world would I have abandoned the verdant and soft naïveté with which I was anointing Uncle Edward.

'Edward,' said my aunt kindly, appearing in the doorway with her bag of sweets in her hand, 'don't get excited, dear, no doubt he fraternizes in Jesus Christ, he fraternizes in the spirit of love of one's neighbour.'

'No,' I stubbornly insisted, 'he just fraternizes, pure and simple, and that's all there is to it. It's just schoolboy fraternization!'

'So he is a pervert, then?' Uncle Edward exclaimed.

'Not at all, he just fraternizes, without any perversion. It's nothing but boyish fraternization.'

'Boyish fraternization? Boyish fraternization? *Mais qu'est-ce que c'est* boyish fraternization?' Uncle Edward said idiotically. 'Boyish fraternization with Bert? With Bert, in my house? With my servant under my roof?'

He lost his temper and rang the bell.

'I'll show him boyish fraternization!'

The young lackey came in. Uncle Edward went towards him with raised hand. Perhaps he was going to give him a short, sharp slap in the face, but he stopped short, his head reeled, he was unable to hit Bert, make contact with Bert's face—in these circumstances. Hit a boy because he was a boy? Hit him because he 'fraternized'? Impossible. And Uncle Edward who did not mind striking a servant for serving a cup of coffee clumsily, dropped his hand to his side.

'Get out!' he shouted.

'Edward!' exclaimed my aunt kindly. 'Edward!'

'Hitting him won't do any good at all,' I said. 'On the contrary, it will only encourage the fraternization: my friend's crazy about men who get hit.'

Uncle Edward blinked, and made a gesture as if to shake a worm off his waistcoat; this virtuoso of worldly irony, ridiculed from below by my irony, was rather like a fencer attacked by a duck. The most curious thing was that, in spite of his experience of the world, he did not for one moment suspect that I might be on Mientus's and Bert's side against him, and that I might perhaps be enjoying his baronial shudderings. This blind confidence in the members of his own social set, this refusal to admit the slightest possibility of disloyalty on their part, was characteristic of him. Old Francis came in, complete with livery and side-whiskers. He was very upset, and stopped in the middle of the room.

Uncle Edward, who had let himself go somewhat, promptly resumed his normal, rather free-and-easy manner.

'What is it, Francis?' he said loftily, but nevertheless with a trace in his voice of the servility which an old servant, like an old wine, inspires in his master. 'What is it, Francis? (Francis looked at me, but my Uncle made a gesture to him.) Well, Francis, what's the matter?'

'You have spoken to Bert, sir.'

'Yes . . . I've spoken to Bert, Francis, I've spoken to Bert.'

'I only wanted to say, sir, that you did well to speak to him, sir. Sir, I wouldn't keep him here a moment longer, I'd throw him out at once. He has become too familiar, sir. Below stairs, sir, they are starting to talk.'

Three servant-girls ran across the courtyard, showing their bare thighs, and a lame dog chased them, yapping.

'They're starting to talk? What are they talking about?' asked Uncle Edward.

'About their masters, sir.'

'About us?'

Fortunately the old servant did not specify.

'They've started talking about their masters, sir. Bert has become familiar with the young gentleman who arrived yesterday, and now, saving your presence, sir, they have started talking about their masters and against their masters without the slightest respect, sir. Particularly Bert and the kitchen-girls, sir. I heard them myself, sir, talking to the young gentleman late last night, sir. They talked like mad, sir, they stopped at nothing, sir, they said such a lot of things that I couldn't say myself, sir, what they were talking about. But what I do know, sir, is that I'd throw that young rogue out straight away.'

The butler in his magnificent livery went as red as a beetroot. Oh, that old flunkey's blush! A flush spread subtly over his master's face and provided a silent answer. Uncle and aunt went on sitting in silence; it would have been unseemly to ask questions, but perhaps the old butler was going to say something else. They hung on his lips, but he said nothing.

'All right, Francis, you may go,' Uncle Edward said eventually.

And the old servant went as he had come.

'They are talking about their masters.' That was all they had found out. Uncle Edward confined himself to remarking bitterly to my aunt:

'You're too weak with the servants, dear, and they take advantage of it. But what do you suppose they can be talking about?'

236

They changed the subject, and for quite a time exchanged commonplace remarks and futile questions. 'Where is Isabel, I wonder?' and 'Has the post come?'

They trifled in this way to avoid showing that Francis's reticent story had touched them on the quick. They went on like this for a good quarter of an hour before Uncle Edward stretched, yawned, and started walking slowly in the direction of the drawing-room. I realized what he was doing; he was looking for Mientus. He must find him and talk to him immediately, he was under the imperious necessity of having this thing out with him straight away. Doubt had become insupportable. My aunt went out behind him.

But Mientus was not in the drawing-room; the only person there was Isabel, with a *Manual of Rational Cereal Culture* in her lap. She was sitting and watching a fly on the wall. Mientus was not in the dining-room or in the boudoir either. The house was dozing in the quiet of the afternoon snooze. Outside the chickens were prowling about and scratching on the dried-up lawn, and the fox-terrier was playing with and pretending to bite the basset-hound's tail. My uncle and aunt glided into the house again, each by a different door; dignity did not allow them to admit that they were looking for anything. But seeing them like this, apparently casual and unconcerned but in reality on the war-path, was more alarming than the most bloodthirsty chase would have been, and I tried in vain to think of some way of averting the bedlam that was ripening like a boil on the horizon. I could no longer talk to them, I could no longer get at them, they had moved out of my reach, had retreated into themselves. Passing through the dining-room, I saw my aunt stop outside the kitchen door, from which there emerged as usual the voices, the squeals, and broad laughter of the girls engaged in washing up. My aunt stood there thoughtfully, pricking up her ears, in the typical attitude of a mistress spying on her servants, and her usual kind expression had vanished. When she saw me, she coughed and went away. Just at that moment my uncle walked past outside in the garden, in order to be nearer the kitchen, and he stopped under the trees. When the cook looked out of the window, he called out sharply to the gardener:

'Nowak! Nowak! Tell Zielenski to repair this pipe!'

He started walking slowly down the avenue of poplars. Nowak followed him, cap in hand. Alfred appeared. He came up to me, and took me by the arm.

'I don't know if it has ever happened to you to fancy a slightly *passée* old woman, but these peasant women, when they're slightly high, have a terrific effect on me. It was Henry Pac who started the fashion, I love them, *je les aime*. A fat peasant woman just past her prime! Very tasty! Very tasty indeed!'

Oh! Oh! Oh! He was afraid that the servants might have started talking about his old woman, the widow Josephine, with whom he hid himself in the bushes down by the pond; and so he produced the vagaries of fashion as an excuse and invoked the name of Henry Pac. I did not answer, seeing that the family were now well away and that there was no more stopping them; once more the lunatic star was rising over my horizon, and recalled all my adventures since Pimko had made me my arsicule. But this latest adventure threatened to be the worst of all. Alfred and I walked out into the courtyard, where we ran into my uncle emerging from the avenue of poplars, followed by Nowak, the gardener, cap in hand.

'What a magnificent day!' my uncle exclaimed in the diaphanous air. 'Magnificent!'

This was true; it certainly was a magnificent day; the golden-russet foliage of the trees rustled against a background of distant blue, and the fox-terrier was still flirting with the basset-hound. Mientus, however, was nowhere to be seen. My aunt appeared, with two mushrooms in her hand. She held out the mushrooms for us to see, and shot us a sweet, kind smile. We gathered at the front door and, as no one was willing to admit that we were all looking for Mientus, exceptional friendliness and delicacy prevailed among us. My aunt asked kindly if anyone felt cold. Some crows had come to rest on the trees. Some children had stopped at the entrance gate and were wiping their faces with their dirty fingers; they whispered, looking at their masters, until Alfred stamped his foot and sent them scurrying away. A moment later they started staring at us through the fence, and Alfred scattered them again, and Nowak the gardener, threw stones after them. They ran away, but they were soon peeping at us again, this time from the well. Uncle Edward sent for some apples and started ostentatiously eating one, throwing away the peel. He was eating against the children.

'Ta-ra-ra-boom-te-ay,' he grumbled.

There was still no sign of Mientus, a fact to which no one drew attention, though we all felt an urgent need to find him and have a word with him. If this was a chase, it was an incredibly lumbering and lethargic and practically immobile chase, and for that reason an alarming one. The master and mistress of the house were in pursuit of Mientus, but they hardly moved. However, it seemed pointless to remain any longer in the court-yard, particularly as the children were still peeping at us through the fence, and Alfred suggested going round to the back of the house. 'We'll show you the stables,' he said, and there we went, unhurriedly, as if going for a stroll, Uncle Edward still followed by the gardener, cap in hand. The children scampered from the fence to near the barn. After we had passed through the gate, the mud started, and the ducks went for us, but the overseer hurriedly shooed them away; and the dog showed his teeth and growled, but the lodge-keeper quickly silenced him. The mastiffs chained beside the stables started barking and howling, irritated by our exotic clothes—I was wearing a grey town suit, collar, tie, and shoes, my uncle a raglan, my aunt a black, fur-trimmed weeper and a small brimmed hat, and Alfred plus-fours. It was a *via crucis*, and how slow a one, the most agonizing walk I have ever had in my life. One day I shall tell you about my adventures in the desert and among the blacks, but darkest Africa was nothing in comparison with this expedition to the backyard at Bolimowo. Nowhere could there be more concentrated exoticism, more fatal poisons, nowhere a more luxuriant blooming of phantasmagoria and rare flowers, nowhere else were these orchids and super-oriental butterflies to be found, no humming-bird from distant lands could compare in exoticism to a duck our hands had never touched. For nothing here had ever been touched by our hands, neither the stable-lads in the stables nor the farm-girls near the barn, nor the cattle, nor the chickens, nor the hay-forks, nor the harness, nor the chains, nor the sacks. Wild chickens, wild horses, wild girls, and wild pigs! Only the stable-lads' faces were touchable by my uncle's hand; and only my aunt's hand was touchable by the faces of the stable-lads when they planted on it their tamed and rustic kisses. Otherwise it was an expedition into the unknown. While we were thus advancing on our heels, there was an irruption of cows into the yard, and.one of them, driven by the children who were spying on our movements, invaded our path, and then we were sur-rounded by the strange and unknown quadrupeds.

'*Attention! Laissez les passer!*' my aunt called out.

'Attansionlessaypa!' the children mimicked her from behind the barn, but the lodge-keeper and overseer hurriedly chased away both children and cows. The wild, native girls in the poultry-yard struck up a country ditty . . . tra-la-la . . . but the words were inaudible. Were they singing about the young master? The most disagreeable thing, however, was the way in which the people seemed to spoil and pamper and make a fuss of their masters. Though the latter reigned over, dominated and economically oppressed them, looked at from the outside it all looked tender and affectionate, as if the plebs were caressing and fondling and making a fuss of them. The overseer in slave-like fashion carried my aunt in his arms over the puddles, but his gesture resembled a caress. Economically they sucked the people's blood, but this economic sucking was accompanied by another kind of sucking—an infantile kind—for they sucked milk as well as blood, and in vain did my uncle sternly and virilely reprimand the farm-hands, and in vain did my aunt allow her hands to be kissed with matronly and matriarchal kindness—neither the latter nor her husband's sternest orders prevented the master from being the people's baby boy and the mistress from being their baby girl.

Not far from the hen-roost the tenant-farmer's wife was stuffing food down the throat of a big turkey, overfeeding it in honour of the baronial palate, preparing it to make a tasty dish for her masters. Outside the farrier's shop a prize filly was having its tail cropped—to give it more distinction—and Alfred patted it and looked at its teeth, for this animal was one of the few things the young master was allowed to touch; at this the unknown and blood-sucked girls sang at him with redoubled vigour—tra-la-la-la-la. But this put him off, the memory of the evening before prevented him from playing the role of the young master; he dropped his hand from the filly's neck, and looked suspiciously in the girls' direction, to see whether by any chance they were mocking him. An old, dried-up peasant, equally unknown and rather blood-sucked too, approached my aunt and kissed the approved part of her body. We came to the end of the buildings. Beyond it was a path and a chequerboard of fields, space. In the distance a blood-sucked labourer noticed us, stopped his plough for a moment, then whipped up his horse again. The wet earth permitted us neither to sit down nor to remain standing. To the masters' right were ditches, corn-fields, fences, patches of woodland; to their left the prickly green of the evergreen forest. There was no sign of Mientus. Wild domestic chickens scratched away among the oats.

Suddenly, not a hundred yards away, Mientus emerged from the wood; and he was not alone, for the little lackey was with him. He did not see us. Spellbound and absorbed by his stable-lad, he was totally oblivious of the world about him. He did not see anyone or anything. He came dawdling and bounding along in a solemn, clownish fashion, and kept taking the lackey's hand and looking him in the eyes. The lackey kept mocking him with his great, rustic laugh, slapping him familiarly on the back. They walked along the edge of the small wood. Mientus with the stable-boy; no, the stable-boy with Mientus accompanying him. Under his spell Mientus kept putting his hand in his pocket and giving something, no doubt small change, to the lad, who kept familiarly slapping him on the back.

'They're drunk!' my aunt muttered.

They were not. The declining sun illuminated everything and left no doubt. The lackey gave Mientus a playful tap on the cheek in the light of the declining sun.

'Bert!' Alfred shouted.

The little lackey vanished into the wood. Mientus, snatched out of his dream, stopped in his tracks. We started walking towards him across the corn-field, because he started walking towards us. But Uncle Edward did not want the confrontation to take place in the open fields, as the urchins were still watching us from the yard and the blood-sucked labourer was labouring.

'Shall we take a turn in the wood?' my uncle said to him with exceptional affability. We walked across the field and entered the dark little wood. Peace and calm. The confrontation took place among the thickly planted pines. We were cramped for space, we all had to stand on top of one another. Uncle Edward was trembling inside, but redoubled his affability.

'I see that you take great pleasure in Bert's company,' he said with subtle irony.

'Yes, I do!' replied Mientus, in a sharp and hate-filled voice.

He was hidden under a prickly pine, his face concealed by the branches, like a fox cornered by the pack. Two yards away from him, among the prickles, were my aunt, Uncle Edward, and Alfred. My uncle said coldly, with barely perceptible sarcasm:

'It seems that you are fra . . . ternizing with Bert.'

'Yes, I am!' came the answer; it was a howl of rage and hatred.

'Edward,' my aunt butted in gently, 'let's go, it's very damp here.'

'This plantation's too thick,' Alfred said to his father. 'We must cut down one tree in three.'

'Yes, I am!' howled Mientus.

He had not expected to be condemned to this torture. So it was for this they had brought him into the little wood, so that they might pretend to be deaf? So it was for this that they had spent such a long time pursuing him, to scorn him after they had found him? What had become of the great confrontation scene, in which everything was going to be explained and made clear? They had treacherously changed roles, they were no longer interested in him; so great was their pride, so all-embracing their contempt, that they had even abandoned their desire to have things out with him. They talked about trifles they behaved as if everything were normal, they ignored him. Oh, base and villainous masters!

'You climbed the gamekeeper!' he yelled, losing all control of himself. 'You climbed the gamekeeper, because you were afraid of the boar! I know! Everyone knows! Ta-ra-ra-boom-te-ay! Ta-ra-ra-boom-te-ay! And old Mother Josephine!' he added.

Uncle Edward pursed his lips, but said nothing.

'We shall have to get rid of Bert,' Alfred said coldly to his father.

'Yes, we shall have to get rid of him,' Uncle Edward answered coldly. 'I'm sorry, but I'm not in the habit of keeping depraved servants.'

So they were revenging themselves on Bert. Oh, their cold vileness! Not only did they not condescend to answer him, but now they were going to sack Bert, they were going to hurt him by way of Bert. Had not old Francis behaved in the same way in the kitchen when he had given Bert and the girl a dressing-down without saying a word to him? The pine-tree trembled, and Mientus would surely have leapt at them had not a game-keeper suddenly emerged from among the trees at that moment, in his green uniform, with his gun slung over his shoulder, and saluted the company respectfully.

'Climb him!' Mientus shouted. 'Climb him! The boar! The boar!' And, having taken leave completely of his senses, he started running desperately through the wood. I ran after him.

'Mientus! Mientus!' I shouted, but he took no notice, and the pine branches struck me and scratched my face. I didn't want him to be alone in the woods for anything in the world. He fled, leaping the ditches, mounds, roots, and holes. When we emerged from this little plantation and plunged into the wood he redoubled his speed; he ran and ran, like a raging boar.

Suddenly I saw Isabel beguiling her boredom by looking for mushrooms. We were making straight towards her, and I was afraid that in his rage Mientus might do her some harm.

'Look out!' I shouted. 'Look out!'

There must have been urgency in my voice, for Isabel turned and fled, and Mientus saw this and started chasing her. I called on my last strength to catch up with her before he did, but fortunately he tripped over a root and fell, so I caught up with him.

'What is it?' he groaned with his face in the moss. 'What is it?'

'Come back to the house!'

'The masters!' He spat the word out. 'The masters! Go away! Go away! Yer one of 'em yersel'!'

'I'm not!'

'Yer tarred with t'same brush. Yah! Master! Master!'

'Come back to the house, Mientus, that's enough of this, it'll lead to something dreadful. Stop this, make a clean break, we must try again some other way!'

'The masters! The masters! Doan't do this! Doan't do that! Doan't do t'other! And yer sold to 'un too!'

'Stop it Mientus, that's not the way you speak! Why are you speaking like that? Why are you speaking like that to me?'

'Give 'un to me! Give 'un to me! Oi shan't give 'un up! Doan't touch Bert! 'ey wanter throw'un out! Bert! Moi Bert! Woan't allow that!'

'Come back to the house!'

It was a shameful retreat. Mientus cried, groaned, despaired, burst out into rustic lamentations.

'Oah! Oah! What a loif! What a loif!'

In the yard the girls and the men-servants were dumbfounded to see a master complaining in their rustic fashion. Night was falling by the time we reached the house. I told Mientus to wait in our first-floor room, while I went off to talk to Uncle Edward. In the smoking-room I found Alfred pacing up and down with his hands in his pockets. The young master was outwardly stiff and inwardly furious. I learnt from his dry replies that Isabel had come back from the wood more dead than alive, that she seemed to have caught a cold, and that my aunt was just taking her temperature. Bert, who was back in the kitchen, had been forbidden access to the rest of the house, and was to be sent away next day. Alfred was careful to explain that he did not hold me responsible for 'that gentleman's' excesses, though in his opinion I ought to choose my friends more carefully. He regretted that he would not be able to enjoy my company for a longer period, but did not believe that in the circumstances we would wish to prolong our stay at Bolimowo. The Warsaw train left at 9 a.m., and the chauffeur had already been ordered to take us to the station. As for dinner, no doubt we should prefer to take it in our own room; Francis would see to this. Alfred spoke in a manner which permitted of no reply, he was speaking on his parents' behalf.

'As for myself,' he said, 'I shall react differently. I propose to punish the gentleman for his insulting behaviour towards my parents. I am a member of the Astoria Club.'

And he made the gesture of slapping a face. I saw what was in his mind; he wished to disqualify a face which had been slapped by a common hand, remove it from the list of honourable, gentlemanly faces.

Fortunately Uncle Edward came in and overheard this threat.

'What *gentleman* are you talking about, my boy?' he exclaimed. 'Whose face is it you want to slap? The face of a stripling who's still at school? It's his behind that's in need of correction!'

Alfred blushed, and hesitated in his honourable proposal. After what my uncle said he could no longer slap Mientus's face. At the age of twenty plus he could not honourably strike a boy of seventeen, particularly after the latter's youthfulness had been drawn attention to in this way. The trouble, however, was that

Mientus's age was an age of transition. The masters could regard him as an unlicked cub, but in the eyes of the people, who mature faster, he was already a fully grown gentleman, and in their eyes his face had all the prestige of a gentleman's face. It was a strange position. Mientus's face was mature enough to be a gentleman's when Bert hit it, but not mature enough for a gentleman to be able to obtain satisfaction from it. Alfred looked at his father, furious at this injustice on the part of nature. But Uncle Alfred refused to admit that Mientus was anything but a snuffle-nosed minor, though at lunch he had treated him as man to man, and had sent for a special bottle of old wine to toast his assumed homosexuality. But now he repudiated all affinity with him, treated him with contempt as a minor. His pride, his ancestry, forbade him to do anything else. His ancestral blood was up. The remorseless march of history was robbing him of his wealth and his power, but he still preserved his blood intact, both mentally and physically, and above all physically. He could tolerate agrarian reform and the general levelling in public and political life, but his blood boiled at the idea of private, physical, corporeal equality, at the idea of fra . . . ternization between man and man. Levelling assailed him here in the darkest depths of his personality, in his ancient, ancestral undergrowth, defended by the instinctive reflexes of repulsion, revulsion, detestation, and fear. Let them take his fortune, let them carry out their reforms, but the master's hand must not seek out the hand of the peasant, the master's cheek must not seek out the vulgar paw! How could anyone of his own free will develop a predilection for the vulgar, betray his blood, fawn on a servant, be full of naïve admiration for the limbs, the movements, the awkwardness of a lackey, become enamoured of a farm-hand's inner being? What is the position of a master whose servant is publicly and plainly the object of such attentions by another master?

'No, no,' he said, 'Mientus is not one of us, but the victim of a childish mania influenced by Bolshevik propaganda. I see that young people at school nowadays are being affected by Bolshevik ideas,' he repeated, as if Mientus were an ordinary young man with revolutionary impulses and not a lover of the people.

'What he needs is a good thrashing,' he said with a laugh.

Through the half-open window we suddenly heard noises and giggles from the bushes near the kitchen. It was a warm Saturday afternoon. The farm-hands had joined the kitchen-girls, and things were warming up. . . . Edward leaned out of the window.

'Who's there?' he called out. 'It's not allowed.'

Someone hid in the bushes. There was a loud laugh. A stone, thrown with violence, landed outside the window, and from behind the bushes a disguised voice bawled:

> *A bloody great swoip*
> *On t'gennleman's jaw,*
> *Haw! Haw!*

There was another giggle and more laughter. The news had spread in the village. They knew. The kitchen-girls must have told the farm-hands. That was only to be expected, but the insolence of this singing under his windows was too much for my uncle. He ceased taking the matter lightly, angry red blobs appeared on his cheeks, and he silently took out his revolver. Fortunately my aunt appeared at that moment.

'Edward!' she exclaimed kindly. 'Put that thing down! Put it down at once! I can't stand loaded weapons! If you insist on carrying that thing about with you, unload it!'

And just as he had just previously made light of Alfred, so did she now make light of him. She kissed him, and he, revolver in hand, allowed himself to be kissed; and she straightened his tie, which effectively inhibited his revolver, she shut the window because of the draught, and made a number of other, similar gestures, with an increasingly restricting and diminishing effect. She threw into the balance all the roundness of her person, which exuded a gentle, maternal warmth, wrapping everything in cotton-wool. She took me aside, and surreptitiously gave me some sweets from her bag.

'What have you done, you naughty boys!' she said, in an exceedingly kind rebuke. 'Isabel's ill, and uncle's angry! You and your idylls with the people! You have to know how to handle the servants, you mustn't permit familiarity, you have to understand them, they're not educated, they're primitives, they're children! James, Uncle Stanislas's son, had the same mania for the people,' she added, looking at me, 'and you take after him a little, there, round about the nostrils. All right, I'm not angry with you, darling, but don't come down to dinner, Uncle doesn't want you to. I'll send up some preserves to cheer you up. Oh, and do you remember how Ladislas, our old servant, beat you because you said he was crazy? Horrid man! I still shudder to think of it. Beating my little darling, my little angel!'

In a sudden burst of affection she kissed me, and gave me more sweets. I rapidly took my leave, with the taste of the childish sweets still in my mouth, and on my way out I heard my aunt asking Alfred to feel her pulse; and Alfred, looking at his watch, felt his mother's pulse, while she lay on the sofa, staring into the void. With sweets still in my mouth I went back to our room, and felt unreal, but my aunt made everybody unreal, she had the extraordinary gift of dissolving people in kindness, plunging them into all sorts of illnesses, and mingling parts of their bodies with those of other members of the family . . . perhaps out of fear of the servants? She was kind, because she suffocated people. As she suffocated people, how could she be anything but kind?

The situation was getting dangerous. They were each taking things lightly against each other, my uncle out of pride and my aunt out of fear, and it was thanks only to this that no shots had been fired, that Alfred's hand had not struck Mientus's face, that my uncle's ammunition was still in his pistol. I was relieved at the thought that we were leaving next morning.

I found Mientus lying on the floor, his head between his arms—he had got into the habit of surrounding, hiding, enveloping himself with his arms. He did not move when I came in, but went on moaning and lamenting in youthful and rustic fashion, with his head buried. 'Oh, lack a day! Oh, lack a day!'

he blubbered disconsolately, and went on incoherently muttering other expressions as grey and crude as the earth, as green as foliage, young, country, peasant expressions. He had lost all sense of shame. When Francis came in with the dinner he did not interrupt his tender complaints and rustic lamentations; he had crossed the threshold beyond which no shame is felt at aspiring to be a servant in a servant's presence, or in sighing for a young lackey in the presence of an old butler. Never before had I seen a member of the educated classes in such a state of degeneration. Francis did not even look in his direction, but when he put the dish on the table his hands were trembling with indignation, and when he went out he slammed the door behind him. Mientus would not eat anything and remained disconsolate—something was murmuring and lamenting, weeping and wailing, inside him, he was sighing for something, grumbling at and wrestling with it, it was impossible to tell exactly what was going on in him; and then again a boorish rage seized him by the throat. He put all the blame for his failure with the stable-boy on my uncle and aunt. It was the masters' fault, the masters'; if they had not put their spoke in the wheel, he would certainly have succeeded in fra . . . ternizing with Bert. Why had they thwarted him? Why were they sacking Bert? In vain I told him that we should have to leave next morning.

'Woan' go!' he said. 'Woan' go! Let 'ey go if 'ey wanna! Oi stay where Bert be! Oi stay wi' Bert! Wi' moi Bert! Moi stable-boy!'

I could not make him see sense, he was totally immersed in his stable-boy, all worldly considerations had ceased to exist for him. When he finally grasped that it was impossible to remain here, he took fright, and started begging me not to abandon the stable-boy.

'Oi woan' go wi'out Bert!' he said. 'Oi woan' leave Bert! We'll take 'un wi' us, oi'll go out an' work an' earn a livin'. Oi'd rather doi than leave 'ere wi'out Bert! Boi all that's 'oly, Johnnie, oi woan' leave wi'out moi Bert! If 'ey turns we out,' he added viciously, 'if 'ey turns we out, oi'll go an' live wi' the widder!

'ey can't turn we out o' the village! Anyone can live i' the village!'

Here was a pretty kettle of fish. I couldn't think what to do. He was perfectly capable of going to live with Alfred's old woman—the 'widow', as the stable-boy called her, compromising my uncle and aunt by denouncing the secrets of the manor-house in the language of the people . . . traitor and spy . . . to make the yokels laugh.

At that moment a monumental smack resounded in the court-yard down below. The windows shook, and the dogs started barking like mad. We looked out. Uncle Edward was silhouetted in the moonlight, gun in hand, trying to pierce the darkness with his eyes. Once more he raised the gun to his cheek and fired— the detonation resounded in the night like a rocket and lost itself in the darkness of space. The dogs broke loose.

' 'ey be foirin' at Bert!'

Mientus gripped me convulsively.

'Bert! 'ey be troyin' to kill 'un!'

Uncle Edward fired to frighten. Had the servants been talking again? Did he fire because he had grown so nervy that he could stand it no longer and had some ammunition in his pocket? Heaven knows what was going on inside him! Was it arrogance and pride that inspired this terroristic gesture? Was the angry master proclaiming far and wide by these detonations that he was awake, on the alert, and armed? My aunt appeared in the doorway, hastily offered him sweets, put a scarf round his neck, and took him inside. But the detonations were beyond recall. When the watch-dogs of the home farm fell silent for a moment I heard the distant answer of the village dogs, and in my mind's eye saw what must be going on in the minds of the villagers —the man-servants, the farm-girls, the labourers all saying to one another:

'What's up there, I wonder? What are they shooting for up at the house? Is that the master shooting? What's he shooting for?'

And the talk about the blows in the face that the young gentleman had taken from Bert spread from mouth to mouth, set free by this fantastic and ostentatious firing. I could no longer control my nerves, I decided to flee immediately; I was afraid of another night in this noxious, feudal house, full of poisonous emanations, I decided to leave instantly, but Mientus refused to go without Bert. So, to save time, I agreed that she should take him with us; he was going to be sacked next morning in any case. We ended by deciding to wait till the whole household was asleep, and that I should then go and find Bert and persuade him to run away with us or, if necessary, order him to. I should bring him back to our room and the three of us should then hold a council of war to decide how best to make our getaway. The dogs knew Bert. We should spend the rest of the night in the fields, and take the train to town next morning. Town! Town! In town man is smaller, better situated among his fellows, more human. Each minute lasted an eternity. We packed our belongings, and tied up in a handkerchief the dinner which we had barely touched.

After midnight, when I had made sure that darkness reigned in the house, I took off my shoes and crept down the little corridor on my bare feet in order to reach the kitchen without making any noise. After Mientus had shut the door behind me, depriving me of the last ray of light, after I had set out on the enterprise and started groping my way about the sleeping house, I saw how senseless and unreasonable was this whole idea of launching myself into space for the purpose of abducting the stable-boy; it is only by action that the full madness of madness is demonstrated. I advanced step by step, every now and then a floor-board creaked under my feet, over the ceiling rats jostled each other and scurried apart. The rustic Mientus was in the room behind me; ahead, on the ground floor, were my uncle and aunt, Alfred and Isabel, whose servant was the objective of all these endeavours. I advanced in death-like stillness and on bare feet. He was straight ahead of me, in the kitchen. I must be very careful. If anyone discovered me like this in the dark corridor, I should be hard put to it for an explanation. What paths lead us to these tortuous and abnormal actions? The normal is a tightrope over the abyss of the abnormal. What lunacies lie hidden behind the daily routine—you can never tell when or how you may be impelled by the course of events to abduct and run away with a stable-boy. It would have been better to abduct Isabel; if anyone was to be abducted, she was the obvious, natural, normal, and obvious choice. Why not abduct Isabel instead of this fatuous and idiotic stable-boy? And in the dark corridor I was tempted by the idea of abducting Isabel, the sensible and rational idea of abducting Isabel. Oh, the sensible and rational idea of abducting Isabel.

Oh, the thought of maturely, nobly, aristocratically abducting Isabel in the manner of so many abductions of the past. I had to fight off the idea, demonstrate to myself how ill-considered it was but the farther I advanced along the treacherous floorboards, the greater the attraction of normality became, the more I was tempted by the idea of a normal and natural abduction as against the involved and complicated abduction of the stable-boy. I tripped over a hole, there was a hole under my feet, a hole in the floor. But where was it? Because I knew it, it was my hole, years before I had made it myself. My uncle had given me a hatchet for my birthday, and I had made the hole with it. My aunt had come hurrying along, and here, standing at this spot, she had scolded me; I still remembered the remonstrations, the tone of severity. Then I had hit her leg with the hatchet. 'Ow! she had called out. 'Ow!' Her cry still lingered here. I stopped as if the scene had caught me by the foot, though the scene was now non-existent but nevertheless existed at that moment and at that spot. I had hit her leg with the hatchet, and in the darkness I clearly saw myself doing it, without knowing why, without wanting to, and I heard her cry out; she had cried out and jumped. My present and past actions, preterite and pluperfect, were mingled and intertwined, suddenly I started trembling and clenched my teeth. Heavens, if I had been stronger I might have chopped her leg off, thank heaven for my weakness! But now I had strength. Instead of looking for the stable-boy, why not go to my aunt's room and chop off her leg? No, no, what childishness, what childishness! But in heaven's name was not the stable-lad childishness too? One was as childish as the other, so why not chop my aunt's leg off? Oh, childishness, childishness! I felt the floor with my foot, carefully, for a creak might have betrayed me, but it seemed to me that it was a child that was groping his way forward like this. Oh, childishness! I was afflicted with triple childishness—if it had been merely single childishness, I might have been able to to defend myself against it. In the first place there was the childishness of this expedition in search of the stable-boy. Then there was the childishness of my memories of life here years ago; and finally the childishness of this feudal household, and as part of it I was childish too. Oh, there are plenty of more or less puerile places in the world, but a country house is perhaps the most puerile of all. Here both masters and people turned themselves into children, preserved themselves by turning themselves into children, they were children to each other. Advancing barefoot along the corridor under the mask of night, I seemed to re-enter my aristocratic and pre-pubertal past; and the sensuous, physical, incalculable world of childhood absorbed and inveigled me. Blind actions. Irresistible impulses. Atavistic instincts. Puerile baronial fantasies. I succumbed to the anachronistic idea of a gigantic super-slap—an idea at one and the same time infantile and in accordance with immemorial tradition—a gigantic super-slap which should simultaneously liberate both master and child. I felt the banisters down which I had once slid, enjoyed the automatism of the slide from top to bottom. Child, infant, infant-king, Mr Grown-Up Child of the present day, oh, if I struck my aunt with an axe now, she wouldn't get up . . . and I was terrified at the idea of a child's possessing a man's strength. What was I doing here on this staircase, where was I going, and what for? Once more the abduction of Isabel struck me as the only possible excuse for this foray, the only possible manly, mature justification for it. The abduction of Isabel, the manly abduction of Isabel. I fought off the idea, but it tickled my fancy, kept buzzing in my head.

Down below in the lumber-room I stopped. All was quiet, they had all gone to bed at the usual time, just as they did every day, my aunt had undoubtedly packed them all off to bed and tucked them in. But tonight there was the difference that they were not really resting under the bed-clothes, but chewing over the events of the day. Not a sound came from the kitchen either, only a gleam of light showed through the crack of the door, behind which the young manservant was cleaning shoes. I could see no change in his face; everything was normal there too. I went in quietly, with my finger to my lips, closed the door behind me, and with infinite precautions whispered my arguments into his ear. Quick, pick up your cap, drop everything, and come with us to Warsaw, we're going to Warsaw. It was a horrible role to play, I should have preferred almost anything to these idiotic proposals, which had to be whispered into the bargain. Particularly as the lad wouldn't agree to them. I pointed out that he was going to get thrown out next morning in any case, and that from his point of view it would be better to go a long way away, to Warsaw, where Mientus would help him. But he would not, could not understand. 'Woi should oi go?' he replied, with an instinctive mistrust of all upper-class fantasies, and once more I had the impression that Isabel would respond more easily, that midnight whisperings to Isabel would be less inexcusable. But time was pressing, and made it impossible to prolong the argument. I struck the lad in the face and ordered him to follow me, and then he obeyed. But I hit him through a dish-cloth; I held a dish-cloth against his left cheek to deaden the sound of the blow, and oh! oh! oh! it was through a dish-cloth that I slapped him in the middle of the night. But he obeyed, though the dish-cloth must have roused some suspicion in his mind, for the vulgar do not like departures from routine. 'Come along, you son of a bitch!' I ordered him, and went out into the lumber-room, with him behind me. Where was the staircase? Pitch darkness.

A door creaked, and my uncle's voice said:
'Who's there?'
I took the lad's arm and pushed him into the dining-room.

We hid behind the door. Uncle Edward slowly approached, and entered the dining-room too; he glided past quite close to where I was standing.

'Who's there?' he asked cautiously, to avoid looking foolish if nobody was there. After launching this question he advanced a step farther into the room and stopped. He had no matches, and the darkness was impenetrable. He turned, retraced his steps, stopped again and lay doggo, he suddenly lay completely doggo. Had he detected in the darkness the *sui generis* odour of the stable-lad, had the master's delicate skin sensed the presence of paws and mug? He was so close that he could have put out his hands and touched us, but that was why he did not put out his hands, he was too close, proximity held him in its grip. He froze into immobility, and this immobility, which started by being slow, rapidly accelerated and condensed into an expression of fear. I don't think he was a coward, in spite of the story of how he climbed the gamekeeper; no, it wasn' this inability to move that made him afraid, for once he had immobilized himself, for reason of pure form each second that passed made it harder for him to start moving again. But fear entered into him, and now it had started taking shape and suffocating him; his fine, baronial Adam's apple had gone up his throat. The stable-lad did not move, and so all three of us remained standing within a foot of each other. Our skin woke up. I did nothing to interrupt. I waited for Uncle Edward to recover his self-control and go away, which would enable us to resume our flight through the lumber-room to the staircase, but I failed to take into account the paralysing effect on him of fear . . . for now, I could tell, an interior change and transformation was taking place in him, and from being afraid because he could not move, now he could not move because he was afraid. I could divine on his face the grave, concentrated, highly serious expression proper to fear . . . and I in my turn started feeling afraid . . . not of him, but of his fear. If we had retreated or made the slightest movement he would have been able to go for us. If he had had his pistol, he would have been able to pull the trigger, but no, we were too close, it was a physical but not a psychological possibility because, before a man can pull the trigger physically, he has to pull it internally, in his mind, and for that there was no room. True, he might plunge forward with his hands out, but he did not know what was in front of him or what his hands might meet. We knew what he looked like, but he did not know what we looked like. I felt like clearing up the whole situation by saying 'Hello, uncle!' or something of the sort, but after so many seconds perhaps even minutes, it was impossible, it was too late, how was I to explain having kept silent for so long? I felt I was going to laugh, as if someone had tickled me. I had a sense of growing, growing enormous in the dark. Growing enormously in the dark. A sense of becoming enormous, gigantic and simultaneously a sense of growing smaller, shrinking and stiffening, a sense of escape and at the same time a kind of general and particular impoverishment, a sense of paralysing tension and tense paralysis, of being hung by a tense thread, as well as of being converted and changed into something, a sense of transmutation and also of relapse into a kind of accumulating and mounting mechanism, as if on a narrow plank being hoisted to the eighth storey, with all one's sense alerted; and also of sub-tickling. The sound of footsteps came from the lumber-room, but nobody budged. Alfred appeared in his slippers.

'Who's there?' he said. He took a step into the dining-room, said 'Who's there?' again, and then froze into immobility, having sensed something. He knew that his father must be somewhere around, for he had heard him moving about and then asking questions. But why didn't his father answer? Because he was inhibited by ancient fears and terrors, oh he could not, because he was afraid. And the son was inhibited by his father's fear. He was afraid because of the quantity of fear that had already been generated, and fell silent, as if for centuries. Perhaps he felt rather lost at the outset, but the very indefinite-ness rapidly assumed a most formidable definition, and grew by itself. The sense of growing, swelling, becoming huge, started all over again, lengthened and broadened, swelled and multiplied itself to the hundredth power, became tense, acute, stretched to bursting point, strain and tension, a sense of stifling monotony, tension, endless, boundless, infinite, a sense of submergence above and below, with Alfred a little further away. A sense of being throttled, yet not throttled; obstacle; hold one's head high, disintegration, explosion, being slowly stripped, repetition, ejection and penetration, transformation and tension, tension, tension. Did this last for minutes or for hours? What was going to happen? Whole worlds flew through my head. I remembered that it was at this spot that I used to lie in wait for my nurse in order to give her a fright—it nearly made me laugh. Hush! Where did that laugh come from? But enough of this, I must stop this, do something, what would happen if my childishness were exposed, if after all this time I were found with the stable-boy, which would be a strange and inexplicable discovery indeed? Oh Isabel, to be with Isabel, to have to hold one's breath with Isabel instead of with the stable-boy! With Isabel it would not be childish. Suddenly I insolently moved and stepped behind the curtain, feeling certain that they would not dare to budge, and sure enough they did not budge. The result was that something like lethargy was superimposed on the fear prevailing in the darkness, for now it was more than just impossible, it was also awkward and embarrassing to break the silence. Perhaps they wanted to, perhaps they thought about it, but they did not know how to set about it. I am referring to their silence, for by my movement I had broken my own silence. Perhaps they were thinking only about the outward formalities of the situation, perhaps they were concerned with appearances, looking for some external pretext or excuse. The worst of it was that the presence of each paralysed the other, and the two thinkers remained standing, powerless to put an end to the situation or to interrupt it, while suspense and repetition still remained ceaselessly at work. Having recovered my own ability to move, I decided to grab the stable-lad and hustle him quickly into the lumber-room, but no sooner had I come to this decision than a gleam of light appeared, casting a slight reflection on the floor, and there was a creaking of floorboards and the sound of foot-steps, Francis was coming with a lamp, and the silhouette of my uncle's leg stood out, plain for all to see. Luckily I was behind the curtain. But the old flunkey mercilessly threw a light on the others and all that was going on in the dark—my uncle, his hair slightly dishevelled, standing only a pace away from the stable-lad, their noses were almost touching, and Alfred planted like a stick only a little way away.

'Is anyone here?' Francis asked crossly, illuminated by the light of the little petrol lamp. He asked the question belatedly, however, merely in order to justify his appearance, because he could see the three of them as plainly as if they were in his hand.

Uncle Edward moved. What would Francis think, seeing him so close to the young manservant? Why were they together there like that? He could not withdraw altogether, but he moved, and thus broke the link connecting him to Bert; then he stepped to one side.

'What are you doing here?' he shouted, changing the fear inside him to fury.

The lad didn't answer; he couldn't think of anything to say. He stood there with a great deal of naturalness, but his tongue failed him. He was alone with the masters; and the inarticulate-ness of this child of the people, his lack of education, cast a suspicious shadow. Francis looked at my uncle. . . . What were the masters doing with Bert in the dark? Was the master being familiar with him too? A flush started slowly spreading over the old servant's face as he stood there stiffly with the lamp in his hand, and soon his cheeks were aglow with the brilliance of a sunset. 'Bert!' Alfred exclaimed. All these exclamations were not well placed in time. They were blurted out either too late or too soon, and I cowered behind my curtain.

'I heard someone here,' Alfred started saying, lamely and incoherently, 'I heard someone here . . . Someone. What were you doing here? What were you doing? Speak up, I tell you! What were you doing? Speak up, damn it!'

There were horrible discords in his excitement.

'It's obvious what he was after,' said the flunkey, who was as red as fire, after a long and ghastly silence. 'It's obvious, sir!'

He stroked his moustaches, and went on:

'The silver is in the drawer, and tomorrow you were going to send him packing, sir. So he was going to . . . steal the silver.'

So he had been going to steal the silver! This was the plausible explanation that they wanted, the lad had been caught red-handed while going to steal the silver. Everyone, including Bert, felt a sense of relief. Uncle Edward moved away from the young manservant, and sat down at the table. He resumed his normal, baronial attitude towards the stable-boy, and recovered his self-confidence. So the lad had been going to steal the silver!

'Come here!' said Uncle Edward. 'Come here, I tell you! Come here, quite close to me!'

He was no longer afraid of proximity, and he was obviously enjoying no longer being afraid.

'Nearer!' he said. 'Nearer!'

Bert, heavily and mistrustfully, went nearer him—still nearer—and when he was nearly touching him Uncle Edward raised his arm and struck his face, first forehanded and then back-handed, like Mene, Mene, Tekel and Upharsin.

'I'll teach you to steal!' he shouted.

Oh, the joy of striking out like this in the light after the fear in the dark! Oh the joy of striking the face which has been the cause of the fear, of striking within the limits laid down by the precise, the definite, idea of attempted robbery! Oh, the pleasure of normality after all the abnormality! Alfred, following his father's example, struck the lad in the teeth, like the hanging gardens of Semiramis. He struck the boy hard and repeatedly. Behind the curtain I writhed as if transfixed on a skewer.

'I didn't steal!' the stable-boy said, getting his breath back.

This was what they had been waiting for; it enabled them to exploit the appearance of attempted robbery to the utmost.

'You didn't steal?' said Uncle Edward, leaning back in his chair, and delivering another blow.

'You didn't steal?' said his son, to the accompaniment of a

short, sharp blow. 'You didn't steal?' they kept repeating. 'You didn't steal?' And each time they said the words their hands relentlessly sought and found the lad's face, delivering a shower of blows as if mounted on springs. Mingled with the short sharp blows were broad resounding swipes.

'I'll teach you to steal! I'll teach you to steal!'

Oh, they were well away. Oh, accursed night, oh accursed, treacherous darkness, without this bath in the shadows none of this would have happened! The country nobility was riding high. Under the pretext of attempted robbery it was striking out and getting its own back for its blushes, for the fraternization with Mientus, and for everything that it had suffered.

'This is mine, mine!' Uncle Edward kept repeating. 'Mine, damn it!'

And gradually, the meaning of the word 'mine' changed; you could not tell whether he was referring to the silver, or his body and soul, his hair, his customs, hands, distinction, culture, breeding; it seemed rather that in striking and hitting the lad he was trying to impose on him, not what he owned and possessed, but himself, not his goods and chattels but his own person. He was imposing himself. Terrorize him, terrorize him, use violence upon him, impose yourself on him, so that never again will he dare to fra . . . ternize, or gossip about his masters, or laugh at them, but accept them like gods. With his delicate, gentlemanly hand Edward nailed himself to the lad's face.

Behind the curtain I rubbed my eyes, wanted to scream, shout for help, but could not. And Francis stood there, illuminating the scene with his little lamp. My aunt! My aunt! Did my eyes deceive me, or did I see her for a moment standing in the doorway, with her bag of sweets? I had a flash of hope that perhaps she would save, mollify, neutralize the situation. She raised her hands as if to cry out, but instead smiled senselessly, made an equally meaningless gesture with her arms, and withdrew to the smoking-room. She pretended she hadn't been there, the dose was too strong for her, she couldn't stand it, so she inwardly dissolved herself backwards, or rather spread herself backwards, in such nebulous fashion that I wondered whether she had really been there at all. Uncle Edward started weakening, but once more sprang forward to impose himself—while Alfred sprang forward at his side, and he too imposed himself, imposed himself, imposed himself with all his power and strength. Between their teeth they muttered phrases such as: 'So I climbed the game-keeper, did I? Climbed the gamekeeper, did I?' 'So you wanted to fra . . . ternize, did you?' 'So I've got an old woman, have I?' And to wipe these things out of existence they struck, not the lad's back or his legs, but his face. They did not fight him, oh no, they did not fight him, they just struck him in the face. And this was perfectly permissible. Meanwhile old Francis illuminated the scene with his lamp, and when their hands weakened he said tactfully:

'The masters will teach you, the masters will teach you!'

At last they stopped. They sat down, and the stable-lad got his breath back; his ear was bleeding, his face and head were dreadfully knocked about. The masters offered each other cigarettes, and the old flunkey leapt forward, match in hand. It looked as if it were over. But Alfred blew a smoke ring.

'Bring us brandy!' he said and, helping themselves abundantly to a fine old bottle, they set about breaking in the stable-lad, to make a fine old servant of him. 'We'll teach you! We'll break you in!' And it started all over again . . . to such good purpose that I thought my senses were deceiving me. For nothing is so deceptive as the senses. Hidden behind my curtain, with bare feet, I was not sure whether the scene going on before my eyes was reality or a prolongation of the shadows. Can one see reality with bare feet? Take off your shoes, hide behind a curtain, and try! Look, with your feet bare. What an ignoble scene! 'Bring this! Bring that!' they shouted. 'Small glasses! Napkins! Bread! Rolls! Ham! and be quick about it!' The stable-lad hurried here and there, faithfully doing whatever he was told. And they started eating in front of him, imposing baronial eating on him. 'Your masters drink,' Uncle Edward announced, emptying a small glass of old brandy. 'Your masters eat,' Alfred chimed in, 'I eat my food. I drink my drink. This is my food and my drink. Not yours!' 'Learn to know your masters,' they shouted at him, putting their persons under his nose, imposing all their peculiarities on him, so that to the end of his days he should lose all desire to criticize or have doubts about, or mock at, or be surprised at them, so that he should accept them as a thing in itself, a *Ding an sich*. And they shouted: 'Do what you're told!' and gave him orders, proliferated orders, which he carried out and kept on carrying out. 'Kiss my shoe!' He kissed it. 'Throw yourself at my feet!' He did so, and Francis like a trumpet provided a tactful accompaniment:

'The masters will show you! The masters will teach you!'

Sitting at the brandy-stained table, by the light of the little petrol lamp, they went on teaching him and breaking him in. And this was permitted and permissible, because they were training and breaking in a stable-boy, turning him into a domestic servant. I wanted to shout no, no, stop! But I couldn't. I was ashamed to see what was going on in front of my eyes, I did not know whether I could believe them, whether what I was seeing was true, how much of my own I was putting into the horrible scene; perhaps with my shoes on what I saw might have been different. And I shuddered at the thought that the eye of some third party might be upon me, regarding me as an integral part of the scene. I cringed under the shower of blows on the stable-lad's face, under the blows of my own despair and terror, and at the same time wanted to laugh, I laughed without wanting to, as if my feet were being tickled. Oh, Isabel, if only Isabel were here, oh to carry off Isabel, oh, to run away with Isabel, maturely, like a man! Meanwhile they continued, in baronial fashion from behind their glasses of old brandy, breaking in the immature stable-lad, breaking him in elegantly, even stylishly, sitting in their chairs behind the table and sipping their old brandy. Mientus appeared in the doorway.

'Leave 'un alone! Leave 'un alone!'

He did not shout, but said the words sharply and shrilly, and advanced on my uncle. I suddenly saw that we were not alone, that the whole scene was being observed, that innumerable eyes were on us. Outside the window there was a crowd. Stable-boys, farm-girls, labourers, village men and women, yokels male and female, farm servants and domestic servants, were all watching us. The shutters were not closed, and they had been attracted by the noise in the middle of the night; and they were respectfully watching their masters ordering Bert about, breaking him in, teaching and instructing and training him to become a servant in a smart household. 'Look out, Mientus!' I shouted, but it was too late. Uncle Edward just had time to turn his back on him contemptuously, and to give the stable-boy one more blow in the face. Mientus went and put his arm round the lad and drew him close to him.

' 'e's moin!' he said. 'Doan't 'it 'un! Doan't 'it 'un! Leave 'un alone! Doan't 'it 'un!'

'You young puppy!' Uncle Edward shouted. 'You young puppy! Just you wait and see what you're going to get on your backside!'

Mientus's juvenile yappings made him and Alfred lose their temper, and they went for him, to ridicule him on his backside, wipe out the value of his fra . . . ternization by chastising him on it in the presence of Bert and of the vulgar outside the window. 'Aow! Aow!' Mientus yelped, cringeing in strange fashion and jumping behind the stable-lad. And the latter, as if his courage in the face of his masters had been restored by Mientus's fra . . . ternization, suddenly fraternized on Uncle Edward's face.

'What does thee think thee's doin'?' he exclaimed vulgarly.

The charm was broken. The servant's hand had fallen on the master's face, and the master saw stars. So unexpected was the blow that he went down like a log. Immaturity spread everywhere. There was the sound of broken glass, and the light went out; a stone thrown from outside shattered the lamp. The windows gave way, and the populace surged in, the darkness was populated with parts of rustic bodies. The atmosphere was as heavy as in the bailiff's office. Paws and hands . . . no, the vulgar have no hands . . . paws, an enormous quantity of big, heavy paws.

The people, roused by the exceptional immaturity of the scene, had lost all sense of respect, and wanted to fra . . . ternize too. I heard Alfred and then Uncle Edward yell . . . they seemed to be holding the two together in some way and to be clumsily and lethargically starting on them, but it all was invisible in the dark . . . I jumped out from behind the curtain. My aunt, my aunt! I remembered my aunt! I ran on my bare feet to the smoking-room and grabbed her: she was lying on the sofa, pretending not to exist. Into the fray with her, into the fray! 'My child! My child! What are you doing?' She implored, and struggled, and offered me sweets, but like a child I dragged and dragged her towards the fray. Into the fray with her, into the fray. That's it, they've got her! I dashed from room to room . . . not running away, only running, running, running, after myself, sounding the general alarm on my bare feet. I ran to the front gate. The moon was emerging from behind the clouds, but it was not the moon, but a bum, a great bum spreading itself over the top of the trees. A childish bum over the world. Bum and nothing but bum. Behind me they were all wallowing in the *mêlée*, and in front of me was this great bum. The trees trembled in the breeze. And this great bum.

Mortal despair seized and held me in its grip. I had become childish to a degree. Where was I to run? Back to the house? There there was nothing but the wallowing and floundering in the *mêlée*. Where was I to go, what was I to do, how find myself a place in the world? I was alone, almost alone, reduced to childhood. But it was impossible to remain alone, unattached to anything. I ran down the path, jumping like a grasshopper over the dry branches, looking for contact with something, for a new dependence, a new link, even if only a temporary link, in order not to remain in the void. A shadow glided from behind a tree. It was Isabel. She had caught me!

'What's happening?' she asked. 'Have the peasants attacked Mamma and Papa?'

I took her by the arm. 'Let us flee!' I said. We fled together across fields bathed in the remote unknown, and there she was, abducted, and there was I, the abductor. We ran down a path through the fields until we ran out of breath, and spent the rest of the night in a meadow by the waterside, hidden away among the reeds, shivering with cold and with our teeth chattering. The grasshoppers chirred. At dawn another huge bum, red this time and a hundred times more dazzling, appeared in the sky, and flooded the world with its rays, forcing everything to project long shadows.

I did not know what to do. I could not explain and describe to Isabel all that was happening up at the house, because I was ashamed and, moreover, words failed me. No doubt she guessed more or less what was happening, but she too was ashamed and did not know what to say. So she remained seated among the reeds, and coughed, because she was feeling the damp. I counted my money; I had nearly fifty zlotys and some small change.

Theoretically we should have walked to the nearest house and asked for help. But how were we to explain, present the matter? Shame made it impossible. And I felt I should prefer spending the rest of my life among the reeds to telling anyone the whole story. That was something I could never do! Better admit having abducted Isabel, which was much more assimilable, better say that we were running away together from her parents' house, which was far more mature. Once I had made the admission, no more explanations would be necessary, for women are always ready to admit that one is in love with them. This would provide a pretext for us to make our way surreptitiously to the station and take the train to Warsaw, where we would start a new life in secret, the secrecy being attributable to the abduction.

And so I kissed her on the cheek and declared my passion, asking her forgiveness for having abducted her; and I explained that her family would never have consented to the match, because my position was not good enough, but that I had fallen in love with her at first sight, and had felt that she reciprocated my feelings.

'There was nothing for it but to abduct you, Isabel,' I said. 'There was nothing for it but for us to run away together.'

At first she was rather startled, but after half an hour of these declarations she started simpering and looking at me (because I was looking at her) and moving her fingers. She forgot all about the peasants up at the house, and became genuinely convinced that she had been abducted by me. This flattered her inordinately, as hitherto she had done nothing but embroidery, or studied, or had just sat looking at something, or been bored, or gone for walks, or looked out of the window, or played the piano, or busied herself philanthropically with the Solidarity Society, or sat for exams in agriculture, or flirted and danced to music, or gone to the seaside, or made conversation and said something. Hitherto she had lived only in the expectation of meeting someone to whom she could belong. And now, not only had she met such a person, but he had actually abducted her. That was why she called on all her capacity for loving, and loved me—because I loved her.

Meanwhile the super-bum mounted higher in the sky, sending out its dazzling rays by the million over a world which was a kind of imitation of the world, a paper world, painted green and illuminated from on high by blazing light. Following remote paths and avoiding villages, we made our way towards the station, and we had a long way to go . . . about thirteen miles. She walked and I walked, I walked and she walked, we walked together, each supporting the walk of the other, under the rays of the pitiless, shining, glittering, sparkling, puerile and puerilizing super-arch-bum. The grasshoppers hopped, the cicadas stridulated in the fields, the birds flew from tree to tree. But Isabel insisted that she knew the way, for she had passed this way thousands of times by car, landau, or cart. The heat was stifling. Fortunately we were able to refresh ourselves by sucking the milk of a solitary cow. Then we set off again. And the whole time, in view of my declaration of love, I had to go on talking of love and behaving gallantly, helping her over little bridges, for instance, chasing flies away, asking whether she were not tired, and paying her numerous other little attentions and making sentimental demonstrations. She responded by asking me whether

266

I were not tired too, by chasing flies off me, and by paying me similar attentions. I was dreadfully exhausted. Oh, when I got to Warsaw I should get rid of Isabel and start living again! I only wanted to use her as pretext and cover, to enable me to escape with some appearance of maturity from the *mêlée* at the house and to get to Warsaw, but for the time being I had to take an interest in her and, in a general way, keep up this intimate conversation of two beings who are happy in each other's company. And Isabel as we have seen, subjugated by my demonstration of feeling, grew more and more enterprising. And the super-bum, shining with improbable brightness and elevated to an altitude of a thousand million square miles cubed, flooded the valley of the universe with light.

She was a country young lady, brought up by her mother, my aunt Hurlecka, *née* Lin, and by the servants; and hitherto she had studied a little at the Horticultural College, where she had peeled some fruit, she had cultivated her mind and heart a little, had sat down a little, worked as a supernumerary in an office, played the piano a little, walked a little, and talked a little, but above all, she had waited and waited and waited for a man to turn up and fall in love with her and carry her off. She was a great specialist in waiting, passive and shy, and that is why she suffered from toothache, for she was made for a dentist's waiting-room, and her teeth knew it. So that now, when the object of all this waiting had at last appeared and carried her off, now that the great day had come, she became intensely active, and started showing herself to her best advantage, simpering, smiling and skipping about, making eyes at me, showing me her teeth and her happiness, gesticulating, or humming tunes to me under her breath. Moreover, she made the most of and accentuated the more pleasing parts of her body and did her best to conceal the others. And I had to look at her and pretend to be interested . . . and the arch-bum suspended loftily over the world in the incommensurable blue of the skies shone, gleamed and glowed, and warmed, burned, and dried up the grass and other vegetation. And Isabel, knowing that when one is in love one is happy, was happy; she looked at me with clear and tranquil eyes, forcing me to look back at her; and she said:

'I wish everyone were as happy as we are! If everyone were good, everyone would be happy!'

Or:

'We are young, we are in love. . . . The world is ours!'

And she rubbed herself tenderly against me, and I had to do the same to her.

And then, convinced that I was in love with her, she opened up and started telling me her secrets, talking to me sincerely and intimately, which she had never done to anyone before. For hitherto she had been afraid of men and, having been brought up in a certain aristocratic isolation by my Aunt Hurlecka, *née* Lin (now lost in the *mêlée*), and by the servants, she had never confided in anyone, for fear of being criticized or misjudged, and she was undefined, uncrystallized, indeterminate, unsure of herself and uncertain of the impact that she made on others. She had a great need of kindness, couldn't do without it, could talk only to someone whom she knew *a priori* and in advance to be well disposed towards her. And now, seeing that I loved her, seeing that she had managed to secure an ardent admirer *a priori* who would lovingly accept whatever she said because he was in love with her, she started confiding in me and revealing herself, disclosing her joys and sorrows, her tastes and inclinations and enthusiasms, her illusions and disappointments, her hopes and aspirations, her sentimentalism, her memories, and all the trivial details, for at last she had found a man who loved her, a man to whom she could show herself as she was, sure of impunity, sure that everything would be accepted with love and warmth. And I had to fall in with this and accept it, and go into ecstasies about it . . . and she said:

'People should try to perfect their minds and bodies, be always beautiful. In the afternoon I like holding my forehead against the window-pane and shutting my eyes. I like the cinema, but I like music better.'

And I had to acquiesce; and, knowing that her nose could not be an object of indifference to me, she whispered to me that when she awoke in the morning she always had to rub it, and she burst out laughing, and I burst out laughing too. After this she said sadly:

'I know I'm not pretty!'

I had to deny this. And she knew that I denied it, not in the name of reality and truth, but because I was in love with her, and she therefore accepted my denial with delight, enraptured at having found an unconditional, *a priori* admirer who loved and accepted everything with graciousness and warmth.

Oh, the agony through which I went to keep up at least the appearance of maturity along these paths through the fields, while, back at the now-distant house, masters and plebs made shameful play with their hands and the super-arch-bum suspended at the zenith terribly and mercilessly spat forth the lances of its rays, its thousands of arrows . . . oh, insipid charm, oh, deadly tenderness, mutual admiration, love! . . . Oh, the insolence of these females so greedy of love, so eager for amorous harmony, so willing to be the objects of adoration! . . . How dared this soft, empty, and insignificant creature consent to my blandishments and accept my homage, and batten ravenously on it? Does there exist in the world under the ardent and burning rays of the arch-bum anything more appalling than this sweet feminine warmth, idolatry and tender snuggling? And to make matters worse, to requite me and complete the cycle of mutual admiration, she started expressing admiration of me, and asking me questions about myself, not that she was really interested, but as a matter of tit for tat, for she knew that the greater interest she took in me, the greater interest I should take in her. And she in her turn stuffed me with adoration, snuggling amorously against me, whispering that she liked me so much, that I had made such an impression on her at first sight, that I was so bold, so brave . . .

'You carried me off,' she said, intoxicating herself with her own words. 'That's not a thing anybody could do! You fell in love with me, and abducted me without asking anybody's permission, without being afraid of my parents. . . . I love those brave, fearless, feline eyes of yours!'

And I writhed under the blows of her admiration as under Satan's whip, while overhead the huge, infernal super-bum, the great super-arch-bum, the hall-mark of the universe, the key to all problems, the essence and common denominator of all things, shone brilliantly and piercingly. Warmly and shyly she snuggled against me, cajoled and wheedled me, mythologized in her lethargic fashion; and I felt her adoring my qualities and peculiarities, searching and finding, warming up and consuming herself. She took my hand and started stroking it, and I stroked her hand, while the infantile and infernal super-arch-bum reached its zenith and apogee, vertically probing with its fire the very depths down here below.

Suspended at the very tip and summit of space, it launched its rays of gold and silver over the whole of this valley and in all directions. Meanwhile Isabel snuggled more and more tenderly against me, united herself with me more and more, and introduced me more and more into herself. I wanted to go to sleep. I could not go on walking, or listening, or answering. We walked through I know not what fields, and in those fields the grass was greenly green and verdant, abounding in yellow camomiles, but the camomiles were shy, and hid themselves in the grass, which was slightly damp and slippery, steaming under the cruel fire in the sky. Poppies appeared on both sides of the path, but they were rather anaemic poppies. A little farther on, on the hillsides, there were a lot of melons. On the water in the ditches were water lilies, pale, discoloured, blanched and delicate, tranquil under the heat beating down from above. And Isabel snuggled still more tenderly against me, and continued with her confidences. And the arch-bum still transfixed the world. The texture of the dwarf trees was anaemic and rickety, they were more like mushrooms, and they were so timorous that when I touched one it broke. There were a multitude of chirping sparrows. Overhead there were fat little reddish, bluish and whitish clouds, which looked as if they were made of silk paper, sorry and sentimental-looking. Everything was so vague and confused in outline, so silent, so chaste, so full of waiting, so unborn and undefined, that